"Past life therapy is undoubtedly the most effective approach to help patients recover from the unfinished emotional wounds of this life. The remarkable stories that come from Chuck's patients help us sense the powerful methods so well described. The time has come for this technique to be sought by both patients and physicians."

    —C. Norman Shealy, M.D., Ph.D.

    Author, *Illustrated Encyclopedia of Healing Remedies*

"I highly commend Dr. Charles V. Tramont's unique courage and foresight, as well as his hard pioneering work, in exploring reincarnation and its healing power, that he documented in his book: From Birth to Rebirth… His book takes us out of the medical box and transports us far away, into a wondrous universe of real health and self awareness, toward what all beings are intent to be—their true selves, the prerequisite for total fulfillment…"

    —Adrian Finkelstein, M.D.

    Author, *Your Past Lives and the Healing Process*

"Enjoy this narrative depicting the rollercoaster life of a successful obstetrician, who transitioned from saving infants' lives in the delivery room to discovering past lives through hypnotic regression. Dr. Tramont meticulously chronicles past life memories of his subjects, many of which could be historically validated, and describes how healing occurs through hypnosis and past life regression therapy. Dr. Tramont approaches life and reincarnation with a heart of a lion and with his book, delivers a new understanding of the human soul."

    —Walter. A. Semkiw, M.D.

    Author, *Return of the Revolutionaries*

From Birth to Rebirth

Gnostic Healing
for the 21st Century

Charles V. Tramont, M.D.

Swan•Raven & Co.
An Imprint
of Granite Publishing

Library of Congress Cataloging-in-Publication Data

Tramont, Charles V., 1937-
From birth to rebirth : gnostic healing for the 21st century / Charles V. Tramont.
p. ; cm.
ISBN-13: 978-1-893183-42-1 (pbk. : alk. paper)
ISBN-10: 1-893183-42-4 (pbk. : alk. paper)
1. Tramont, Charles V., 1937- 2. Physicians--United States--Biography.
3. Reincarnation therapy. 4. Rebirthing. 5. Hypnotism in obstetrics.
6. Hypnotism--Therapeutic use.
I Title.
[DNLM: 1. Physicians--psychology--Personal Narratives. 2. Spirituality--Personal Narratives. 3. Burnout, Professional--psychology--Personal Narratives.
4. Hypnosis--Personal Narratives. 5. Religious Philosophies--psychology--Personal Narratives. W 62 T87771F2008]

RG76.T73A3 2008
618.20092--dc22
[B]
2008001473

Final Manuscript Editor: Brian L. Crissey
Book & Cover Design: Pamela Meyer

Printed in the United States of America on recycled paper.

Address all inquiries to:
Swan•Raven & Co.
An Imprint of Granite Publishing
P.O. Box 1429
Columbus, NC 28722
granitepublishing.us

Dedication

This book is dedicated:

—— To those Gnostics who had the courage to publicly uphold their beliefs for which they paid the ultimate price, of torture and death, rather than ascribe to the mandated religion of their time;

—— To those individuals of the past, present, and the future, who refuse to be confined to mainstream thinking;

—— To those who maintain an open mind; for without an open mind this book would not have been written, nor will it be read.

Table of Contents

PROLOGUE

It is the 21st Century. Humankind continues to surge ahead technologically, yet millions of humans on our planet continue to die from disease, starvation, and the ravages of war. Inhumanity flourishes in every corner of the world. Have we really come so far? I think not. Times have changed, but many people remain unchanged, still ruled by fear, greed, anger, jealousy, and other negative emotions that haunt their personalities, dictating how they conduct their lives and how they treat other human beings. Still through this curtain of darkness there shines a beacon of hope, a bright light of spirituality, spreading its loving illumination with such intensity that it touches and sets ablaze the flickering but never extinguished flame of our Creator that burns within each of us.

What does this dismal account of the obvious stagnation of humanity's progress towards a better world and the mention of hope in the form of spirituality have to do with me, a medical doctor? To answer this question I must first review my life as a physician. In doing so, I feel a great sense of pride as I am one of thousands of physicians who have been waging the war against disease in the frontline trenches of medicine. I've had the privilege of bringing close to 5,000 new lives into this world, as well as performing many thousands of surgeries on grateful patients. My peers gave me a vote of confidence by electing me to prestigious hospital positions. And I've also had the honor of serving my country during two wars. Like most physicians I've found that practicing medicine well comes at a high price. Sacrificing family time becomes a way of life as the needs of the patients become overwhelming. Being a medical doctor was much more than a profession; it was a vocation, an art, and a labor of love. I was able to cure people of disease, afford safe entry into this world, and repair damaged bodies. More importantly

I was able to befriend my patients and truly help them in many ways with their personal problems. I gave it all I had, and some days it showed. The hours were grueling, the stress never-ending, and the absence from home and family unbearable. In spite of all this, I still felt immersed in a rewarding, healing profession, one that was very much interwoven within the human fabric. Yet, in the midst of this self-propelled, noble but chaotic, life-style as a physician, I discovered that I could no longer ignore a nagging emptiness, a void in my life that made its haunting presence known to me in different ways.

Day-to-day living seemed to be filled with rich and rewarding accomplishments—providing for my family, diligently practicing medicine, maintaining a religious and social life , etc. As I listened more carefully to the plights of my patients, I became ever more frustrated as I could not always answer their questions regarding life and death. As the years went by, I found myself blanketed by many of my own questions for which I had no answers. Many of these concerned not only life and death, but also our origin, destination, and especially our purpose on this Earth, or for that matter, in the universe. I was beginning to feel as if my daily experience with reality was very superficial and actually a very small part of something much bigger, something on which I could find no handle.

Such was my life during those many years in practice. Then I discovered late in my career that events occur for a reason, and not by coincidence. As it happened, my wife encouraged me to investigate the use of hypnosis in my practice. Following a course given by a physician who exclusively practiced medical hypnosis, I found that I was utterly fascinated and taken back by this powerful and very effective modality. Within a short time I had incorporated the use of hypnosis in my OB/GYN practice and made it a permanent part of my therapeutic armamentarium. Being an avid reader of New Age material, my wife soon led me to such authors as Roger Wolger, Dick Sutphen, Adrian Finkelstein, Raymond Moody, and Brian Weiss. I thus had my first introduction to the subjects of past-life regression and reincarnation. At this stage in my life I had not formulated any opinion on these topics. My initial comment, delivered in a joking fashion, was that this sounds like subversive literature; however, as I waded into these and other books on past-life regression, I became profoundly impressed with the validation of these lives and the healing effect the sessions had upon the patients. As I continued to read, I became progressively more excited and enthusiastic over the therapeutic value of hypnotic regressions and soon conducted my own.

I found that terminal patients were comforted by being given a sense of being eternal. I was able to treat anxious and depressed patients without drugs and relieve others of their phobias and nightmares. Following each past-life regression I spent considerable time researching historical events, dates, names, and places. What I uncovered literally blew me away, especially the validation that included the nuances that only someone there could have known. This was indeed very exciting; I was hooked. I was becoming truly enlightened and found myself embarking on a journey that can only be described as evolutionary and spiritual.

I have now concluded that open-mindedness and the ever-rising tide of spirituality have escalated to the degree that they are now forces to be reckoned with in the sea of medical technology and have led to new and exciting alternative medical treatments. I now believe that by allowing ourselves to listen to our intuition, the voice of the soul, and to expand our minds beyond what our superficial senses tell us, we are able to avoid the restraining boundaries of focal vision and rise above the deafening, insignificant clatter of our daily life. Only in this way can we properly formulate what we need to ask of our universe. This spiritual tide has encouraged many to search for answers to questions such as, who am I? Where did I come from? Where am I going? Why am I here? In looking for these answers, these individuals leap forward in expectation of a closer relationship with their Creator. In finding these answers, they learn to look deeply within themselves. In doing this, they discover that their mind and heart become one, only to communicate the true message of the soul, namely love and compassion.

I was being led from the narrow constraints of conventional medicine to a higher calling, one that enabled me to help patients in a much more comprehensive way, a way that exposes and identifies the origins of physical and emotional disease so healing can take place, a way that will soon take its place among the mainstream methods of alternative medicine. This is my story.

1

FLASHBACKS

THE HEART OF A LION:
A PREREQUISITE FOR OBSTETRICIANS

I see myself gowned and masked in a sterile-appearing delivery room breathing heavily as I desperately struggle to save the life of an infant who remains imprisoned in his mother's pelvis. As my recall of this moment takes on an eerie uncanniness, I once more begin to smell the antiseptic and once more experience the overwhelming sense of frustration that comes from watching a human life slip away, regardless of your efforts to save it.

This memory took on a life of its own as I began to remember every detail and reexperience every emotion in spite of the many years that have passed. I was making evening rounds on the surgery patients during my last year of residency, when the stillness of evening was abruptly interrupted by an emergency page from the operator. There was an emergency in Delivery Room 2, and I was at the other end of the hospital. I sprinted and then broke into an open run through the hallways. Reaching the delivery room I immediately read panic all over the first-year resident's face as he was catheterizing his patient's bladder. She was moaning loudly and contorting her body within the stirrups as she writhed in pain. The nurse gowned and gloved me as the resident filled me in. His patient had labored over two hours with a fully dilated cervix when the fetal heart rate became irregular and dropped precipitously. The new resident suspected that the baby's head was not in a normal anterior position, but he could not be sure. The head nurse had by now taken up a position by the mother's abdomen and began monitoring the fetal heart with a

1

fetoscope. I instructed her to tap her index finger with each beat so I could see it clearly. As I gave the go-ahead to the anesthesiologist to take the patient down with general anesthesia, I looked at the clock on the wall and memorized the time. I instinctively knew that I would be racing against minutes and that the gas anesthesia would only further compromise the infant if I didn't get him out quickly.

Rushing through the pelvic exam, I judged the baby's firmly embedded head to be in a persistent posterior position (facing the ceiling). I thought it would be possible to do an emergency delivery this way with forceps, but it would be difficult and would probably injure the infant. If I could rotate his head to an anterior position (facing the floor), I could then get him out more easily and safely with forceps.

Making a large episiotomy incision in the mother's perineum, I gave myself enough room to place my entire hand on the side of the baby's head so I could rotate it manually. I pushed and tugged and angled my hand to no avail, as sweat dampened my mask and gown. My frustration grew as I reapplied my hand and found I could still not budge the infant's head. I glanced again at the clock and picked up the forceps, as perspiration now poured from my forehead. I placed the blades of the forceps on the infant's head as fast and as gently as I could, without injuring the mother or baby. Locking the forceps into position I again attempted to rotate the head with the forceps, and again I was deprived of any movement.

The resident fidgeted and cleared his throat, and at that moment I felt a stifling feeling of dread fill the room. Looking up at the nurse monitoring the heartbeat, I could see that her finger tapping had slowed to a sickening pace, telling me soon all would be lost. Anxiety swept over me as this nurse then shouted, "The fetal heart is below 60!" With her sense of urgency still ringing in my ears I took a deep breath, carefully reapplied the forceps blades, and placed more pressure on the baby's head so as to dislodge it from its seemingly immobile position.

Movement! I felt movement of the head! "Hallelujah!" I screamed to myself, as I went through the maneuver of rotation. Mumbling "Thank God," I removed the forceps and reapplied them to the baby's head while holding it in place so it would not swing back to its prior position. I then gently but firmly delivered the baby's head and suctioned his mouth and nose. As I delivered the infant's full limp body, I saw that five minutes had elapsed. Quickly clamping and severing the umbilical cord, I literally ran the baby over to the bassinette, where the anesthesiologist and nurse were waiting to resuscitate. Returning to the mother to deliver the placenta and put a stop to the bleeding, my eyes fell upon an irregular lump on the umbilical cord. It was a knot, a true knot in the cord. Showing this to the resident, I explained that as the baby descended into the pelvis, the umbilical cord would stretch and cause the knot to tighten, thus shutting off the baby's blood supply and adversely affecting his heart rate. I emphasized that these true knots are often fatal.

While concentrating on massaging the mother's uterus, I could hear the distress in the voices of those working on the baby. As I turned my head slowly towards them, my eyes immediately became fixated on that motionless pale body lying in the bassinette. I soon found myself praying hard for that tiny human being. The seconds slowly passed, and the scene became surreal as time almost stood still. Then my heart jumped as I noticed a pink hue envelop his ashen torso. Seconds later a wonderful, familiar cry emerged as the child began to wave his arms and legs. I could see smiles around me beginning to form as a sense of peace descended upon the scene. The young resident patted me on my hand and thanked me. As I wound up the episiotomy repair, I felt a wave of relief wash over me and yes, thankfulness.

As the images of this harrowing memory faded, I reflected on all that had taken place on that stressful evening. The baby did quite well and was able to have a circumcision performed the following day. This case was one of many hundreds of emergency deliveries that I had managed throughout my career. The vast majority of them

3

resulted in healthy babies with grateful parents, a very positive side of obstetrics indeed. Unfortunately, the negative aspects of the stress involved do take their toll on the obstetrician.

THE MANY FACETS OF MEMORY

Memory shines forth its brilliance as does a precious diamond, exposing its many facets all at once, but sparkling in only a few. In a like manner, each facet of memory reflects a specific emotion which was present in a particular moment in time, but only some of these will be powerful enough to dominate the memory and allow it to surface when a similar emotion is experienced in one's present life.

Putting down on paper the events of one's life is very much like listening to music from years ago. The memories that surface are sometimes replete with deep-seated emotions that once again bring back to life in strikingly realistic images a time that has long-since passed. My days as an obstetrician seem far removed from my present life. It reminds me of peering through a veil in a dream. Those days were filled to the brim with the full essence of life that my specialty exuded. This brought me great pride and joy. Still, the stress was built-in; and the other side of the coin made its presence known in many ways, bringing the two polarities of obstetrics together, namely, the positive joy associated with bringing a new life into the world, and the negative tension and anxiety associated with the responsibility and concern over possible outcomes. Fortunately, these many heart-pounding moments of long ago stay locked up in the forefront of my subconscious mind; however, when present circumstances trigger the recall of this memory and allow these moments to move into conscious thought, they bring with them a plethora of emotions that is difficult to hide.

The vivid memories of those all-too-frequent tense moments seem to hang in the balance, and, in doing so, they dilute and mar the joyous times when I helped to bring life into this world. It's as if these anxious moments in time leave one with a negative imprint upon his memory which is not easily erased, a kind of battle fatigue that is unending.

INSPIRATION

Becoming a doctor was something I wanted very badly, especially in my early years as a young boy. My father's oldest brother was a general practitioner in a small Ohio town. He had been a radio announcer before he became a physician and had been offered a glamorous, lucrative medical practice in New York City, caring for the stars at NBC.

He turned this down and decided instead to practice in Mount Vernon, Ohio, where he could treat many more patients who really needed his services. I remember stories of him receiving a bushel of apples as his fee, or just a thank-you. The dedication that my uncle exhibited, and the respect he received in return, made an early, deep impression on my young mind. My desire to become a doctor underwent a jump-start when my sister was born in the late forties. I was ten years old and had a difficult time understanding why she had brain damage following her birth. I was told she didn't breathe for a short time after birth. The result was cerebral palsy. This event changed my life; and as I think back, the impact was much more than I realized.It was a devastating blow to my parents, and they soon settled into a life of care, revolving around my sister. I also shared in this care giving and, as in many situations like this, it became a way of life, bringing with it a defensive attitude.

My desire to be in medicine remained strong throughout high school, as I focused on courses that would prepare me for college and a medical career. Following acceptance to a Jesuit university, I eagerly looked forward to starting a premedical curriculum; however, I soon found out that good grades did not come easily in a Jesuit school. The 'Jebbies," as we affectionately called them, made sure that we worked hard for everything we received. I remember arriving very early and leaving very late on a daily basis and putting in an unbelievable amount of hours studying and preparing for tests, which were almost daily. I also recall peering out the laboratory windows and seeing the happy-go-lucky, unstressed business students leaving for home in the early afternoon, as usual. There were over 120 of us premed students starting out in freshman year. By graduation, our numbers had dwindled down to 16, 8 of whom were accepted to medical schools. I was fortunate enough to be accepted to two medical schools, one in Chicago and one in New York City. I chose New York.

THE HELLACIOUS YEARS OF MEDICAL SCHOOL

It was a hot, humid day in August of 1958 when I arrived in New York City, ready to take on the rigors of medical school. My emotions were volatile, alternating between fear and excitement. Here I was, 20 years old, newly married, and starting medical school, in one of the busiest cities of the world. The welcoming lecture by the dean was one in which he indicated that the person next to you probably won't be there next year. This was not what I expected to hear. Being accepted to medical school was tough enough, especially coming out of a Jesuit university where good grades were hard to come by. As I mentioned previously, the premed students in undergraduate school dropped out like flies as the years progressed. Eight of us were fortunate enough to be accepted into med school. Now I am being told that the idea that you're home free, once you've landed in medical school, is a fable. I was not happy; the pressure was still on, only I didn't realize how much.

My biggest hurdle that year was anatomy. I remember thinking "This is like memorizing and picturing a 3-D road map of the world." We were divided into groups of four and assigned our cadaver for the year. We named our cadaver "Lester," and how well I remember working on him, late into the night, with nothing more than a gooseneck lamp and sixty of his brethren lying nearby. The chairman of the anatomy department wrote and memorized his own book on human anatomy. When he chose to describe an organ, he never missed a beat, as we followed him in his rather extensive book. Passing his exams was more like a crapshoot, since his exam consisted of one question, "Describe the function and relations of a particular structure going through a particular area of the body." The Herculean effort put forth at attempting to outguess the Master was phenomenal. There were constant lists made up of the fifty most likely questions to be asked. It was maddening. Finally, you would come to the conclusion that the number of questions that could be asked is astronomical, and the only solution is to study everything and hope you're lucky.

I made it to sophomore year, which was purported to be the toughest, with different courses and a lineup of rather nasty faculty. To say med school was rough would be like scalding yourself with boiling water and saying, "It's a little warm." I learned that you had to stay focused, keep your sense of humor, and be able to handle anything and everything that comes your way. Were some professors sadistic? You bet, especially in sophomore year. Replete with rationalizing statements, such as, "If you can't handle the pressure, you won't make a competent physician," what they really meant was, if you can't handle the pressure, you won't make it through medical school to become a physician. On many occasions, I bore witness to a medical school student's dignity being trampled by a professor bent on embarrassing him. As for constant pressure, how about only posting a list of medical students who are in danger of failing the course? Being on the list obviously meant that you're in trouble; if you're not on the list, you may have already failed. That particular clinical pathology professor took great delight in keeping the students guessing by not releasing any test scores. However, a clandestine student tradition filtered down from the junior class to the suffering second year students, allowing them an opportunity to see their grades. This traditional caper was affectionately known as "the old soft shoe," or "the night patrol." It involved the steady nerves of several brave medical students who would take the elevator to the eighth floor in the early morning hours; and with commando-like precision, post guards at the elevator and stairwell, while the one who chose the short straw stealthily made his way to the professor's office, which was conveniently left unlocked, with the light on, and the student file cabinet laying open and waiting.

Such nerve-wracking endeavors were more the rule than the exception as the tone of the med students, in this particular New York school, was quite aggressive when it came to grades. This professor was a fox. His "In Danger of Flunking" list kept the pressure on; however, at the same time, he was able to satisfy the students' voracious appetite for grades while never having to tolerate the usual barrage of harassing complaints and questions regarding his exams. It was a clever but malicious system, one which could have resulted in an expulsion if the student were caught. Such a situation nearly occurred in the class prior to ours. It seems that a middle-of-the-night autopsy interrupted the night patrol and an abandoned student was left behind but remained hidden in an office closet. His student partners in crime returned for him several hours later. I understand that he was a basket case when they found him.

As a sophomore, it became obvious that the dean meant what he said on our first day of school. We had lost half of our class, which were, by this time, replaced. The long hours in laboratories came to a screeching halt in our junior year, being replaced by long lectures and multiple clinics. Yes, we were now actually seeing patients in different hospital clinics, with supervision, of course. This brings to mind a very big problem, parking in Manhattan. One of my classmates insisted on always double-parking and received in excess of 100 parking tickets. He eventually went to court and was asked that fateful question by the judge, "Are you a doctor?" His answer was a classic response, "They call me Doctor."

Senior year was a whole new wrinkle. We were given white intern outfits and forced into slave labor, at least that's what it felt like. Our official title was that of being an "extern;" our senior group staffed our plush Manhattan hospital and our not so plush Spanish

Harlem hospital. We were under direct control of the resident staff who took over our training as we rotated through the services. Some residents were unbelievably great and were responsible for a good part of our training. By the same token, there were a few residents who mostly used us for scut work and gave us zip for training. I lucked out in surgery and learned a great deal. The Emergency Room in Spanish Harlem was always jumping and afforded us a great amount of suture time. We also found ourselves staffing ambulances, which covered a large part of Manhattan. This was an exciting episode, to say the least, especially when the ambulance driver would hand you a black bag, drop you off at an accident in Harlem, and lock the door following your exit from the ambulance. Harlem was a dangerous place in those days, and it was a known fact that both the ambulance and the doctors who manned them carried drugs.

Midway into my senior year, I was still unsure of what specialty I was leaning toward. OB rotation was coming up, and I had mixed feelings about it. I had seen my classmates who had gone through the OB service, and they looked bad. The number of deliveries on this service was many hundreds per month. The shifts were 36 hours on, and 12 hours off, and they weren't kidding.

My starting day finally came, and I witnessed my first delivery. It affected me in a very profound way, more than I can ever express in words. The rampant emotion, that of indescribably joyous exhilaration, that swept over me like a tidal wave, was brought to even a higher level when I delivered my first infant, only now it was intermixed with feelings of pride, honor, and gratitude for being given the privilege to assist during the final stages of God's greatest creation. That miraculous moment cemented itself into my very being and became indelibly highlighted in the memory banks of my soul. I knew immediately that this specialty was speaking to me in a very loud voice. Here, a doctor could actually give God a hand in bringing a new human life into this world.

As the weeks passed, and I had delivered close to thirty infants, I found that I didn't mind the grueling schedule and that my legs felt like lead. There was a lot to be mastered in this noble art; however, once you have experienced the challenge and overcome the obstacles; once you have felt life springing forth in a tiny limp body, and once you have looked into a new mother's appreciative eyes, you cannot walk away. The feelings that well up in you following a successful completion of a delivery are not only overwhelming, they are addictive. I was hooked. This was indeed to be my life's work.

Looking back on those difficult years in medical school, I find that I have mixed emotions. It's unfortunate that academics was the main criteria to keep one in school, as I had witnessed many potentially good physicians drop by the wayside. As far as the nonsensical idea of keeping you under pressure, to keep you focused, I feel that the professors' true motivation was control so as to advance their ego, rather than simulate the pressure of medical practice as they would often emulate.

Graduating from medical school was a big deal, with diplomas being handed out in Carnegie Hall. We were now called "Doctor" because we had earned the right, and not just because we wore white coats.

2

PRACTICE MAKES PERFECT

INTERNSHIP:
A FORM OF INDENTURED SERVITUDE

With the nightmare of medical school behind me, I found myself embarking upon a new adventure: internship, a full year of slavery-type servitude, with a salary to match. My fourth year of medical school externship prepared me well for this experience, only now, I had an "MD" behind my name. The types of internships varied according to what you were interested in. I did things a little differently. Feeling that I had a wealth of experience in surgery and in obstetrics, I decided to immerse myself in the areas I felt weak in, namely internal medicine. So I signed on for a mixed medical internship, being on call every day and every third night. Of course, within a few months, I also signed on to moonlight a few nights a week at an affiliated hospital that did only obstetrics and gynecology. I was hungry for experience, and it showed.

Eugene Stark, a fellow intern, became a good friend of mine, and one day, while chatting in the on-call room, we pondered over the military draft status, as the Vietnam War was still raging out of control, and we had heard that many physicians were being called in to serve. I told Eugene that the uncertainty of draft status was driving me crazy, and I was going to call the draft board now. Eugene argued with me and exclaimed that it was better not to remind them that we're around! I ignored him and made the call. Reaching the draft board, I meekly asked if I could find out what my draft status was. As the voice on the other side of the line asked for my name, my knees went limp, and I blurted out, "Eugene Stark!" The voice on the phone said, "You're second on the list to be called." I then summoned my fleeting courage and asked about Charles Tramont. The response was, "He's first on the list, next to be called up." The not knowing was no longer a problem; it was just a matter of days until we were drafted. The internship was almost over, and we had both signed contracts for three-year residencies at the same OB/GYN hospital. Within two weeks I received notice to report for submarine service in the United States Navy. One week later, Eugene was drafted by the Army. Our hospital pleaded undue hardship and was able to retain me for the residency. Eugene left for Army training.

RESIDENCY:
AN ADVANCED FORM OF SLAVE LABOR

I was the only first-year resident at St. Ann Hospital in Cleveland, which was a private OB/GYN hospital, and the training was going to be very different from anything I had known before. As an extern in New York City hospitals, I had massive experience with indigent patients, supervised by a guy with one or two years' seniority, namely, the resident who after a year or two of this type of training was in my estimation entirely too insensitive and rough with patients. His experience was extensive, but somewhere along the way he lost his compassion, possibly because of the manner in which these patients treated him, namely, being uncooperative, unappreciative, and often unable to fully comprehend their medical situation. I felt that a private-patient OB/GYN practice would require private-patient OB/GYN training, a decision I have never regretted. The training was unique in that I was exposed to a large number of attending physicians, private OB/GYN doctors with large practices, and a wealth of information to be had. I ended up managing their patients, delivering their babies, and following up with rounds and circumcisions. My last year of residency was spent in two hospitals, where I assisted during the GYN surgery and picked up the varying techniques of many surgeons. Within a short time, I was doing the surgery myself, being assisted by the private physicians.

MILITARY SERVICE:
AN OPPORTUNITY TO SERVE AND PRACTICE YOUR CRAFT

In my last week as chief resident, Eugene Stark came aboard to begin his residency. The war was still on, and I had heard nothing from the draft board. I decided to hire on as a chief resident, month to month, at another hospital, and not start up a practice, as I felt convinced that the armed forces would soon pick me up again. Three months later I was drafted by the United States Air Force, and a few weeks later found myself training in Texas as a Captain in the Strategic Air Command. Being assigned to a SAC Missile base in Missouri, I found that my voracious appetite for experience had not abated. As chief of OB/GYN, I soaked up an unbelievable amount of experience, including giving my own spinal anesthetics.

In 1968 I was discharged and returned home to Ohio to practice in a small town. By now I had developed my own techniques and preferences for the many and varied surgery and delivery situations. I was ready for the rigors of private practice.

3

The Trenches of Daily Practice

Getting My Feet Wet

The practice of medicine is truly a mixed bag of triumphs and fears. The first days of practice were unbelievably sweet. I was the new kid on the block; I had a lot to prove, and I loved the challenge. As I looked back on those years, I can truly say I wore an invincible suit of armor. I found that, deep down, I really did have the heart of a lion, ready and willing to handle anything that came my way. I even went out of my way to take on greater responsibilities and even tougher cases. I found myself being drawn into the stereotypical quagmire called "the busy physician." This was OK, I thought; actually, it felt great to practice this artful profession that I worked so hard to master. I enjoyed the respect and increasing income that followed, but as the practice expanded I found that I was becoming too busy to spend extra time with patients.

I always looked forward to talking and listening to my patients in the office. This was time I had enjoyed and valued. What I didn't realize was that my patients valued this time even more. As my practice grew, I was required to be at the hospital much more often, and my time in the office became less. Seeing more patients at the office in shorter periods of time caused the entire office to be immersed in a hurried and hectic atmosphere. At first I began to see disappointment in the patients' faces. It wasn't until a patient confronted me directly that I truly empathized with them and came to the realization that they were being shortchanged and rushed through their appointments without my taking sufficient time to listen to all their problems, physical as well as personal. It was a rude awakening for me, and I'm glad it came early, about my second year

14

in practice. I felt embarrassed and ashamed that I allowed myself to be sucked into this successful-practice entrapment syndrome; however, I was grateful for that patient's comment and was determined to change the program and allow sufficient time for office patients to be seen properly, another decision I have never regretted.

THE DAY THAT CHANGED MY LIFE

It was Wednesday as I pulled into the doctors' parking lot at the hospital. A typical, cloudy March day, I thought, as I entered the hospital and headed down the long hallway to the surgery department. Peering at the calendar in the doctors' locker room, I pulled on my scrub suit and saw that it was the 24th of March, 1971. I then thought, "Boy, I've been in practice for a good two and a half years." Hurrying to the operating room, I was completely oblivious to the life-changing events that were about to unfold. After greeting the patient and reassuring her that she would be fine, I began my scrubbing ritual at the sink and focused on the upcoming case, for it was one in which a new technique was to be used.

The surgery lasted an hour and a half. As I placed the last suture in the skin, I was told that I had a call. Quickly removing my gown and gloves, I picked up the nearest phone. The voice on the line identified himself as an emergency room doctor at a hospital in a Cleveland suburb. He then mentioned my father's name, and followed with, "He has expired...." The voice continued on about identification and releases, but none of these words registered as my subconscious took over and went through the motions of the phone call. Barely hearing the click of the receiver as I hung up, a feeling of overwhelming loss began to wash over me, like a wave that leaves a pool of frightening thoughts in its wake.

My father was my best friend, and I loved him more than I could ever say. We shared a lot, including the joy that my sister had brought to our family and the sadness that she evoked in us as we watched her grow up while missing so much in life that most people take for granted. She was now 22, and it was obvious that she would never walk, talk, or care for herself in any way. My father knocked himself out giving her as big a chunk of life as possible. She not only loved him, but also depended upon him completely.

At that moment, she was at the Cerebral Palsy Center in downtown Cleveland waiting to be picked up by my father. He had barely dropped her off at the center and gotten back on the freeway when he suffered a fatal heart attack. He evidently took the time to slow down and stop his car in the right-hand lane before he slumped over and died. My sister immediately sensed that something was wrong when a close friend of mine picked her up and brought her to my office. Telling her that our father was dead was the toughest thing I've ever done. As I uttered the painful words, my sister's eyes widened and stared off into space. Her body then stiffened into an exaggerated spastic posture as if I had stabbed her in the heart. She remained quiet for a few moments and then a pathetic whimper found its way out of her clenched and grimaced mouth. I had often said I would be glad to take her pain for her. This was one of those times.

As my mother was emotionally and physically unable to care for my sister, I took on full responsibility for her care, which entailed hiring various people to care for her, driving to where she was, carrying her to the bathroom and feeding her. This demanding situation continued for over a year, until I was able to place her at Camp Echoing Hills, which was run by Rev. Cordell Brown, a talented administrator and motivational speaker, who also had cerebral palsy. His words ring in my memory; "We all have handicaps; mine is just a little more obvious." Even though I knew that I would be visiting her as often as I could, I was unable to hold the tears back when I left her at the residence. While this tore at my heartstrings, I knew deep down that I needed to be a full-time physician.

While at Echoing Hills, my sister fell in love with another resident who also had cerebral palsy but could speak. They wanted to get married, and even though I initially did not encourage this, my family did, and they worked hard to plan the wedding. Finally their big day arrived, and with assistance they took their vows in their wheelchairs nestled next to each other at the altar. There wasn't a dry eye in the place.

Sixteen years have passed, and my sister and her husband remain happy in their own little house while being cared-for 24 hours a day by a company that employs the kindest and most compassionate people I have ever met. My sister and brother-in-law have definitely cut themselves a bigger piece of life than I could ever have envisioned for them, and they have eloquently put it into words of inspiration in their upcoming book titled, *Through Our Eyes*.

THE COMPLEXITIES OF CAESARIAN SECTIONS

As the years passed, I retained my fortitude, but more cautiously. In those days I found that I allowed negative emotions to run amok within me, and yes, fear was a big one. Was I fearful of poor outcomes? Sure I was, especially when complicated cases would come my way, and this was all too often. I discovered that courage has nothing to do with being fearful. Courage has to do with moving forward in spite of fear, doing your best in an unwavering fashion, under the most adverse circumstances. That often meant staying focused and moving rapidly but carefully. Time was often my enemy, and I had to beat it if we were to have a good result. That result was often a live baby, unscathed by brain damage. I can vividly recall emergency C-sections in the middle of the night, when I was very much alone. Patients with severe pelvic adhesions (tissues and organs densely adherent to each other) from a variety of causes, such as previous surgery, pelvic infections, or endometriosis, often required emergency C-sections for fetal distress. Operating on such individuals presented an unbelievable challenge, since the densely adherent tissues required very delicate separation in the face of a speedy delivery for this compromised infant. In order to accomplish this feat, the rapidity of the surgery had to be tempered with a meticulous dissection of the adhesions, so as not to endanger the mother.

17

Another nightmarish situation was the patient who presented with a prematurely separating afterbirth. The ensuing hemorrhage from the uterus permeated the musculature of the uterus, causing it to easily tear like wet paper. As these scenarios unfolded, I would become extremely frustrated as I quickly placed suture after suture in an attempt to put a stop to the incessant bleeding, only to see them pull through the mushy tissue or bleed more from the needle holes. Emergency C-sections were often fraught with unexpected problems, such as when a large infant's head became stuck in a tight pelvis. During such moments I found myself quickly glancing at the clock ticking off precious minutes, perspiring profusely while struggling to dislodge the infant's head from a narrow maternal pelvis. Often I silently prayed for divine help to intervene and loosen that solidly wedged-in head. It seems that Higher Powers always came through for me, as I would find myself greatly encouraged and breathing much easier when I finally detected some head movement. After surgery I often pondered over everything that had occurred, especially while dictating the operative report, and I would often think of an old World War II movie titled "God is my Copilot" that made an impression on me as a small boy. "Well," I thought, "when I'm under fire in surgery or carrying out a difficult delivery, God is beside me, guiding my hands and calming my mind and heart."

A C-section is one of the few major surgeries in the world to which the patient's partner is invited to observe. Having the father present during his child's delivery evolved during the late '60s, along with the return of the trend of natural childbirth, and it eventually spilled over into the surgical scene. This is fine, as long as everything goes smoothly during the delivery. However, when problems erupt unexpectedly, more stress than necessary is compounded into the delivery scene. The obstetrician must now calm the father and explain what is occurring, in addition to solving the problem. Add hysterical emotional reactions from the father or the patient, who is often awake and very verbal, and you have an unusually tense and sometimes explosive situation that is not easily quelled. Regardless of your preparation and instructions prior to the procedure, sometimes the father must be ushered from the room. He may be worried, but understanding; or he may be in a panic, kicking and screaming all the way. I once had a father faint during a routine C-section. The dull thud that I heard was his head hitting the operating room floor. I winced but then divorced my mind from the situation and continued with the operation, that is, until the mother began crying uncontrollably, as she saw his unconscious body being carried out of the operating room.

Such disruptive and unusually stressful scenarios are the exception rather than the rule, thank God, but when they do occur, they leave a bad taste in your mouth for the whole idea. Whenever I asked a general surgeon if he would routinely subject himself to the ordeal of having a spouse or significant other present during major surgery, a typical answer I received was, "Hell, NO! You OB/GYNs are crazy! Surgery is no place for the general public, especially an individual with a personal relationship to the patient!" People are not medically sophisticated enough to understand what is happening in surgery, and thus may easily misinterpret what has occurred, even to the point of mistaken malpractice.

THE TRUE ART OF OBSTETRICS

The true art of obstetrics resides in performing vaginal deliveries. The stress involved in managing difficult labor and delivery cases more than makes up for the majority of easy deliveries that one encounters. However, in spite of the many problems that an obstetrician may run into when managing such cases, the miracle of childbirth never loses its luster.

The most challenging obstetrical deliveries include breech presentations (wherein the baby is delivered feet or buttocks first), which certainly are very dramatic and often difficult, especially when involving large babies. My greatest nightmare was the thought of the baby's head becoming stuck in the pelvis following delivery of the baby's body. Having witnessed such a disaster in residency while assisting another physician, I found myself programmed to be ultra cautious in such cases. Twins often presented as breeches, and sometimes it was even necessary to convert them into a breech presentation. This often was the case following delivery of the first twin. In this situation, it became necessary to then break the water of the second twin and feel for a presenting part. Once you were convinced that the second twin was not coming down head first, you would feel around for a foot, get a good grip on it with your fingers, and pull this baby down as a single or double footling. Time was of the essence here, as the uterus would begin to clamp down on the baby following release of the fluid from the second bag of water. It seems that we were always working against time.

Because of the increased morbidity, or damage to the infant, from vaginal deliveries, C-section became the method of choice for delivering primigravida, or first babies with breech presentations. As the years wore on, I not only delivered all my primigravida breech presentations by Caesarian but also the majority of breech presentations that occurred in patients having subsequent babies.

Another all-too-common situation was the persistent posterior presentation. In these cases, we needed to rotate the baby's head to facilitate a faster, safer, and more physiologic delivery. The finely-honed skill of using forceps often allowed us to shorten an otherwise long, painful labor, or more importantly, to quickly and safely deliver a baby in acute fetal distress. An obstetrician usually favors one or another type of forceps and learns to use them very well. I was no exception, and I felt I could accomplish a safe and rather slick delivery with Tucker forceps. Unfortunately, the malpractice climate worsened to the point where just picking up the forceps automatically put you into a bad light, liability-speaking. If the outcome was poor, or there was any problem with the baby, forceps would be blamed, so midway through my practice I made the painful decision to stop using forceps altogether, which meant I had to rotate the infant's head manually or wait for it to occur spontaneously, which also meant that I had to use the MityVac, or vacuum extractor, to facilitate a more immediate or emergency delivery. However, this procedure, even if used properly and gently, was also subject to risk, namely intracranial hemorrhage. As you can see from this brief glimpse into the world of obstetrics, surprises lurk around every corner, and outcomes can be unpredictable, as you precariously skate through a virtual malpractice minefield.

GYNECOLOGICAL SURGERY

A large part of gynecological surgery will always be performed through abdominal incisions, especially hysterectomies and removal of large tumors and cysts, such as the ten-pound ovarian cyst I once removed. As time passed, endoscopic surgery, especially abdominal laparoscopy, became popular, mostly due to the fact that it was minimally invasive. Another physician and I were among the few groups in the country to pioneer the use of laparoscopic procedures. We had our share of problems, especially with the early "Model T" type equipment, however, as we became comfortable with the instruments, we became quite good at it. Later, as TV cameras were introduced, we had to orient ourselves to operating while watching a screen. We were accomplishing unbelievable feats with the scope, such as removing tubal pregnancies, performing appendectomies, and many GYN procedures. As my children would say, it was definitely cool.

Performing surgery through a vaginal approach made OB/GYN surgery very different from other surgical specialties, especially general surgery. Vaginal hysterectomies enabled us to lessen patients' time in the hospital and minimize their discomfort. Vaginal procedures were common, encompassing hysterectomies, an array of biopsies, tightening-up procedures often related to bowel and bladder, and the proverbial D & C, which the old-timers referred to as a "dusting and cleaning." D & Cs in obstetrics were frequently performed following miscarriages and were often associated with excessive vaginal bleeding. Some of those incomplete miscarriages in the early morning hours were unbelievably stressful. Bleeding was very heavy when the patient arrived at the hospital and worsened when instruments were used to scrape out the remaining segments of afterbirth from the uterus. I remember thinking "God, it's like I turned on a faucet!" I had many such operations, and always I marveled at how this "faucet" turned off as soon as all the placental tissue was removed. Once the emergency was over, the important work of emotionally supporting the patient began.

Before I leave this subject I feel compelled to say that GYN surgery or, for that matter, any surgery, is invasive and carries the potential for severe complications. Surgeons therefore must carefully weigh their indications for surgery as well as their options; and in doing so, be very sure that a particular operation is necessary for the welfare of the patient.

THE "LACK MONSTER"

The telephone kept close company with me throughout my career. If I had to personify it, I would have it represented by a lack monster: lack of sleep, lack of food, lack of fun, lack of life. It seemed that I never attained a deep sleep, as I always grabbed the phone before the first ring was completed. I then immediately cleared my mind so as not to miss anything the nurse was telling me. I could then give her accurate and concise verbal orders, an ability that comes about only after much interrupted sleep.

One particular night was preceded by several nights of back-to-back sleepless torture, involving tubal pregnancies, emergency Caesarians, and an array of assorted but interesting deliveries, including twins and a breech presentation. I barely dragged myself home that evening and was even stopped by a local town cop, as I slowly drove through his village. It seemed my car was weaving, and he thought he was catching a drunk. Bed felt awfully good that night, until I was once again awakened by that horrible ring. Whipping up the receiver as I normally did, I heard the nurse speaking to me; however, it

22

occurred to me that something was wrong. I could hear her voice, but I wasn't able to put together what she was saying. It might as well have been in Arabic. My brain wasn't working! I knew I was desperately tired, but I couldn't even communicate that. After a few minutes of a frustrating one-way conversation, I forced myself to tell the nurse that I would call her back. This dull feeling, this inability to jumpstart the cognitive function of my conscious mind, was not just weird, it was downright scary. I began to pace around my bed in an attempt to bring myself to a higher level of alertness, which I finally achieved in ten or fifteen minutes. I then called back and could finally focus on the issues. I'm very thankful that this exasperating and rather frightening experience happened to me only once in my career. We OB/GYN physicians have enough problems skating through liability minefields and certainly do not need the added worry of misunderstanding nighttime communications due to excessive fatigue.

SO YOU WANT TO BE A PHYSICIAN

The nurses were good at what they did, so when I could detect a sense of urgency in their voice when they called me from the ER, I knew there was a major problem waiting for me. Unfortunately, this was often the case in the early hours of the morning. I would dress and be out the door and on my way within minutes. As I pushed my car beyond its usual limits on country roads, I would be preoccupied with a multitude of thoughts ringing in my mind. Had I missed anything? I went through mental checklists as my speedometer crept up to 90. I thought of what might be awaiting me: a woman in cold shock with a belly full of blood, difficulty getting the right blood type, a Jehovah's Witness declining blood, a ruptured tubal pregnancy, and on and on. My mind was racing, filling me with all kinds of emotions, both positive and negative. Sure, I felt a sense of confidence from my extensive training, and yes, I understood that enough experience can make handling a difficult situation second nature. However, I also knew that things can happen that are beyond my control, causing my

23

patient's condition to deteriorate rapidly. My hospital did not have a resident physician or intern staff, so as a solo physician on call, I was just that: solo. Everything that was going to happen was up to me. I was the man, the captain of the ship. In the early morning hours, the only other physician around was the ER doc, who was usually of no help in obstetrical or surgical situations.

In a typical case, I arrive with spring in my step and hurry to the ER, where I evaluate the patient and come up with a tentative diagnosis of acute abdomen (extremely painful and tender abdomen) and hypovolemic shock (inadequate blood volume from probable hemorrhage, causing rapid pulse and decreasing blood pressure). Since the patient has a positive pregnancy test, I am betting on a ruptured tubal pregnancy. Time is now critical, as I quickly complete preparations for surgery, which includes speaking to the family and having them sign the consents if the patient is unable to do so. The patient is rushed to surgery, blood is started, and as I scrub, I hear the sad tale from the anesthesiologist about how the patient just ate a full meal within the past few hours. Add one more problem to the list, I'm thinking, as I make an incision. I'm also thinking those ruptured tubes bleed like hell, that is, until the blood pressure drops too low. How's that for a paradox? As I enter the abdomen I'm greeted by massive blood clots. We suction like crazy until I can finally see and feel the enlarged, bleeding fallopian tube and place a clamp on the pumping artery. Everyone now breathes a little easier, and the pace slows down.

With another case wrapped up, I head for the shower and dressing room, clean up, make rounds, and head back to surgery for my scheduled morning cases, grabbing a few graham crackers and coffee on the way — standard hospital supply that has sustained me through the years. Office hours start at 1:00 PM, so I try to look fresh and wide awake. It doesn't work. The schedule is brutal and twice a week extends into the evening to help working patients. Finishing up about 9:00 PM, I drag myself to my car and drive slowly home with my windows open to keep me awake. All the way home, I'm hoping that my

24

OB patients that are due will hold off a few more days. I grab a late dinner and fall into bed, seemingly just in time to hear that awful ring again. As I pick up the phone I hear, "Mrs. So and So is in early labor." All of a sudden I'm wide awake and have to make a decision. Do I go to bed and wait for another call and head into the hospital when this patient is in active labor? I would love to put my head on my pillow right now, but I probably would not be able to sleep, knowing that patients in labor are full of surprises, that the phone might soon ring again, and knowing that I would then have to practically fly to the hospital. So once again, I am up and on my way, yawning all the way to the hospital and hoping to get a few hours of sleep there before my daily schedule begins.

This stressful life-style that every dedicated obstetrician understands and fully accepts when he or she chooses this specialty, continued on in this vein year after year with no letup. Only rarely did I finally concede and cancel office hours to get some sleep. Would you say that this type of life led to constant interference with my family and social life? Absolutely. I soon learned never to buy tickets for anything ahead of time. My family said they understood, but I heard much in the way of complaints when I missed birthday parties, first communions, school plays, football games- you name it.

WELCOME TO HOSPITAL POLITICS

Practicing in a hospital almost guarantees your involvement in hospital politics, even when you attempt to maintain a low profile as I did. My first "stick to your principles" experience with this malady occurred in my second year of practice. The hospital was young and for the most part run by family doctors known as GPs, or general practitioners, who delivered the majority of the babies. I was one of a few OB/GYN specialists in the area that would be called upon to take over complicated cases for the GPs. After my first year in practice, it was obvious to me that one of the GPs was not well trained and was actually downright dangerous in the delivery room. I bore witness to this abomination of the delivery room process and couldn't believe my eyes at the time. The nurses were very aware of the situation and were constantly complaining. During a monthly physician staff meeting, this problem was brought up by the OB department but was immediately watered down by the GP staff. At that moment I threw caution to the wind and did the unspeakable. I stood up, addressed the entire staff of family doctors and voiced my objection. I remember my words as if they were carved in granite, because when I boldly uttered them, you could hear a pin drop, along with my standing among the GPs: "Why do all of you protect an incompetent?" In spite of the shake-up at the staff meeting, I was able to start the ball rolling, and by the end of that year, that particular GPs OB privileges had been revoked, an action that was applauded by doctors and nurses alike.

As the years passed, I was elected to various staff positions. A few months before I was to become the new chief of obstetrics and gynecology, I found myself in an awkward situation, one where I had to blow the whistle on a chemically dependent colleague who had been acting strangely at the hospital on several occasions. There was virtually no choice in the matter, when the OB nurse paged me in a panic and insisted that I scrub in on a C-section he had just begun. It seems that he was acting peculiarly and operating in a bizarre and unacceptable manner. Within minutes of my scrubbing in on the case to assist him, I had to relieve him of instruments and take over the surgery. This was a difficult undertaking but extremely necessary, as the patient was bleeding profusely from unnecessarily rough handling of her organs. I was able to stop the hemorrhage and deliver the infant uneventfully. This doctor's hospital privileges were suspended while he entered a detoxification program and began his rehabilitation.

THE UNSPEAKABLE HAPPENS

During my fifth year in practice I was elected president of the county Medical Society; however, that year is burned into my memory for a much more important reason. It was in that fateful year that I

26

had a maternal death, something about which every obstetrician has nightmares.

It was a relatively quiet evening in the hospital as I slept in the doctors' room, while one of my patients labored. This particular patient was a registered nurse in labor with her third child. She made a rather unusual comment to me when she was admitted, saying she had a feeling that she would not live through this delivery. I reassured her that everything was fine and figured that as a nurse, she was much more aware of the problems that could develop and therefore was overly nervous.

The nurse on call awakened me in a panic and breathlessly cried out, "Your patient went into convulsions when the anesthesiologist injected the caudal anesthesia! Come quickly!" I dropped the phone, grabbed my shoes, and ran down the hall, my heart racing. The nurse and anesthesiologist had already begun to move the patient's bed into the hall. I joined them, and we literally ran the bed into the delivery room. The patient slipped into respiratory arrest as we got her onto the delivery table. The nurse then reported, "There's no heartbeat!" We began resuscitation and continued until I came to that awful real-ization that the mother was not coming back. In seconds I opened the abdomen and removed the baby by postmortem C-section. The lack of maternal bleeding was eerie, as I handed the limp infant to the nurse. Soon, the baby was breathing and pinking up. We had a live baby, but one with brain damage. As I later found out, it was cerebral palsy - the terrible, permanent physical disability that will overshadow the indi-vidual's life, and change everyone's life around him. My blood ran cold with this prospect as scenes from my own personal life flooded my mind, scenes of my own sister growing up with this same life-altering condition.

People exhibit a variety of behavior in the presence of a handi-capped person, especially a severely handicapped person. I recall my high school buddies speaking loudly to my sister, thinking that she would understand them better. Many people assumed she was mentally retarded as well, but nothing could be farther from the truth. My parents and I took an affront to such assumptions and became quite intolerant of people's ignorance of such conditions, causing us to pick and choose our friends accordingly. As I looked back, I realized how unreasonable and unnecessary our protective attitude was. I can also understand how families of handicapped children become entangled with false fears involving strong negative emotions, such as guilt, blame, and anger. These are traps that await the families of handicapped children as these children grow up; and this negative emotional entrapment will often affect the entire family. This destructive force places undue strain on their relationships, the consequences of which may last a lifetime.

These deeply engrained memories dimmed as I refocused on the present case I had just been involved with. The words maternal death struck deeply into my heart and mind. The next several days were brutal, as I tried desperately to shake off depression and lack of confidence. In my heart I knew I had done everything that I could, and I had done it right. As I later found out, the anesthesiologist had used a new drug that later became linked to many maternal deaths. It was discovered that when this medication was administered in a bolus (a large amount at one time) during conduction anesthesia, the patient would respond with convulsions, respiratory arrest, and finally, cardiac arrest, which was exceptionally resistant to resuscitation. The anesthesiologist was sued for malpractice, and as per usual, the plaintiff's lawyer shotgunned and dragged the hospital and me into the lawsuit. Several decades later I still empathize with the child's father and feel his pain, for I know that story well.

THE PRAGMATIC CHIEF

As chief of surgery in my later years of practice, I often found myself in departmental meetings settling political disputes and petty arguments among the surgeons. One of my most humorous yet very pragmatic contributions to the department of surgery was to eventually convince the hospital administration to have food available in the surgeons' lounge. My surgical peers had a good time poking fun at my "great accomplishment." Actually, they were very appreciative, and this food was a godsend, as surgery often went over the scheduled time, leaving the surgeon starving and late for the office.

THE SEDUCTION OF DRUGS

In my first few years of practice, when I decided to not rush patients through office hours, I also made a vow that I would not just throw medicine at them, but rather listen and talk with them. These courteous, caring, and compassionate thoughts regarding patients stayed with me throughout my career and did not falter, even in the face of growing pressure from patients who felt that they must be given drugs in order to feel better. The growing power of the drug companies and the idea of a pill for everything was beginning to really annoy me. I thought to myself that people may just want to stop numbing their perception of life with drugs and medicines of all kinds. They may just want to experience reality to the fullest, with a heightened sense of awareness, not a drug-induced dullness. They may just want to open their clouded, tranquilized minds to clearly see the things that really count in life. In short, they may want to choose joy, happiness, and good health as their life-style and not give in to the hypnotic seduction of drug commercials.

The unbelievably wealthy drug companies pour billions of dollars annually into advertising media with the express purpose of indoctrinating the public into believing that they cannot live without these drugs. Every day millions of people fall prey to the heartfelt jargon that comes across the TV screen in the form of drug commercials. The actors are chosen for their look of sincerity so that every word they utter rings with unembellished truth. The public is enticed into believing they have ailments they can't even pronounce.

Drug stores are becoming more common than gas stations. The demand for drugs is great. The media has made sure of that. Over-the-counter and prescription drugs seem to be the in thing. We cannot envision a healthful, contented life without them. Many doctors have also fallen in line for the drug companies. The thinking now is that every problem requires a medicine, pills of some sort, and the drug salesmen are only too happy to unload plenty of samples on the doctors. This kind of reasoning is unfortunately encouraged by managed care, which severely limits the time that a physician can spend with a patient.

Patients have come to expect to leave the doctor's office with several prescriptions for various medications. If they don't, they feel cheated. Many physicians understand this present-day attitude of patients and cave in to their demands. Others go along with the program because they have very little time in which to see a large number of patients, and it's easier and quicker to prescribe medications that the patient has already decided he needs than to get into long discussions about why he thinks he needs them. Fortunately, there still are some physicians who are holding the line by refusing to give in to the pitfalls of managed care and the drug companies' enticement. There are physicians who feel they ought to be just that, a physician. They will take the time to listen to their patients and give them the benefit of their experience and knowledge. Medications are important and often very necessary, but there is a lot more to practicing medicine than dispensing drugs, and sometimes it is better not to dispense them at all.

MANAGED CARE: THE NEW PURGATORY

Managed care has become a breeding ground for increasing malpractice cases. Insurance company reimbursements are a fraction of what a physician would normally receive for services. Appointment schedules allow less time for the individual, and are filled completely so enough income is available to justify the massive overhead, the largest chunk of which is malpractice insurance. The amount of time spent with a patient has become inversely proportional to the amount of malpractice cases filed. If patients feel they have lost their individuality and are merely numbers, they are not going to be very forgiving of mistakes. However, if they have a good rapport with their doctor and know that he cares about them and will take time with them if they need it, they will be much less likely to sue for malpractice.

Having been there myself, I can appreciate the predicament that physicians find themselves in. If you spend more time with patients or decrease your load of patients, your income suffers, and you may have trouble meeting your overhead. So what's the answer? There are no simple answers; they're all tough! I can only speak from experience. I handled this situation by allowing a set amount of time for each patient but took extra time when I saw that it was necessary. After a while the patients in the waiting room would await their turn without complaining, knowing that they would also be given extra time with their doctor if they needed it. This would sometimes result in longer waiting periods for patients and longer hours for me. My secretaries and office manager would frequently talk to the patients in the waiting room to keep them abreast of how my schedule was running. Knowing the patients and having a rapport with them was the key to a successful and less liability-prone practice. The patients somehow knew that my office represented kindness, care, and compassion, and that made the difference, even when my appointments were frequently interrupted with deliveries, emergency surgery, or calls from the hospital. In spite of these many disruptions in my schedule, I very much enjoyed and looked forward to the time I spent in the office seeing my patients.

TIME TO HANG IT UP

A common thread that often runs through our thoughts is that we live forever. The same kind of thinking exists in most doctors' minds when it comes to how long they will practice their craft. I was one of these physicians who felt that I would be doing surgery and delivering babies until I dropped dead in my tracks. This was for two reasons: one was financial survival, and the other reason was that this is what I do, what I trained for, and yes, it's still a labor of love.

31

Little did I know that my last year in practice was fast approaching. I had begun to have numbness and paresthesia (pins and needles feeling) in the fingers of my left hand. This symptom was soon followed by sharp left-shoulder pain, which became worse as the cold, wet winter progressed. My orthopedic buddies diagnosed severe degenerative cervical arthritis. I remember that the X-rays of the cervical vertebrae were so obviously involved with arthritic changes that even I could make the diagnosis. Actually, it looked as if someone had whitewashed my neck with a paintbrush. In spite of physical therapy and medication, the problem worsened with the flexion of my head, which occurred almost constantly during surgery, office exams, and paperwork.

My thirty-second year in practice was a tough one. I found myself running into unbelievably unusual situations, especially in obstetrics. A case in point was a laboring patient with placenta acreta, a rare condition in which the afterbirth is fused to the musculature of the uterus and cannot cleanly separate after delivery, causing massive hemorrhage. I had managed such a case for a family doctor in my third year of practice. By the time I was called, the patient had lost tremendous amounts of blood. In those days we placed blood pressure cuffs over the plastic bags of blood and pumped the blood into the patient as fast as possible as we performed the surgery. That particular day I was pretty proud of myself in that I was able to get into this patient's belly and stop the bleeding before the shock did her in. There was no choice in the matter; her uterus had to be removed, the usual treatment rendered in these situations.

I ended up with three of these rare placenta acreta cases that year, all proven pathologically. I was able to save the uterus in two of the cases by temporarily packing it with several cloth packs that I tied together and fed directly into the uterus through the incisional opening from the C-section. According to the literature, this technique was rarely successful, however I chose to try it, hoping to give these young women another opportunity to have more children. As it happened, we lucked out both times.

Thus my last year in practice was exciting and oh, yes, full of hospital political drama. I had been elected vice-chief of staff and was immersed in the usual political upheavals of the day. I was being groomed to be the next chief of staff, however the pain and paresthesia continued to worsen, forcing me to make the big decision that most doctors dread. Within a month I chose to throw in the towel and move to a warm, dry climate, another choice I will never regret. Little did I know that a new profession awaited me there.

4

TRANSITION TO TRANSCENDENCE

Having developed an avid interest in hypnosis during my last ten years of practice and following training in this discipline, I discovered that it was not only interesting, but also downright fascinating. Working with the subconscious mind was something that was totally foreign to me; however, as I continued to delve further into this new and exciting world of altered consciousness, I sensed that there was a great potential for treating many medical conditions or for augmenting the usual conventional treatment for these conditions. Besides helping alleviate anxiety, fears, and phobias, I was able to rid patients of harmful habits and addictive tendencies. Within a short time I was using hypnosis to relieve the pain of labor and delivery for those patients who were eager to try this. I was also able to alleviate various forms of chronic pain, for which surgery was no longer an option. Cases of sexual dysfunction and chronic nausea and vomiting of pregnancy underwent remarkable improvement. As I became more and more astonished with the results that I was seeing, I found myself stepping back and taking another look at the power of the mind.

Just as I was attaining a strong foothold into the use of this surprisingly powerful medical modality, the Gulf War began, and my Air Force Reserve unit was placed on alert status. Within two weeks my squadron was activated, and I was gone from my practice. This came as a shock to many of my patients, as they had to be immediately referred to other doctors for prenatal care, upcoming surgery, and an assortment of GYN-related problems. I felt uncomfortable about leaving my medical practice in such confusion; but I was fortunate to have my wife and daughter stay on top of things and keep the practice together as much as possible. They fielded the many phone calls and assisted a good-Samaritan gynecologist who offered his kind help and saw my patients three evenings a week following his grueling days in surgery. This generous help was above and beyond the call of duty, especially since he drove a considerable distance and had to substitute fast food for good dinners at home in the process.

Returning home several months later I found that I was only able to devote a minimal amount of time to hypnosis, since I had to rebuild my practice by extending my hours in two offices. I also came home to a financial crisis, since my income had decreased dramatically while my overhead had remained the same. As the following months passed, my practice grew and again became quite busy. I once more regained my enthusiasm for hypnosis but by now I had read enough about past-life regression that I felt comfortable in taking the plunge and conducting my own sessions.

As it turns out, I was astounded at the number of patients who displayed an open mind in regard to reincarnation and were extremely eager to undergo a hypnotic regression into the past so as to help explain the present. The therapeutic effects were unmistakably beneficial. Several patients with various forms of terminal cancer appeared to find an inner peace by discovering that their present life was just one of many lives that they had lived and will live. They saw themselves die and be reborn over and over; and this realization instilled a great comfort within them, for now they had a sense of knowing without reservation that their soul lives on forever as it sheds its temporal physical body from lifetime to lifetime.

My passion for past-life regression grew in leaps and bounds and markedly accelerated when I found that I was able to validate many of these lifetimes. I discovered that the most opportune time to carry out regression sessions in my main office was after hours on the days I didn't work late. I also figured out that I could use my time wisely on weekends while waiting for patients who were laboring in the hospital. This worked out quite well, since my main office was adjacent to the hospital, and I could set my beeper on vibration.

In my remaining years of practice, I found that hypnosis and past-life regression therapy were invaluable tools for my patients. I also sensed that I was undergoing a metamorphosis, a steady and unwavering transformation into someone I knew a lot better, someone with a very different outlook and different aspirations from the person that I knew before. As I conducted more regressions, I had the feeling that I was opening a door to the unknown, to places that could help unlock the mysteries of the mind or, for that matter, the universe.

Engendering the same strong sense of purpose and unfettered motivation that I displayed in the early years of my medical training and practice, I began to hurl myself wholeheartedly into this captivating discipline which I now considered a virtual treasure-house of help and healing for many people. This forceful endeavor was extremely difficult to accomplish in the face of a full-time solo OB/GYN practice, so I reluctantly tempered my enthusiasm and incorporated the use of hypnotherapy and past-life regression therapy whenever I felt it was appropriate to do so.

In order that you gain a better understanding and appreciation of the process of regression, I will expound on some of the fine points of its basic components, namely, hypnosis, hypnotherapy, and past-life regression therapy. In addition, we will look at twin conceptual doctrines that are inherently related: reincarnation and karma.

DISCOVERING THE POWER OF HYPNOSIS

How shall we define hypnosis? The definition I prefer is an altered state of consciousness which is induced by another person; it resembles sleep but is not sleep. It is characterized by the presence of profound mental concentration, extreme physical relaxation, an increased susceptibility of the subconscious mind to acceptable suggestions, and access to memories long since forgotten.

In actuality, the subject is hypnotizing himself while being directed by the hypnotherapist. There are many misconceptions regarding hypnosis, so let's dispel them:

- The subject will lose control. Absolutely not! The subject is always in control.
- Will I be asleep? No; the hypnotic state resembles sleep. The conscious mind is fully awake and all senses are functioning.
- The subject can be made to do anything. Wrong! The subject's conscious mind is fully aware of what is transpiring and can refuse to carry out suggestions that seem inappropriate.
- What if the subject can't awaken? It won't happen; however, the relaxation is often so enjoyable that some decide to enjoy it for a few moments longer. If the hypnotherapist leaves the hypnotized subject alone indefinitely, the subject will awaken spontaneously or will fall asleep, then awaken naturally.
- Strong-willed subjects cannot be hypnotized. Not true! Good subjects are not only strong-willed but intelligent and imaginative.
- There may be dangers involved in hypnosis. This is never true as long as the subject is not a threat to himself or others originally. I always eliminate this remote possibility by interviewing my subjects prior to hypnosis.
- Unpleasant experiences may occur during regression. This is not the case, since I invoke suggestions prior to the regressions that help the subject to avoid emotional or physical discomfort and negative feelings.
- A person can be hypnotized against his will. No. A subject's cooperation is necessary for hypnosis to occur.
- The subject's will power will be weakened. This can never occur. Hypnosis intends to help the individual in a positive way.
- Do repeated sessions increase the hypnotizability of the subject? Yes. The extent of relaxation and depth of trance will improve as the number of sessions increases.

- What qualities should the subject strive for in order to be hypnotized? Motivation and cooperation.

In my experience approximately 90% of those hypnotized will experience recall of a past life or a spiritual experience. With persistence, practically everyone can be hypnotized; however, an individual will not be hypnotized if he does not wish to be.

Hypnosis sets the stage for healing to occur through the process of hypnotherapy and regression. It allows the subconscious to take center stage within the spotlight, and at the same time removes the conscious mind from the stage and gives it a front row seat in the audience. The stage is now set for healing, using the power of the more intuitive and protective subconscious mind.

The little-known proven fact that a woman's breast size can be increased by hypnotic techniques suggests that we are altering cellular growth with our subconscious mind. How powerful is the mind? More powerful than we could ever imagine, and I firmly believe that hypnosis is the key that will eventually unlock that mystery and benefit humankind beyond its wildest dreams.

Hypnosis needs to be recognized for the massive good it can accomplish. It needs to be extracted from its abomination as stage entertainment and rightfully take its place in medicine as an exceptional healing modality. Its potential has been too long ignored.

PAST-LIFE REGRESSION HYPNOTHERAPY

Hypnotherapy utilizes hypnosis as a therapeutic tool to confront and eliminate the subject's fears and phobias, as well as his anxieties, addictive tendencies, and habits, which are undesirable and pernicious in regard to his vitality and his emotional and physical health. This therapy can be successfully accomplished, employing deep hypnosis in combination with positive suggestions to the subconscious mind; however, if past-life regression techniques are incorporated into this regime, the cure rate of emotional and physical problems esca-

38

lates dramatically. Why is this so? Simply because the subconscious mind is a virtual reservoir of complete and intricately detailed memories of one's life experiences, regardless of whether they occurred in the present or the past. These experiences are like computer programs that condition our physical and emotional responses to everything life has to offer, everything that comes into our consciousness through our physical senses.

The subconscious mind not only recalls every moment of every life but also integrates this information so that it interacts with — and many times overrides — our conscious thoughts by giving us a specific attitude and emotional feeling about everything in life, thus laying the groundwork of our personality and giving credence to the idea that we are presently the sum total of all of our previous personalities. Of paramount importance here is the fact that the distinction of time when an event took place is conspicuously absent when the subconscious files memories away. In some ways we are like robots, giving in to the easier thought which may have been laid down for us centuries ago.

I believe that the energy that we call our soul or consciousness carries this subconscious memory with it into the spiritual realm when we experience physical death, thus allowing the soul to carry out its life review. Everything that occurs in this afterlife dimension occurs in the Now: the past and the future are indistinguishable from the present, since there is no *time* in this realm. The subconscious memories of the soul become "knowing" as the soul's energy takes on full expression, unlike its "compressed" status in the physical body. I further believe that the subconscious retains this afterlife quality of the soul that does not distinguish time and carries this over from lifetime to lifetime. Therefore, recall of a negative incident which happened hundreds of years ago will affect the subconscious to the same degree as one which has just occurred, thus allowing faulty negative programming to dominate a person's present life without really relating to it. On the other hand, *time* appears to be a logical construct of

39

physical life on Earth, one which is necessary for an individual's consciousness to make sense of its human sensory input. It fits well in this dimension of sunrise and sunset and interfaces propitiously with our mortality as physical beings.

Skeptics love to throw cold water on anything that occurs outside the so-called *normal* box. Past-life regression is no exception. Some skeptics look at these lives as stories made up to impress the hypnotherapist. Others consider these lives fantasy, or bizarre or highly imaginative memories. Still others believe them to be mental images which are similar to dreams and are somehow related to one's aspirations, desires, and fears. The criticisms are many and diverse and as extreme as they are incongruous. Truly, where do these 'lives' come from? I have asked myself this question many times in my earliest experiences with regression. As Dick Sutphen often states during his seminars, "Your experience is your reality." My experience tells me that yes, these lives are authentic and fulfill the criteria of truth for that individual. I believe the subject either lived that life, was a partial essence of that soul, or somehow tapped into that life within the Akashic records. We are unaware of the universal laws that govern other realms, so we must be open-minded enough to view these events with basic common sense and not fully expect to prove the existence of these lives scientifically, using the physical laws of nature as we know them. I would be hard-pressed to believe that the hundreds of thousands of past-life regressions and future-life progressions that have been carried out over the last twenty-five-plus years are all products of talented screenwriters or prize-winning novelists. The stories that come through in moment-to-moment drama or in an overview style depict the true human condition on this Earth with all its ramifications of raw realism. This is especially true, since the subject has all of his physical senses involved and is experiencing a full-spectrum of emotions that is occurring in that lifetime. Some subjects are better than others in recalling past lives; however, a subject will usually tend to increase his awareness within those lifetimes as he undergoes more regressions. A favorite comment among subjects is "Where did that come from?" In my mind, there is no mistaking that this memory came from the subject's subconscious mind.

After conducting thousands of past-life regressions, I have come to believe that every cell in our physical body and possibly the most minute of subatomic particles within our body retain the subconscious memory, replete with the emotional impact of the moment. This so-called 'cell memory' — a term used by several authors, is often thought to be related to various maladies of one's physical body that occurred during a past lifetime. This is especially true if the injury was serious or resulted in the death of that individual in a prior lifetime. It seems that the area of the body that was involved in the injury or death blow now becomes a target for pain in one's present life. The pain in that specific area of the body can be brought on by a person, place, thing or event related to that prior lifetime, thus allowing the cell memory to subconsciously surface along with the pain and its attendant emotions. In my experience I have observed this entire scenario, resulting from the subconscious recognition of a person from that life or something as minor as an odor, a sound, or a word that serves as a catalyst that triggers the subconscious recall of this emotionally-laden cell memory.

Scientific proof regarding the presence of subconscious cell memory will not be easily forthcoming; however, a proof of sorts has surfaced from research done on heart and other organ transplant recipients. Many of these recipients have reported all types of changes in personality, including preferences for music and food. What's remarkable is that these changes in preferences of the personality parallel those of the deceased donor. Paul Pearsall, Ph.D., a psychoneuroimmunologist and author of *The Heart's Code*, reported on the case of a nine-year-old girl who was the recipient of an eight-year-old girl's heart. The 8-year-old donor had been murdered. Following the transplant, the 9-year-old heart recipient began to have lucid dreams about the crime and was able to identify the murderer, who was subsequently apprehended and convicted.

My experience in taking subjects back to the cause of physical problems related to certain parts of the body has convinced me that the "cell memory" referred to in transplant research is actually subconscious cell memory, which is fully retrievable by the subconscious mind under hypnosis.

Following physical death the conscious mind appears to be fully aware of the details of the transition into a spiritual dimension. Thus the conscious awareness in the afterlife is similar and at the same time different from that which is present in the physical body. One's higher consciousness appears to prevail, thus causing attitudes and emotions to differ from those that existed on Earth. Life in spirit form is dominated by love, truth, wisdom, and an overwhelming feeling of belonging. Appearances, communication, travel, and many other facets of life in the spirit world are dictated by the laws that exist in that realm, most of which are unknown to us.

Sneak previews giving a glimpse of life in the afterlife have been afforded us by brilliant and courageous authors who have pioneered the afterlife experience. These authors include Dr. Raymond Moody, with his landmark work on near-death experiences, and Michael Newton, Ph.D., in his book *Journey of Souls*. My experience in regressing subjects into the afterlife appears to coincide with the work of these authors.

As a physician, I am both intrigued and enthralled by the therapeutic use of past-life regression, and so I would like to expound on my thoughts in this area. Some of my beliefs may coincide with those of other authors who have fearlessly pioneered this heretofore unexplored territory of the mind and brought forth a methodology which, according to conventional medicine, is unorthodox and smacks of metaphysical overtones. These very astute and intuitive authors realized the value and potential applications inherent in such inquiries into the subconscious mind and soon began to promulgate past-life regression therapy as a successful alternative treatment for many conditions for which conventional medical treatment was only partially helpful at best.

I personally feel that the applications of such therapy are potentially limitless. Modern-day medicine acknowledges the presence of an emotional component in certain illnesses such as asthma, colitis, and ulcers, to name a few. I contend that all illnesses have an emotional component, affecting it in one way or another, and patients have the potential to improve more rapidly and completely with conventional treatment when such regression therapy is instituted and followed by positive suggestions to the subconscious.

Negative thinking may have its origins in current thoughts or from deep-seated negative programming of the subconscious mind from centuries ago. Either way, the effect is the same, causing havoc in one's reality and a virtual eruption of negative emotions which in turn has a detrimental effect on many organ systems in the body, often leading to illness. Thus, past-life regression therapy affords us the opportunity to eliminate this entire negative process that can lead to illness and to avoid this succession of events in the future.

The use of past-life regression therapy is extremely beneficial when preceded by nonspecific instructions from the hypnotherapist designed to help the subject understand more completely what is restricting joy, peace, and growth in his present lifetime. The regression process gives permission to the subconscious mind to retrieve these vivid memories of the past and at the same time allow the subject's conscious mind to be totally aware of the process he is going through. In this way observations and judgments can be made regarding the timing, content, and often cathartic emotions involved in the past experiences, which may have occurred in one's present life or in a past life.

A unique aspect of the regression process is that there is also a second conscious awareness present, one that existed at the time the life experience first occurred, before the memory was filed away into the subconscious mind. When regressed, the subject soon finds himself immersed in an extraordinary reality wherein he is functioning within the framework of two separate conscious states, which appear to compliment each other as they integrate and interact under the orchestration of the subconscious mind and under the direction of the hypnotherapist. The subject's current state of consciousness is fully cognizant of his other conscious awareness which is bearing witness to all aspects of the past time being recalled, including the subtlest and most delicate of feelings. Such a state of consciousness compels the subject to truly believe that he is actually there in that past life, perceiving reality through his five senses, reacting through the full spectrum of emotions, and making rational judgments then, much as he is now, in his present state of consciousness. This duality of awareness allows one's present consciousness to not only observe but also be objective in its interpretation of these events occurring in the past, and, in doing so, easily identify negative patterns that relate to one's current life. At the same time, he may achieve a sense of whether or not he is progressing as he should. For many individuals, this unique form of 'time travel' is an overwhelming experience; for most subjects, it is an unparalleled experience, one that profoundly affects their lives in a positive way.

When specific instructions are given to the subject's subconscious mind under deep hypnosis with regard to the cause of physical and emotional problems, great strides can be made in his treatment. The subconscious mind is very protective of the individual and will often zero in to the precise event or events that contributed to the negative programming responsible for the particular problem being examined. Often the emotions encountered are very strong, and occasionally physical discomforts can be very real. I purposely invoke protective suggestions to avoid such emotional or physical discomfort, or for that matter, extreme sadness. I do not believe it is necessary to concentrate or focus on the degree of discomfort that is programmed into the subconscious memory. Rather, I believe the subject's present conscious awareness will unmistakably understand the relationship that this previously suppressed memory has to his present problem inclusive of the timing and circumstances involved. The rational conscious mind must be made to understand that the subconscious does not make any distinction of time when allowing an emotional or physical effect to evolve from a causal event in the past and impact the present. This revelation usually evokes a response in the form of a conscious thought, such as "this occurred a long time ago and really does not relate to me or my present life now." In this way the subject recognizes that his emotional or physical problem is based upon false beliefs which have come about through misperception and misinterpretation of past life memories that have resurfaced.

Once subconscious programming is recognized for what it truly is, the present conscious mind can now begin the process of releasing the effect that the subject is enduring in his present life, namely, the physical discomfort and emotional turmoil that he has unconsciously chosen to live with. Dr. Adrian Finkelstein adroitly picked up on this process many years ago in his book, *Your Past Lives and the Healing Process*. In his book he says, "Healing occurs when, through one or more processes, a harmonious relationship is effected between the conscious and subconscious minds."[1] Exposing the negative past event or events that are responsible for the subject's problem is often sufficient in itself; however, it may be necessary to forgive oneself or others involved in the event to facilitate a greater degree of resolution of the problem. Dick Sutphen advocates such an approach and further suggests that sometimes the subject may want to do something more in his life so as to release the effect, the so-called symbolic resolution. Such past-life therapy is very effective, often dramatic in its results, and many times surprising to the subject, who never dreamed his problem was rooted in emotionally laden, negative programming that occurred a long time ago.

---

1. Finklestein, *Your Past Lives and the Healing Process*, Malibu CA: 50 Gates Publishing Co., p. 97.

All energy vibrates, and the soul is no exception. The soul is pure energy. It exists at a higher vibration in the spiritual plane without the confines of the physical body. This vibration is further increased as the soul advances in awareness by growing in knowledge and wisdom. This growth can be accelerated when the soul decides to incarnate on Earth again for the purpose of learning lessons, so it may continue to evolve toward its goal of perfection. Earth is often referred to as a kind of school where lessons are learned. The challenges here can be very difficult, putting our free will to the ultimate test; however, the soul can also look upon this incarnation as an opportunity to advance more rapidly and thus look forward to the challenges. By incarnating again, the soul once more chooses its lessons and its parents and lays out a general blueprint for its life which may not be recognizable later, since conscious memory fades following an incarnation and one's free will changes circumstances.

The growth of the soul is bound irrevocably to its karmic responsibilities, the law of cause and effect. It is within this universal framework that an individual's subconscious programming interfaces with his experience so as to initiate the molding of an attitude which is then tempered by his analytical conscious mind and his free will. Such perspectives help make up one's personality and may be a positive or negative influence on his level of awareness in this lifetime.

During human existence an individual must somehow rise above the superficialities of daily living and be curious enough to ask himself, "Who am I, really? Why am I here? Where did I come from? Where do I go when I leave this Earth?" If such questions haven't arisen under normal circumstances of living, these thoughts may become unavoidable when tragedy befalls one and propels such questions to the forefront of the conscious mind.

One must be interested enough to seriously ponder the meaning of the soul and how it relates to life on Earth. When this occurs, the individual will find that he is experiencing a deep frustration and disappointment as he seeks answers from others, from books, and from

46

organized religion. Eventually he will find himself turning inward for answers and in doing so, discover his Higher Self and his intuition, the voice of his soul.

My research has led me to believe that looking within oneself is the only path to discovering Ultimate Truth. Such a quest will lead one to understand that the answers to all questions, including those pertaining to the mysteries of the universe, are to be found within one's very being. These answers flow from the same spark of the Creator that resides in all of us, the spiritual reality that defines our divine origin. The magnificent power of man's soul lies within his knowing, the deep realization that he is an eternal being. His soul lives forever, and therefore nothing can truly harm him.

I have further concluded that this knowing is the spiritual strength that allows the body and mind to heal themselves, using the awesome power of the mind, the extent of which has yet to be revealed. Hypnotic past-life regression therapy acts as a key which can unlock the mysterious domain of the subconscious mind. This in turn allows an individual to tap into his Higher Self, and in doing so, become aware of his roots which are imbedded in spiritual soil, originating from a divine source. Once the subconscious mind is asked to go back in time and search out the cause of a particular emotional or physical problem, the conscious mind is brought into play and is now able to work in concert with the subconscious and thereby make a rational judgment regarding what was brought forth by the subconscious, thus setting the stage for healing to occur.

This account of my observations and conclusions regarding the use of hypnotic past-life regression therapy strikes an uncanny parallel to the beliefs of an ancient religious movement that preceded and followed the life of Christ. This movement was known as Gnosticism, referring to the Greek word, "gnosis," meaning knowledge. The Gnostics held that a broader perspective of reality and other realms could be accessed through intuition and contemplation, which would ultimately lead to introspection. They had little regard for organized religion and conceptual possibilities; instead, they asserted that their reality was based on existence, experience, and knowing. The introspection that followed allowed them to attain spiritual truths, and as such, know God by direct perception, not faith. Such thinking led to their denouncement as a mystical group.

The Gnostic movement became so popular by the 3rd century that the orthodox Christian church leaders declared it a heresy and did everything in their power to denigrate it and persecute its followers. As a result, the Gnostics were forced to go underground and became practically extinct; however, Gnostic philosophy resurfaced in the 20th century when their ancient lost texts and gospels were found. These findings included the Nag Hammadi Library, which was the most comprehensive collection of Gnostic writings ever discovered. These ancient scrolls were found in 1945 in Nag Hammadi, Egypt; however, the translated version was not published until 1978. As these exciting and thought-provoking historical writings were being slowly disseminated, it became obvious that there was a growing resurgence of interest in these works by those who had a void in their lives by organized religion. These Gnostic gospels, written so many centuries ago, painted a very different picture of the Gnostic movement, giving it credibility and reverence, which were long overdue.

Comparing the similarity of the mental processes leading to healing through regression therapy to the Gnostic concepts of introspection, knowing, and the use of power of the mind/soul, has led me to the point where I feel compelled to apply the term "Gnostic Healing" to the remarkable emotional and physical healing that takes place during regressive therapy.

Thus the wisdom of the soul attained through many incarnations can therefore be accessible and within reach should one seek it. Communing with one's Higher Self through hypnosis and witnessing many incarnations affords one the rare opportunity to directly relive prior-life experiences and attain wisdom without years of conscious introspection. Put in another way, hypnotic past-life regression is a shortcut to Gnosis.

In his award-winning best-seller, *The Seat of the Soul*, Gary Zukov speaks of man going beyond his five senses to attain what he terms, "a multi-sensory perception," especially in regard to understanding his soul and its influence upon his personality. With a multi-sensory perception status, an individual will find that he has the tools to recognize that the personality needs to be in balance with the soul to achieve a state of harmony. Zukov states, "Every experience that you have and will have upon the Earth encourages the alignment of your personality with your soul." I feel such an alignment enables a human being to be completely whole and centered in the universe, thus maintaining his footing on the path of life that his soul has created for him.

Sooner or later man may come to the realization that he creates his own reality and this revelation will afford him the wisdom to view life from a vastly different perspective, one in which he will find a greater opportunity to grow in awareness. Those who remain unaware of our spiritual origins will find themselves frustrated with their inability to find true happiness and peace and will thus remain spiritually stagnant throughout this lifetime and find it necessary to incarnate again for the purpose of relearning the lessons of this life.

BASIC DOCTRINES OF OUR SPIRITUAL REALITY: REINCARNATION AND KARMA

According to Webster's definition, reincarnation is the rebirth of the soul into a new body. *Encyclopedia Britannica* calls it transmigration, or metempsychosis in religion and philosophy, rebirth of the soul in one or more successive existences, which may be human, animal, or in some instances, vegetable.

Reincarnation has been referred to as natural law, a doctrine, a concept, a theory, etc. Whatever its perceptual appearance, it will be sure to arouse a spectrum of feelings and emotions in those who contemplate its true meaning. At one time or another, it has been an important part of most religions. Such a statement may invoke a goodly amount of controversy among religious groups; nonetheless, the evidence of its inclusion is rather extensive. Dr. Semkiw gives a sterling account of this very theme in his book, *Return of the Revolutionaries.*[1] He and other authors have virtually exhausted the seemingly endless succession of ramifications that stem from belief in reincarnation. They speak of very different perspectives and world views on hot topics, such as cultural and religious war, discrimination, abortion, homosexuality, world suffering, and the environment, to name a few. I am very much in agreement with what I have read by these authors; however, most of my thoughts on these and other topics are based on my reality, namely, my experience with the many subjects that I have regressed to past lives or progressed to future lives. My commentary on many of these themes is disseminated throughout this book.

Any discussion about reincarnation would be flagrantly incomplete without speaking of its inherent counterpart, the doctrine of karma. The term is derived from the Sanskrit word, karman, meaning deed or act. Sanskrit is the ancient Aryan language of the Hindus of India. Karma is the spiritual law of cause and effect, the total accumulation of one's deeds throughout the many incarnations of his existence and its profound effect in determining his fate.

This "spiritual inheritance" is in reality a balance of energy, equating actions that are good, help others, and bring harmony to the universe, with those that are evil, hurt others, and bring disharmony to the universe. Karma is not an inimical rule to be followed; it is justice in the truest sense, and its message is loud and clear: we are responsible for our actions! Whatever reality we create for ourselves in our present lifetime will be back in kind to haunt us in a future lifetime. Using the modern vernacular: "What goes around, comes around."

---

1. Semkiw, Walter, M.D., *Return of the Revolutionaries*, Hampton Roads, Charlottesville, VA, 2003

The universal law of cause and effect is unwavering. We cannot change the fact that for every action, there is a reaction. However, we can change the action, or better yet, the intention behind the action, and the attitude and thoughts that led to the intention. Sooner or later we come face to face with our mortality and ask those all-important questions about who we are and why we are here. It is then that we begin our ascent into enlightenment. It is then that we look inward for answers and it is then that we discover the most important precept of all: It's all about how you treat others.

Karma is a learning process. It's there to teach us, not punish us. Negative karmic causes in previous lives generate negative karmic effects in our present lifetime; however, I feel, as many authors do, that the understanding that comes from the wisdom of enlightenment along with intentions that stem from love and compassion, can alter and shorten such effects to the point of eliminating them.

When one realizes that he creates his own reality and calls his own shots, he understands that he and only he is responsible for his thoughts, his intentions, his attitude, and his actions. In other words, he is responsible for his life and can only blame himself for what happens in it. This is not what my Christian upbringing spoke of, nor did it mention reincarnation and karma. Thus, early in my transition I found that I needed to rethink and reexamine my belief system, but this time with an open mind.

Exercising free will means that we are making choices in our life. No matter what situations arise, we always have a choice in our reaction to them, even when we say, "I had no choice but to …" When faced with failures in life or unhappy circumstances, we can choose to maintain a positive attitude and push on, or we can choose to be depressed, blame others, and stagnate. Even in the throngs of tragedy we have the option to feel sorry for ourselves and possibly "go under," or step backward, take a deep breath, and look at the big picture with an enlightened perspective and see the tragic circumstances as an opportunity for growth.

51

Knowing that every moment of your life is creating karma should be taken in stride with the proper attitude and perspective. One must not be fearful of taking action because it creates karma. One must remember that it is one's thoughts and intentions that actually create the karma. To not act on an intention that is karmically border-line would still be bringing about negative karma — and possibly a greater degree of it — by not acting. Being afraid to create karma goes hand-in-hand with denying your human nature in order to become more spiritual. This is an exercise in futility, since man can not be separated from his humanistic qualities and therefore should strike a balance with the qualities of the soul if he is to persist in his quest for spiritual development.

EARLY CASES... THE JOURNEY BEGINS

I will describe and discuss a multiplicity of cases throughout this book for which names and other identifiable information have been changed so as to ensure the privacy of the subjects. The only exception is that of Jeffrey Mishlove, Ph.D., who has kindly granted me permission to use his name in conjunction with his regression experiences.

The backgrounds of the many subjects seen were as diverse as the lifetimes they had recalled. The following is a list of occupations of these subjects, which speaks well of this diversity: physicians; dentists; lawyers; a prominent author with a Ph.D. in parapsychology; a college professor with a Ph.D. in music; Registered Nurses; physical therapists; hypnotherapists; massage therapists; Reiki therapists; teachers; a medical school student; a law school student and college students; executives in the fields of mortgage lending, insurance, marketing, real estate, and other various businesses; a policewoman; a Martial arts instructor; a travel agent; secretaries; a metal craftsman; a professional violinist; a professional fisherman; a professional photographer; a world-famous dancer and choreographer; a stage dancer and actress; an exotic dancer; mediums; psychics; housewives; a casino hostess; a plumber, and others too numerous to mention.

The next several cases are among the most interesting of my early cases of regression. Where possible, they are immediately followed by an historical perspective for purposes of validation.

CASE ONE

Evelyn was a 48-year-old legal secretary who came to me with recurring nightmares for over ten years. The nightmares were becoming worse and more frequent, causing her to wake up screaming. She could not remember details of the dreams, only that they were very sad. She was becoming progressively more anxious and had several phobias in addition to this problem. The phobias included fear of guns and fear of horses. Case One includes the following several regressions:

Mistress to a Druid King

Evelyn easily went into a deep trance on her first visit. "Shhh, I hear screams, men are raiding the village… they're Vikings! We must hurry and hide in the woods. Oin, oldest and wisest, is giving his life and will distract them." The year is 975 A.D. Her name is Aelish; she is 35 years old. She and a large group of villagers are escaping from a Viking raid. She and her people are Druids, and their coastal village is described as Hibernia, an ancient name for Ireland. Advancing her in time, she then said that she had been a mistress to Brian Boru, who in her words, became the "King of All Ireland" and was the last of the Druid Kings. Aelish died at a very old age in Dublin. She felt that this life had taught her to stand strong, with courage and dignity.

Historically: The Vikings began invading the coastal areas of Hibernia, or Ireland, in 795 A.D., and continued until they, as allies of the King of Dublin, were defeated at the battle of Clontorf, by High King Brian Boru, in 1014. This victory placed all five divisions of Ireland under his reign and gave him the title, "King of all Ireland." He was killed following this battle, at the age of 74, making him the same age as Aelish, his alleged mistress.

The Druids were members of the learned class among the ancient Celts. They acted as priests, poets, teachers, and judges and believed that the soul was immortal and that it passed at death from one person to another, the so-called transmigration of souls. They committed nothing to writing, depending only on their memories. They were vicious in battle, often fighting from chariots and taking heads as trophies.

Since many details from this subject's regression proved to be historically accurate, I found myself armed with an uncanny confidence which motivated me to pursue her remaining regressions with even more vigor.

Traumatic Delivery into Scotland

She is now speaking from the spirit plane, "I am resting at the bottom of the pyramid. The Masters are at the top."

I asked her about animals being present in the spirit plane.

She answered, "The animals are in another area."

She remained quiet for several minutes and then said that she intends to incarnate as a woman.

"I'll do it… I will… I'm being called again."

At that precise moment, Evelyn began squirming and screaming in pain as she placed herself in what appeared to be a fetal position. This was entirely too frightening and was obviously a birthing experience. I immediately rose her above this scene so she could observe it rather than experience it.

She spoke again, this time with no distress in her voice. "I have red hair… my mother is pale… she is dying."

I advanced her to a young woman and asked her name and the date.

She answered briskly, "My name is Mary MacGregor, of course," with a very Scottish brogue.

The year is 1040 A.D. She was married, had children, and lived a long life until her death in Scotland. Asking her what lesson she had learned in that lifetime, her answer was "patience."

The Druid Priestess

On her next visit Evelyn again easily slipped into a deep trance. She spoke, "I am barefoot... in my teens. I am a Druid priestess. My bodyguard, Amen, is here. I recognize him as my brother. Shaun, David, Richard, Brian... are all here. 'Annir duit Grania,'" speaking in Gaelic. She then continued, "Grace is the one... I am holding Grania by the ankles. Grania has volunteered to be sacrificed. She will be opened by Leon and blood will bless the Earth." She remained quiet for several minutes and then spoke again... "He has pulled her heart out... she felt nothing... was given potion... I am asking the gods and the ancient ones to warm the Earth and stop the rain. I am holding up her womb, center of life... only another woman may hold it. None here are married. Those who are chosen will bring forth life." The subject paused for a few minutes and once again continued, "I am a healer and a caller. I speak to the ancient ones that have gone before... the rains have stopped."

Advancing her to her death as a very old woman, she again spoke, "I am old. I will be taken by the ancient ones to Ternog, the land of youth, where I will be young and beautiful again. I have no fear... I will lie down and die." Asking the year, she replies, "1114."

Following her death, she uttered, "Grania is here." She remained quiet for several minutes and began again, "I am in the Great Hall... there are many souls around... a few new souls and many old souls. There are many caretakers and custodians. Never be afraid of dying; those afraid to die may become Earthbound. These souls are ghosts that have to be released by being directed to come here by mortals. Time does not exist in the Hall of Souls."

Historically: the Druid priest and priestess offered human sacrifices from third century B.C. to 1069 A.D., putting her in the right time frame. Also, the Druids believed in another world, imagined sometimes as islands in the sea or under the sea. It was called the "Land of the Young" or the "Land of the Living" and was believed to be a place where there was no old age, sickness, or death, and happiness lasted forever, and a hundred years was as one day.

In addition, many authors agree that extreme fear of death, such as in wartime and before surgery, may cause the soul to become Earthbound and that the soul can only be released by those specifically trained in such paranormal techniques. Also, time is unknown in the spirit plane. Evelyn recognized her brother in that lifetime, another example of soul recognition. Her phrase, "Annir duit Grania" is truly Gaelic and translates into "Grace is the one." This subject was my introduction to the phenomenon of xenoglossy (speaking languages that are not known to the subject).

The Irish Physician

When Evelyn completed her third past-life regression, her nightmares stopped, and she was able to sleep peacefully at night. Often following hypnotic regression the subject may experience flashback memories to other past lives. Somehow, these memories are "loosened" and made more available to the subject consciously following subconscious recovery of previous lifetimes.

Evelyn began to have flashback memories while in a state between sleep and waking, the so-called hypnogogic state that occurs before falling asleep (or the hypnopompic state prior to fully awakening). These flashbacks were vivid and detailed. She saw herself as Dr. Edmund Healy, an Irish physician pressed into service aboard an Irish ship, The Morning Glory. He was born in Galway, Ireland, and graduated from Trinity College in Dublin. His son had volunteered to serve on the same ship and was fatally injured following a fall from the crow's nest, a vivid memory for Evelyn, as she saw the young sailor hanging upside down by a rope that was attached to him. The ship was involved in a skirmish with a French ship, and while Dr. Healey was attending to an injured crew member, a French sailor burst into his cabin and shot him in the abdomen, killing him. The year was 1798.

Evelyn's fourth regression confirmed the details of the flashbacks that she was experiencing. Evelyn has a round birthmark on her abdomen where the musket ball would have entered. Birthmarks related to fatal trauma in previous lives are a common occurrence.

Historically: A series of radical political Irish societies, especially the United Irishmen, were preparing for rebellion that eventually broke out in May of 1798. It was widespread only in Ulster and Wexford. The societies were forced underground and in desperation sought the support of revolutionary France, which, between 1796 and 1798 dispatched a series of naval expeditions to Ireland, many of which were aborted.

Evelyn contacted a friend in Dublin, Ireland, by the name of Margaret Mount, and requested that she research historical documents to validate Evelyn's lifetime as Edmund Healy. Margaret Mount spent many months in this pursuit and was finally able to corroborate that an Eamon Healiegh (which translates to Edmund Healy in modern Irish dialect) was born in Galway, Ireland, and graduated from Trinity Medical College in Dublin.

Margaret Mount was also able to confirm that an Irish warship by the name of Morning Glory was involved in the rebellious activities of 1798. This information was found in the County Wexford Historical Society records, but there was no list of the ship's crew.

The Hungarian Village Girl

Evelyn returned for her fifth regression. She was twenty years old and at a dance at Szolomedja, a small village in Hungary. Her name was Scusca Mikola, and the year was 1843. She again began to speak, "I am in my new red dress... my red boots... my apron... and my ribbons. Stanislous, you look so handsome." The subject began to blush as Stanislous began to speak to her. She then carried on a conversation with him in fluent Hungarian. The subject would speak aloud and then pause, as if she were listening to Stanislous. Her accompanying facial expressions were appropriate and quite dramatic. It seems Stanislous Novak was a foot soldier in the Hungarian army, and they were to be married on October 8, 1843. In an overview statement, Evelyn said that they never married and that Stanislous Novak was killed in the revolution six years later (1849) fighting the Austrians and Russians. She lived until her death at 60 years old in 1883.

Historically: there was a bloodless revolution in 1848, led by intellectuals. It turned bloody and ended in bitter fighting one year later in 1849 when the Austrians and Russians invaded Hungary and were victorious. The dates mentioned were historically correct and were in agreement with Evelyn's age progression. In spite of the fact that Evelyn did not speak any foreign language, this was the second time that she experienced xenoglossy.

The Militant Hungarian Student

During Evelyn's sixth regression she again experienced a life in Hungary. This time the year was 1918, and she was a man. Evelyn spoke in a gruff manner, "My name is Emerick Novak. I was born in 1896, and I am 22 years old. I live in Pest; there are many scattered farms there. I'm a student at the university."

While still under deep hypnosis, Evelyn stood up in a very aggressive manner and began waving her fists while speaking in a loud voice… "Damn the French… they're helping to break up the Austria-Hungarian empire… the Czechoslovakians are just waiting!"

After advancing the subject in time, Emerick gave an overview statement, saying that he died two years later, at the age of 24, after being kicked in the chest by his horse.

Historically: Budapest received its name in 1873 by amalgamating three communities: Pest on the left of the Danube, Buda on the right, and Abuda to the north. The residents continued to use the individual town names for several decades; also, Pest was the only area that was mostly flat farmland. Emerick Novak's behavior and mannerisms as a passionate Hungarian student embroiled in the political upheaval of his time was extremely typical, and his fiery comment, "Damn the French!" was most appropriate in that the French indeed occupied Szegel, a city to the south of Budapest, in 1918. Also, Hungary at that time was referred to as the Austria-Hungarian Empire.

Additionally, the Treaty of Trianon, signed in 1920, allowed the Czechoslovakians to annex large areas of the Hungarian population.

Evelyn no longer has nightmares, since she recognizes that they were subconscious visions of past lives being recalled in her dream state. Her conscious mind now understands why she harbored a fear of guns and horses, as these were instruments of death in previous lives. Recognizing that those events were in her past and are not related to her current life, she has now given herself permission to release those memories and be free of her previous anxieties. She is a much happier person.

CASE TWO

Angel of Mercy soon to become a Spirit Guide

Julie was a 50-year-old patient who was dying of cancer. She wanted to be regressed in spite of the fact that she was very weak from her chemotherapy and radiation. This pale, drawn woman quickly relaxed into a deep hypnotic state and went back to a lifetime during the Civil War. She spoke in barely audible whispers. "I am seeing everything in a bluish hue. I am in a white dress, but I am not a nurse. I'm in my thirties. My dark hair is in a bun, and I'm tall and quiet. I usually keep to myself and my needlework. My name is Lillian."

The subject described a large tent near a battlefield in Gettysburg. She was caring for soldiers in gray uniforms. Again she spoke softly, "There is much blood and screaming for loved ones. Limbs are gone; many are dying. The doctors are in white. I hear heavy cannons in the distance." She held a young soldier's head in her lap and said, "He's screaming. His leg has been shot off."

Advancing her to five years later, she now spoke in a calm voice, "I'm in my kitchen, cooking; it's a small home… I'm alone." Responding to my questions, the patient gave an overview of her life. "I was married in my twenties. My husband's name was Paul Jackson. Two years after we were married, he fell off his horse and was killed. We had no children."

59

Advancing her five years more, Julie informed me that Lillian had died and was buried in her white dress with a little doll. When she was in the afterlife, I asked her about what she had learned in this lifetime. She replied, "I learned the importance of comforting those with great suffering." She then said that she will soon be helping someone on Earth but as yet did not know whom. She is to be a protector, a Spirit Guide.

Postscript: At the time of this session, this patient was eleven months post-op. She had been surgically opened and immediately closed, following discovery of a fulminating advanced intestinal cancer. Breaking the news to her following surgery was among the most difficult tasks that I had to perform as a physician. I remember that day vividly and sadly, as she was a longtime patient who appeared very full of life. I'm afraid I shed a few tears with her that day. She died six months after the session. She was a very special person, and I honestly believe that she will be someone's Spirit Guide.

I feel that the regression experience here was beneficial. When one is facing death, it is comforting to see one's individuality continuing on into the afterlife. This vivid reality in the form of mental images brought forth during the regression process appears to bring with it a sense of being eternal, something every dying person needs to experience. It impresses upon a person the everlasting nature of the soul and the fact that repeating Earth lives is a frequently occurring necessity for the evolution of the soul to continue in its quest for perfection.

CASE THREE

Meaningful Spiritual Experiences

This last case is about an individual I will refer to as Jonathan. He was a personal friend with a terminal case of lung cancer. In order to help him as much as I could, I volunteered the use of hypnotherapy with visualization to instill a strong, positive attitude toward recovery. People with terminal conditions have, on occasion, gone into complete and permanent remission with such therapy or by just having a solid, positive attitude about recovering. It seems this type of outlook fires up the immune system. These people picture themselves as wholesome, healthy, and free of cancer, living a normal life. What's more, they believe it. Many of these cases are labeled 'miracle cures' and continue to confound the medical community.

As a physician I have also seen the reverse situation, whereupon the patient is convinced that his condition is terminal and he is going to die. The oppressive negativity of these patients contributes to the depletion of the body's immune system, allowing these patients to deteriorate and die, as they know they will. Bernie Siegel, M.D., discusses this subject in great detail in his book, *Love, Medicine, and Miracles.*

Several years ago, Jonathan's wife had an affair and decided to leave him. Jonathan was completely devastated, and although he loved his wife very much, he managed to make a life for himself without her. After the divorce, his former wife's affair came to an end, and she now begged him to take her back, threatening to kill herself if he did not. Jonathan refused and his ex-wife committed suicide, which caused him an enormous amount of guilt.

I decided to use regression and see where it would lead. In his first session, Jonathan found himself in a spiritual experience, during which he met a holy man who gave him a mustard seed, telling him to always hold on to it. I am sure this was a representation of his faith.

During his second session he again had a spiritual experience and found himself walking on a moonlit beach. He saw someone familiar calling to him and approaching him. It was his deceased wife. Jonathan remained very quiet for more than ten minutes, except for frequent tears. I softly inquired as to what was happening. He replied, "We're just talking…" He again became quiet and, some twenty minutes later, smiled and tearfully whispered, "We've forgiven each other."

This experience released his guilt and bestowed upon him a certain indescribable peacefulness which remained until his death. Jonathan had fallen in love again, and the loving care that he received from this woman became a great source of comfort to him, as his suffering increased toward the end of his life. Although he insisted he wanted to recover and live, I felt that subconsciously and deep within his heart he did not. This was borne out in subtle ways as he approached his death. I believe that Jonathan had accomplished the lesson that his soul needed to learn, and I am sure that lesson included forgiveness.

The Blacksmith from South Dakota

I did several more regressions on Jonathan before he died. This time, instead of a spiritual experience, he recounted a life in 1898 as Richard Phillips, a blacksmith who lived in Keystone, a mining town in South Dakota. He recalled a time when he was standing in a dusty street with his friends. They soon all left for Barb's Saloon. During that time I asked him to feel the sides of his trousers and to describe what he felt. He indicated that he was wearing a holster containing his side gun, a Colt 44. He and his wife, Carol, and their two children eventually moved to a big city in the east, where his son became a medical doctor.

His life was long, peaceful, and full of contentment. He felt the lessons that he learned were the importance of gentleness, sensitivity, and caring.

Historically: There is an old mining town in South Dakota with the name of Keystone, near Rapid City, the county seat.

The Engineer from Pakistan

A life that Jonathan kept returning to was that of H. R.,[1] the son of a wealthy family from Pakistan. Jonathan made several interesting remarks while reliving this life, such as, "I'm taller, younger, and more robust." H. R. was educated in the United States at U.C.L.A. and went on to become an environmental engineer, who later worked on sewer projects in Pakistan. During the last regression, H. R., his wife,

1. Author has all complete names, which are hidden here for privacy.

62

H., and his seven-year-old son, K., vacationed in Las Vegas, and stayed at the Mirage. The year was 1998.

Following the session, the subject voiced his confusion regarding the dates. It was obvious to him that the other lifetime that he was experiencing under hypnosis was occurring simultaneously with his present life. I explained that this was believed to be a current parallel life, a phenomenon in which the soul splits and occupies two bodies at the same time or overlapping times for the purpose of learning lessons from different perspectives (see "Parallel Lives" on page 135).

Although I was unable to validate any of the details, some of them because of privacy issues, I feel that the authenticity of this lifetime was unimportant. I believe that recalling this life served a purpose in that Jonathan saw himself as a robust and very successful individual, thus bolstering his self image and allowing him to know intuitively that his soul is eternal and that he can choose to experience other physical identities in other times, and in other places, to enhance the enlightenment of his soul. Jonathan felt a certain pride in knowing that the personality of H. R. was also a vibrant part of him. As Jonathan's condition steadily deteriorated, the idea of his consciousness continuing on into the afterlife and in a parallel life in this present day under these more favorable circumstances was both thought-provoking and comforting. Jonathan informed me that seeing himself dying and being reborn, over and over, gave him a sense of being eternal, an extremely worthwhile use of hypnotic regression in terminal patients. He died several months later.

RETIREMENT REDEFINED

Retiring from active practice and leaving my longtime patients was rather difficult; however, the blow was softened by my steadily mounting interest in metaphysics and hypnotic regression. The move to Las Vegas was long and arduous, but I didn't even notice, since my mind was totally absorbed on what was ahead of me. Moving out west was exciting and adventuresome, but nowhere as much as what I had been accomplishing with hypnosis.

Once we were entrenched in our new location, I became certified by the American Board of Hypnotherapy and went into high gear with regard to recruiting new subjects for regression. I was able to absorb a considerable amount of information about the process and techniques of regression by reading what several authors had written about their sessions; however, I wanted firsthand experience. I needed to see this for myself. Thus began my research on hypnotic regression.

Within a few months of arriving in Las Vegas, I became aware of Dr. Raymond Moody's presence at UNLV (University of Nevada in Las Vegas), where he was teaching a series of courses on Consciousness. I had read several books of his regarding near-death experiences and had telephoned him when I was in practice, regarding a patient of mine who required resuscitation. In spite of the fact that the phone call was made twenty-six years earlier, Dr. Moody remembered me and the phone call. I made it a point to visit him at the university. Shortly after learning about my research on hypnotic past-life regression, he invited me to speak to his classes, which I did on two occasions. Following each lecture I would ask for volunteers to help me in my research project on hypnotic regression. The response was overwhelming; it was as if I had opened up a floodgate. Scores of students of all ages eagerly signed up to be regressed hypnotically. The number of subjects increased dramatically as these students referred many of their friends.

I found that Dick Sutphen's idea of taking a subject up to his Higher Self and calling for his Spirit Guide was quite ingenious. Using this technique, I decided to take it a step further and carry on a channeling of sorts with the Spirit Guides, asking them an assortment of questions about the subject. These various inquiries included such questions as whether the subject lived in Atlantis or Lemuria or on other planets, and whether the subject had parallel lives or lives with his Spirit Guide or other individuals in the subject's life. Becoming more creative at this, I started asking a variety of esoteric questions so as to compare the answers. The experimental model that I eventually designed for the Spirit Guides proved to me that the information I was receiving was accurate.

As the number of past-life regressions and future-life progressions mounted, the research seemed to take on a life of its own. I was being handed glimpses into realms that I had no idea existed. I knew now that I must somehow share these revelations. I felt truly compelled to write this book.

Drawing on my Virgo tendencies, I designed a large chart to compare specific topics that were brought out under deep hypnosis by individual subjects. Organizing the massive amount of material that I had gathered allowed me to approach the composition of this book in a somewhat organized fashion. At first it appeared insurmountable, but as I proceeded, I found that it gave me great pleasure to graph out what I was learning. The insights gained from that activity eventually led to a noticeable change in my thinking and how I perceived reality.

Picturing this project in metaphorical terms, I could envision the confining walls of conventional medicine breaking down so as to make way for new methods of healing. With this conventional limitation out of the way, a physician could now make use of his patients' very protective subconscious mind and use it as a healing tool to search out, recognize, and expose the causes of both emotional and physical illnesses at their very core. I have found that once the source of ill health was exposed in this way, most patients would be able to improve in a rapid fashion, some with the help of conventional medicine, and some without, depending on the extent of physical illness present.

It is my hope that this book will be instrumental in expanding the conventional thinking of the medical community and at the same time point out how people can come to terms with, and finally rid themselves of, the many maladies that affect them without resorting to the use of drugs. I cannot help but wonder if this endeavor has helped me focus on the true path and purpose of my present incarnation.

5

BACK TO THE CAUSE OF EMOTIONAL PROBLEMS

**THE CASE OF LAURA MILLER:
RECURRING THOUGHTS OF "HELP ME"**

This intriguing case centered around an energetic and spiritually advanced subject. For the past 20 years she had been plagued
by a thought which resembled an inner voice, saying, "Help me."
She would also utter those words upon waking in the morning. This
emotionally troubling situation began after her mother died over
twenty years ago. During that time a string of physically and emotionally traumatic events occurred signaling a rather dark episode in
her present life. A few months prior to seeing me, the subject had
been regressed to the cause of this emotional plea. She was taken
back to a life in the 1800s wherein she was a male explorer in South
America who died when he was unable to make his way out of a
quicksand bog. Unfortunately, Laura retained this problem and
would occasionally say or think the words, "Help me," and at the
same time have associated shoulder discomfort.

Laura's session had included several issues which needed
work, and this "Help me" issue was the last one to be confronted.
With the previous regression history in mind, I took her back again
to the cause of this emotional call for help and enlisted the aid of
her Spirit Guide. Recounting the same lifetime, we found that the
explorer was also an author and wrote many articles which were
posthumously published as a book. His death in the quicksand

occurred around 1888. The subject became unduly fatigued, and I thought it best to end the session.

Four months later I once again saw the subject. She was still having a sort of panic reaction and repeating the words "Help me." This time I asked the Spirit Guide to take us back to any further causes of this problem. Laura immediately felt herself falling out of a crumbling building during an Earthquake. By taking her further back in time to the day before this incident, I was able to ascertain that this event had taken place in Atlantis. (The subject has had eight lives in Atlantis.) At the time of the tremor, the Earth shook mercilessly as the building began to disintegrate. The subject in that lifetime tried in vain to hold things together using her own energy field, and then attempted this using the collective energy fields of her family and friends. The entire time that she endeavored to keep the building intact, she screamed, "Help me... help me!" She and many others died that day, as the destruction of Atlantis began.

After Laura relived these events, I felt confident that she would be able to release this negative cell memory and its emotional impact; but as always, I prodded the Spirit Guide further in an attempt to uncover any other causes of this rather serious emotional problem. I was promptly told, "Enough for now." I decided that in this instance, discretion was definitely the better part of valor, and I ended the session with my usual positive suggestions and figured I would make use of a timeworn medical phrase: I would put into effect "watchful waiting."

At her following session one month later, Laura informed me that she was improved but still had occasional thoughts of "Help me." I once again invoked her Spirit Guide and asked for his assistance. He then came forward with a dissertation on the mission of Spirit Guides and also spoke of angels. I interrupted him to ask about the mission of Spiritual Warriors. I received no response; however, Laura claimed that she did, in the form of a feeling of strength from her Spirit Guide. I then asked to have the subject return to any further causes of this powerful, emotional appeal that often interfered with her thinking, bringing forth anxiety and often unwarranted fear.

Laura immediately began to cry, as a look of panic overcame her face. The words, "Help me!... God... Why have You left me?" slowly filtered out of her lips. I rose her above the scene and told her to view what was going on from a third-person perspective. She then told me that she was being dragged through the streets and beaten. "The people want to burn me. I have gifts... I can heal...they don't understand, and this frightens them... they feel threatened." Though she was viewing the scene from this objective perspective, Laura still exhibited deep emotions while describing what was happening. I was able to ascertain that she was a 17-year-old young woman about to be killed in a horribly painful manner by 17th-century religious zealots and bigots. Such ignorance and cruelty reigned supreme in that sad era and was responsible for many thousands of intensely agonizing deaths of young, innocent, and gifted women.

The subconscious cell memory of these horrible deaths has surfaced in many present-day individuals in the form of emotional or physical pain. These individuals, much like my subject, are gifted in many ways. Upon seeing themselves persecuted and tortured in those lifetimes, they can easily understand why their present life is so affected and why it is so important for them to forgive in order to release the effect. Laura was no exception, as she now indicated to me that her Spirit Guide purposely delayed recalling this lifetime, as he needed time to prepare her to relive this memory. She also informed me that her Spirit Guide in some way compelled me to ask him about Spiritual Warriors, and the Spirit Guide's response further shored up her protective preparation for what was about to come. Even though she admitted that she subconsciously resisted going back to that life, her Spirit Guide was able to gently lead her back into it with a minimum of emotional trauma, for he knew that she had help from a Spiritual Warrior as she suffered through the burning at the stake.

Her Spirit Guide now impressed upon her the necessity of forgiving all those who participated in this heinous crime, for only then will she be able to release this crippling memory. The Spirit Guide put it very well when he told her, "You must leave your coat at the door before you walk through." I must say that I rather enjoy and appreciate the help of Spirit Guides. I find that they are very protective of those in their care, and in this case, most comprehensively so.

Subsequent follow-up contact with the subject revealed no recurrence of the negative emotional plea of, "Help me, help me!" for over three and a half years.

THE CASE OF LARRY NASH: RUNNING OUT OF TIME

Larry was a 53-year-old man who had been plagued for many years with anxiety over "running out of time." Any situation in life, regardless of what it was related to, seemed to be subject to this uncomfortable feeling of not having enough time, thus producing varying degrees of unnecessary anxiety with all its attendant negative feelings. I had regressed Larry to several lifetimes prior to this session, and he was observed to die early in those lifetimes, but it wasn't until I asked his Higher Self to help take him back to the cause of why he feels that he is "running out of time" that his conscious mind put it all together. Larry practically jumped off the couch as he loudly affirmed, "That's it! I die early in many of my lifetimes... that's why I feel like I'm running out of time. But... I'm fifty-three... I'm home free... I've made it. I don't have to worry any more." Grinning from ear to ear, Larry acknowledged that he felt like a great weight had been lifted from him. I understand that he was literally walking on air for months after that session. Once more, I was totally floored by the enormous influence that our timeless and sometimes illogical subconscious memory can have on our present lives.

Subsequent follow up has shown that Larry has remained free of this problem for well over four years after the regression session.

THE CASE OF VANESSA JACKSON:
DEPRESSIVE THOUGHTS

This young woman was instructed to return to the cause of depressive thoughts, which she has had all of her life. She regressed to a life as Marvin Banks, a private in the Confederate Army. The year was 1865, and Private Banks lay dying in a makeshift hospital in South Carolina, close to his home state of Georgia. Marvin had taken a bullet in the right side of his abdomen and was suffering greatly. The pain became worse with every day that passed. The only time that the military doctor saw him, the blood-soaked, weary surgeon just shook his head and mumbled, "Pitiful," as he slowly walked away.

Marvin was consumed with frustration, anger, and depression, as he lay there waiting to die as he knew he would. Four long weeks dragged on, until his body, wracked with pain, mercifully gave up his spirit. As his beleaguered soul made its way to the light, Marvin still remained embroiled in anger and could not rid himself of the depressive residue from the last weeks of that lifetime. In an effort to soothe his soul, Marvin's Spirit Guide reminded him that his lesson was all about compassion and forgiveness, that it was necessary for him to remove this coat of anger, frustration, and depression, and leave it at the door to the light, for he will need to don it again when he returns to the Earth to relearn this lesson. (This was the second time that I heard this metaphor from a Spirit Guide.)

Following this revelation, I told the subject that she must never forget this lesson; and in order to release this well-engrained memory of depressive thoughts, she must be willing to forgive all transgressions. During a follow-up phone conversation four years later, the subject gratefully acknowledged that she has had no further depressive thoughts since that session. I smiled and thought to myself… one more victory for the power of the mind, and, oh, yes, less profits for the drug companies.

THE CASE OF SHARON PEROT:
FEAR OF FAILURE AND FEAR OF
EXPRESSING TRUE FEELINGS REGARDING MEN

This middle-aged female subject was actually quite successful in business; nevertheless, she constantly fostered a nagging feeling of fear that she will fail at what she is doing. Taking her back to the cause of this fear of failure, she regressed back to a life in Italy in the 1800s. She was born into that life as Francisco, who grew up to become a talented artist. Francisco was even more extraordinary in that he possessed psychic gifts, wherein he was able to see and hear spiritual beings. Making good use of his talent in combination with his unusual abilities, Francisco became absorbed with putting these spiritual forms on canvas. His preoccupation grew to become an obsession as he discovered how to protect himself with light and invite spiritual beings to use his paintbrush. The colorful and strikingly bizarre paintings interested only a few patrons who bought them and infuriated others who criticized his art on moral grounds and brought this "evil" activity to the attention of the local authorities, who confiscated and burned all of his paintings.

Seeing all of the years of effort, joy, love and passion destroyed in a few hours was more than Francisco could bear. Witnessing all of his life's work going up in smoke brought home the harsh realization that the dedication of his life force to the pursuit of this sweet passion meant nothing. Francisco's life was already compromised by his use of alcohol, and his marriage was damaged by the physical abuse that he thrust upon his wife. Now, he was being stripped of the passion that brought him life. This imprint of failure was stamped deeply upon his very being, so much so that Francisco never picked up another paintbrush. The remaining eight years of his life were no more than an existence, until the fateful day arrived when his failing alcoholic liver mercifully allowed him to enter the spirit world that he knew so well.

Sharon also harbored a fear of expressing her true feelings in relationships with men. Taking her back to the cause, she recalled the adolescent years of her present life and a sexual abuse problem with her father. Almost immediately, the subject came to the realization that her relationships with men were laden with mistrust due to their being representative of a father figure to her. This situation led to her subconscious refusal to express her true emotions and feelings and thus kept her living in a prison of sorts. The pieces of the karmic puzzle fell into place as Sharon then informed me that while still under hypnosis she had recognized Francisco's wife in the preceding life as her present father.

Asking her to step back to look at the big picture, I reminded her that she had created this reality and that a karmic balance often exists. In one lifetime you're a 'victim', and in another, you're a 'perpetrator.' It's all about your soul learning lessons. Sharon now understood how the memories came about and could now make a choice to be free of this great weight and experience joy and happiness in her relationships with men. I appealed to her Higher Self to release these memories once and for all by forgiving her father in this lifetime and herself in the life as Francisco. By doing so, she will be free to express love and affection without limitation.

Follow-up three and a half years later revealed that since the session, Sharon has no longer had a fear of failure or a fear of expressing her true feelings in her relationships with men. When I received this report from her, one word dominated my thoughts… "Cool!"

THE CASE OF GINA ROBERTS: REMAINING IN AN ABUSIVE RELATIONSHIP

This subject presented as a woman in her mid-fifties, who, like many battered women, often found herself remaining in an abusive relationship. Taking her back to the cause of this particular problem, her subconscious mind began to convey the unpleasant details of three lifetimes, one of which was her present childhood. Together these life-times appeared to shed light on her innermost feelings about men.

Her early childhood years were filled with mental pictures of her father as a large, looming, ominous figure, who was extremely mean and threatening. He would drink excessively and both emotionally and physically abuse her mother and brother. The subject claimed she was never really hurt but was always afraid that she would be. Gina knew that her father would be drunk if he came home late, and this meant that her mother would most likely be choked and punched. The subject's fear became uncontrollable, even when her father was not around. Gina left home when she was 18 years old.

In the second lifetime Gina found herself in England in the late 1930s. She saw herself as a young teenage girl walking in a wooded forest at night. Seeing a man on horseback coming toward her, she thought to herself, "He is someone in authority; he looks like he's going to grab me." The subject then saw nothing as she proceeded to block out what was happening next. Following further deepening, she continued, "He's dragging me along to a place that has bars, like a dungeon. I stayed there for two days... I feel OK; he did not hurt me... I then went home and remained alone most of the time. I allowed myself to be taken away... I felt fear but I knew I couldn't do anything about it, so I didn't."

In the third lifetime she saw herself as a shepherd girl in her early twenties in the time of Christ. She was observing Roman soldiers who were standing around and remarked, "They are in authority. I feel very lowly next to them. I'm so alone... as I watch these men, I'm thinking how handsome they are and how wonderful it would be to be with one of them or to be one of them."

After hearing this synopsis of experiences that had been brought to the surface by her subconscious mind, I began to meticulously explain to the subject while still under deep hypnosis how the subconscious cell memory pattern that was laid out for her many hundreds of years ago had been broadened and reinforced by certain events of her lifetime in the 1930s and in her present life as she grew up. The unusual combination of emotions brought on by these experiences became part of this subconscious memory, and as such were deeply engrained in a neurogenic brain pathway. Thus current abusive situations would trigger the activation of the brain cells along this familiar, well-worn neurogenic tract and evoke seemingly inappropriate feelings and attitudes, which involved emotions that normally were not expressed simultaneously. In Gina's case, it was obvious that she had carried over this same bizarre blend of emotions, namely, affection and fear, into her present relationships with men, and this was overly complicated by the fact that she inappropriately looked up to these men as authority figures. In addition to this irrational form of thinking Gina harbored a fear of being alone, which would explain why she would remain in an abusive relationship as long as she did.

My explanation included the very important fact that interrupting these neurogenic brain pathways would break the ice the first time, and repeated interruptions will begin to end this distorted type of thinking, putting her back on track with proper emotional responses. Consciously recognizing the causes that contributed to the problem will be its initial undoing; and as more appropriate responses come into play, new neurogenic pathways will be formed and will be responsible for eliciting the proper emotions that will fit the circumstances.

During a follow-up call six months later, Gina stated that she no longer harbored a fear of men or of being alone. She felt that she could now express her true feelings with men.

THE CASE OF GRACE RUTLEDGE: ALWAYS SAYING, "I'M SORRY"

Returning to the source of a constantly apologetic attitude, the subject uncovered four contributory lives. The first life showed her to be a middle-aged English woman in the 1500s, who blamed herself for having a miscarriage.

The second life was in Indonesia in the 1800s. Grace was a teenage daughter of a widower who was always disappointed in her choices of boyfriends. She eventually ran off with one of those boyfriends.

In a third lifetime, Grace was a male living in Montana in the 1700s, who hunted professionally and also for his family's food. His son became ill and needed medical attention. As the father and sole provider, he felt he should have been able to transport his son into the closest town to be seen by a doctor. He did not have the means to do this; and his inability to get his son to a doctor resulted in the son's death. He never forgave himself.

A fourth life found Grace living as a twenty-five-year-old very overweight Tahitian woman, who was very ashamed of her appearance.

Grace's Spirit Guide said that she had many more such lives that also contributed to the memory of this apologetic disposition. Understanding where this feeling of being sorry came from and why it pervaded her daily mental posture gave the subject's conscious mind all it needed to release this subconscious memory and rid herself from routinely saying this annoying and self-defeating statement.

Follow-up three and a half years later found this subject to be completely free of frequently and inappropriately saying, "I'm sorry."

THE CASE OF JEAN COLLINS: DEPRESSION AND FEELINGS OF ABANDONMENT

Jean was an attractive, intelligent woman in her midforties who desired to investigate and eliminate a depression problem. When taken back to the problem source, the subject immediately said in a fretful tone, "I was abandoned on Earth." This statement caught me off-guard.

I countered, "Where did you come from?"

Subject: "I came from a higher realm, a higher vibration... Lemuria."[1]

---

1. See also "Lemuria" on page 151.

Dr. T: "What was your purpose in coming to Earth?"

Subject: "To be of assistance… Earthlings have many problems."

Dr. T: "Were you born into a life on Earth?"

Subject: "No, I came into a physical form as a walk-in, when the host body was seventeen years old."

Dr. T: "Were you in contact with others from Lemuria?"

Subject: "They were around, but there was no contact; however, I was aware of High Masters from other realms who seemed to check on me. I had forgotten who I was and have had this feeling of being abandoned for a long time."

I explained to the subject that knowing who she was and why she was here will be of great value to her. Also, understanding that she was a voluntary walk-in with an express mission to help people on Earth and therefore was not abandoned, will allow her to release the misperceived memory of being abandoned and thus cure her of depression.

Upon waking from this session, Jean was ineffably surprised at this revelation; however, she now recalled that her life took on a more spiritual tone when she was seventeen years old. At that time she began to have the ability to see and communicate with spirit entities as well as to have frequent out-of-body experiences.

I was very happy to hear that she has had no further depression or thoughts of abandonment two and a half years later.

6

BACK TO THE CAUSE OF
PHYSICAL PROBLEMS

THE CASE OF GEORGE DOWNING:
CHRONIC HIP PAIN

I am especially happy with the beneficial results of hypnotherapy in the case of George Downing, a man who was advanced in
years and had been living with chronic right hip pain that started
two weeks after a major surgery. The surgery was performed one
year earlier for an abdominal mass that was found to be densely
adherent to the bowel and was thought to be malignant. Since the
frozen-section biopsy that was initially taken during the surgery
was benign, and since the mass was not causing any obstruction to
the bowel, it was decided to leave it in place. George was discharged from the hospital and returned to his rather limited life-
style, as he required a walker and was almost completely blind.
Within two weeks he began to experience right hip pain, which
required narcotics such as oxycodone and Neurontin. Eventually a
tens unit, a device which gives off an electric current to help
decrease the pain, was surgically implanted near the site of the pain.

When I first saw George I found him to be exceptionally pleasant and outgoing in spite of his chronic pain and blindness. His history revealed twenty years of active duty in the United States Navy,
something he was very proud of. Once we figured out that we
needed to turn off the tens unit, I was able to utilize hypnotic techniques to reduce his pain. Over the course of several sessions I was
able to take George up to his super-conscious mind level, his Higher
Self, and communicate with his Spirit Guide. Using the help of his
Spirit Guide we were able to uncover four incidents that occurred in

his present life that contributed to the negative programming of his subconscious mind regarding the right hip pain.

The cell memory residing in the right hip would surface and manifest when there was an injury in this area associated with a concomitant fear of impending death. Two such situations occurred when the subject was twelve years old. While on active duty in the Navy, the subject again experienced two more life-threatening situations associated with stress to the right hip. The cell memory within the right hip was so often associated with the fear of death, that when George faced the possibility of not recovering from a rather complicated surgery for a probable malignant mass, the cell memory of the right hip was triggered and the pain began.

Discovering the relationship of this right-hip pain to the fear of dying was an important step in George's treatment. His analytical conscious mind now concluded that root causes of his problem were buried in early adolescent memories and were reinforced by his close calls in the Navy, thus setting off the chain of events that led to his present situation.

The medical community might look at this case as an example of the Triple Allergenic Theory, popularized by Brian, Boswell, and others. It has to do with emotional disorders that start off with an initial sensitizing event which is not consciously remembered. Symptoms soon occur when reinforced by a symptom-producing event, which is usually remembered. Finally a symptom-intensifying event occurs, allowing the symptom to intensify and remain.

While recounting his Navy experiences, George mumbled, "I'm not worthy." My thoughts on this pertained to his sense of duty and his macho attitude. I felt that George did not think he should feel afraid, in spite of the fact that he carried out his duty splendidly. Under deep hypnosis, I pointed out why he should consider himself worthy and begin to choose joy and a state of being painfree.

Approximately three years later, George remains much improved.

THE CASE OF DARLENE ZORN:
CHRONIC HEADACHES AND NECK PAIN

This 33-year-old white female has had a problem with chronic daily headaches associated with neck pain for many years. When taken back to the source of this problem, the subject was thrust into a lifetime in the 1800s as a Saskatchewan Indian woman in her thirties. She was a virtual slave to the chief of the tribe and was often beaten, especially on the head, by members of the tribe for not complying with their wishes as they felt she should. Her resistance only resulted in further mistreatment, including isolation, starvation, and more beatings. She would often be found crying profusely while curled up in a fetal position and holding her head. This treatment caused her to become progressively weaker until she became quite ill. Eventually she just gave up and died.

Asked if another lifetime contributed to this chronic headache problem associated with neck pain, Darlene replied yes, and immediately zeroed into a life in England in 1740. She was married to a man who was prominent in politics and very controlling. He would often grab her roughly by the back of the neck and lead her around in this manner so that she could do his bidding. He considered her his prize and his property.

The subject now indicated that there was a final lifetime that contributed to the origin of these headaches and returned to a scene in a lifetime in 1943. She was a six-year-old girl named Sarah, playing on a swing. Several mean-spirited boys wandered by and began to push Sarah's swing higher and higher. They laughed as it became uncontrollable. Sarah cried and tried to hang on, but the swing was completely out of control, and she was thrown high into the air and crashed upon the ground, causing a severe head injury, which shortly resulted in her death.

Still under deep hypnosis and working within her Higher Mind, I employed the basic tenets of past life regression therapy as advocated by Dick Sutphen and asked the subject if she could forgive herself

79

and others involved; and by doing so, rise above this karma, knowing that wisdom erases karma and the law of grace supersedes the law of karma. Darlene was able to recognize that her subconscious cell memory had been negatively programmed by experiencing serious injuries to her head in prior lifetimes. Those injuries were almost always associated with extremely traumatic emotions, and something in her present lifetime caused these same emotions to surface, bringing the physical pain along with it. Her conscious mind now clearly perceived why her present headaches and neck pain manifested but also understood that these occurrences in the past should not affect her current lifetime. Through such awareness and forgiveness, this subject was able to relieve herself of the chronic headaches and neck pain which had plagued her for many years.

Three years later Darlene was still free of this problem.

THE CASE OF SALLY SEVERS: FIBROMYALGIA

This case involved a thirty-eight-year-old female who had been working in a healing capacity for the past several years. Some time earlier she was diagnosed as having fibromyalgia, a disease which is characterized by achy pain, tenderness and stiffness of soft tissue areas, such as muscles, tendon insertions, and adjacent structures.

The onset of fibromyalgia is often related to anxiety, tension, and depression; therefore, it is thought of as strictly psychosomatic by many physicians. Once the disease takes hold, the pain is very real, and damage to tissues can occur. Many of these cases are difficult to manage, and often physicians find that they have no choice but to treat fibromyalgia patients with various forms of pain medication, tranquilizers, non-steroidal anti-inflammatory drugs, and other symptomatic medications.

Personally believing that all illness has an emotional factor involved, I feel that the medical treatment of a disease should include whatever is necessary to satisfactorily handle this emotional component, even if it requires a form of alternative medicine. This particular subject was extremely disillusioned with the conventional medical treatment she had received so far. Instead, she came to me for past-life regression therapy. Working through her Higher Self, I instructed her to go back to the cause or source of the fibromyalgia problem. Sally recalled three lifetimes that contributed to the onset of this disease.

The initial image that she saw in her first lifetime was that of herself as a healer in England in 1843. She was a young girl in her twenties, caught in a raging river current. As she drowned, she felt her spirit leaving her body and saw her deceased mother coming to greet her and guide her to the light. Taking her back in time to determine how she came to be in the river, I found that her husband in that lifetime threw her into the river and drowned her to keep her from healing people – something that embarrassed and annoyed him. He despised her healing power. At that moment the subject's conscious mind interjected that she had a flashback to this death in recent times when a friend had died in a flash flood.

Going back to the second life that contributed to this disease, the subject saw herself bound to a stake about to be put to death by fire for being a witch. This was occurring in France in the 1700s. Viewing her death from a third-person perspective, she could see that she forgave the people for what they were doing to her. As her spirit left her body and was greeted by her son from her present life, the subject wept profusely. In the light she felt much better and reiterated that she did not feel scorn towards those who had put the torch to her and ended her life so cruelly. She had been a healer, but the ignorance pervading society in the 1700s dictated that whatever was not understood could only be feared.

The third contributing life took place in Atlantis around 15030 B.C. The subject was a priestess named Rolana, who carried out healing inside a pyramid. Rolana was androgynous, being both male and female. Others like her existed in Atlantis, but this genetic makeup was especially helpful in her healing efforts. People also came to her for knowledge and in order to advance spiritually and attain longevity. She conducted her healing sessions telepathically or through touch, depending on how advanced the person was spiritually. The healing was carried out in centers within a pyramid, so she could utilize the energy from the many crystals of all sizes that surrounded her chamber. Also, the white-light energy that entered through the center of the top of the pyramid would aid in the healing process. (This description of pyramids is uncannily similar to those given in the sections titled, "Insights from Spirit Guides" and "Atlantis").

The High Council of Atlantis, which controlled the consciousness of the people, became concerned that the priestess Rolana was elevating the consciousness of too many citizens of Atlantis. They felt that they needed to put a stop to this; thus, the Council decreed that the healing would cease immediately. Following this decree, Rolana said that she left Atlantis. I asked, "Where did you go?"

Rolana replied, "I don't die; I just leave. I see myself as etheric; I can go from spirit form to physical form at will. It's a place like the afterlife." The subject was describing what sounded to me like Lemuria, where some Atlanteans were thought to have originated.[1] (See Chapter 16 on Lost Contients.)

In summation, following the recollection of the three lifetimes contributing to her fibromyalgia problem, I told the subject that her present-day healing efforts probably triggered this pattern of cell memory, which was carried forward from prior lifetimes in which she had been prevented from using her healing talent. This cell memory set in motion the recall of physical pain and negative emotions, resulting in a fibromyalgia syndrome, which again was an attempt to put a stop to her healing others. I suggested to the subject that she release this memory, now that she understands how it relates to her present disease. By doing so, and thereby interrupting the neuronal brain-body connection pattern that had originated in the past, she would be able to eliminate the effects it had caused in her present life. I believe

---

1. See also "Lemuria" on page 151.

the subconscious memory carries over from lifetime to lifetime and imprints the current mind-body connection with the same neuronal pattern that was formed in prior lifetimes. While there is a tendency to repeat patterns from lifetime to lifetime, these patterns can be interrupted and dissipated.

Six weeks after the session I spoke to this subject and was happy to hear that she had over 90% less discomfort during the first month following her regression. Soon after that she developed an allergy which brought back some of the pain; however, by her own estimation she still remains at least 30% to 40% improved. In this situation, I feel that phone reinforcement and a repeat session would be extremely helpful in reestablishing the complete release of this devastating negative programming of the subconscious. Further follow up was not possible.

THE CASE OF LOIS LANDERS:
MIGRAINE HEADACHES

When taken back to the cause of her migraine headaches, this young female subject remained silent as she tearfully envisioned herself in an episode as an adult woman in the 15th century, cringing and holding her bloodied head in a village square. People were yelling and throwing rocks at her. She was being stoned to death. It was only after I had brought her out of the hypnotic state that the subject could relate the events to me that she had experienced in that lifetime. I felt that the circumstances of that 15th century incident were so traumatic that they prohibited Lois from voicing the moment-to-moment details as she perceived them during the regression. The revelation that the stoning death was the cause of her migraines was understood by the subject and put into proper perspective by her conscious mind.

Subsequent contact with Lois indicated that she had experienced a great degree of improvement with the severity of her headaches.

THE CASE OF DONALD MAYER:
TMJ DISORDER

This thirty-one-year-old male subject came to me with TMJ (temporomandibular joint) pain. Besides analgesics, the subject was also taking antidepressants. Several years prior to the onset of the TMJ problem, he suffered from a panic disorder, which has since improved. The TMJ has been a direct result of grinding his teeth during his sleeping hours.

Under deep hypnosis, Donald's higher self responded immediately to my request to go to the cause of his TMJ problem. He soon found himself in China in the late 1500s, where he was observing a wild tiger nervously prancing around a young Oriental woman fastened to a pole. In this lifetime, the subject was a middle-aged Oriental man who spoke about a frightened young girl he was looking at. He said, "She is afraid, but I am not."

As I took him back in time so as to make sense of this scene, Donald saw himself on several occasions meeting with a particular man who seemed to be in authority and of royal status. The man wore lavishly ornamental clothing, and the immediate surroundings were very much like a palace, decorated in gaudy colors. This Oriental nobleman would give him tasks to perform, and by doing so would induce immediate flashbacks of the scene with the tiger circling the frightened young woman. The last time he was given a task, he flashed back to a scene where he was fighting the tiger with a spear and was sustaining many wounds from this large, ferocious beast. As he thrust his spear into the excited animal's heart, he could see that the young woman's face was frozen with fear. As the tiger fell dead, he could hear the roar of a large crowd. He stood there proudly, barely able to breathe, with blood oozing from his head and arms. He looked over to the girl, who showed no emotion, not even relief, and then to the crowd, who cheered loudly and applauded. A man soon led him back to a special room, where his wounds were attended to. At this moment, the entire lifetime became very clear to Donald. The man of royalty was the Emperor, who had decreed that the subject, whose name was Chu in that lifetime, face the tiger as a punishment for a crime that he had committed. The Emperor put on this bloody spectacle for his own entertainment, as well as for his people. The subject sensed that Chu was confined to that room, given good food and forced to face the tiger when called upon.

At this point, I asked Donald to go backwards in time to the first moment that he had faced the tiger. He became noticeably frightened as he saw himself in the arena with the tiger for the first time. There was no crowd, just the Emperor and his court. The tiger's trainer was present, and this allowed the animal to exhibit a greater degree of calmness. As a result, the tiger paid no attention to Chu, who stood in the center of the arena, shaking uncontrollably with fear. The Emperor decided to repeat the performance in front of a crowd. This time, Chu had been given a knife and was told to kill the tiger. Again, Chu found himself standing alone in the center of the arena, facing the same trained tiger. The crowd roared in great anticipation of seeing blood spilled (a sickening sound reminiscent of the Roman Coliseum days). Chu was overcome with fright but noticed that the tiger remained docile. Deciding to take advantage of the situation, he suddenly lunged forward and plunged the knife into the tiger's chest. As the tiger's life slipped away, Chu felt great sympathy for the beast and then walked from the arena amidst loud cheers.

The Emperor continued the performances, much to Chu's dismay. The tigers became wilder and Chu's wounds more severe. Sometimes he was given a spear, sometimes a knife. Little by little, his fear began to diminish. In an effort to please the bloodthirsty crowd, the Emperor decided to place a young woman in the center of the arena, tied to a stake. Chu fought many tigers through the years and in spite of his wounds became good at what he did, to the point of becoming arrogant. The pain from his wounds appeared to increase his pride. Chu pleased the Emperor for many years and eventually was given his freedom. Upon leaving, Chu feared going back out into the world; he felt that he would miss the recognition and the security of his food and shelter. The remainder of his life was filled with pain and loneliness.

Speaking with Donald both during and after the session, I emphasized that the chronic doses of intense fear that accompanied that lifetime saturated his subconscious cell memory with an unfathomable amount of negative emotion. Like an explosive booby-trap, this cell memory was set off by something that occurred in his present life and set into motion the destructive nocturnal teeth-grinding as a response to the feeling of overwhelming fear. Another possibility is that the subject may have been having recurring dreams related to that lifetime and not recalling them. I felt strongly that the subject would improve, now that his conscious mind had witnessed and understood these past life circumstances and the mechanism by which they had affected his present life.

A follow-up call approximately two years later revealed that Donald's TMJ pain had diminished significantly for several months following the regression; however personal problems that occurred later added undue stress to his life, with a resultant increase in his TMJ discomfort. I suggested a follow-up session for reinforcement.

THE CASE OF DAN WHITMAN: GASTRIC REFLUX

This middle-aged college professor presented with a gastric reflux problem that required medication almost daily. Pinpointing the source of this problem, his Higher Self revealed that he was unnecessarily suffering from stress that he was creating for himself. The stress was based on his compulsion to please others, to measure up, to be perfect. He was assuming the responsibility for the happiness of others in many of his relationships, primarily with his family and his students. Throughout his life, he had been unable to let go of this perceived responsibility, and as a result, continued to suffer the physical consequences of the stress it inevitably created. Ensuring that Dan thoroughly assimilated what had come through, I then emphasized that he forgive himself for adhering to this subconscious misperception and understand that every person is totally responsible for his own happiness.

Not every person will return to a past-life experience as a causal explanation of a physical or emotional problem. Sometimes the Higher Self, in its infinite wisdom, will lay out the problem in simple terms, without pulling any punches. It will often show the subject's conscious mind how the problem relates to the subject's personality and zeroes in to defects therein. The Higher Self thus exposes these personal defects without any apology or excuse and opens the door for the therapist to suggest solutions to correct the problem. These solutions will often be very logical and not offensive to the subject in the altered state of hypnosis, since he is more open to suggestions which are understandable. This case is representative of this type of Higher Self insight into this particular subject's problem.

A follow-up phone call well over two years later revealed that Dan experienced significant improvement within the first year and complete disappearance of the gastric reflux after two years.

THE CASE OF VICKI LARKIN: IRRITABLE BOWEL SYNDROME

This forty-five-year-old female subject was seen for the first time with irritable bowel syndrome, which she had had for several years. This syndrome is characterized by constipation, colicky abdominal pain, mucus stools, bloating, nausea, and dyspepsia (upper abdominal or chest discomfort, described as indigestion, fullness, gas, or a burning pain).

Vicki easily slipped into a deep state of hypnosis and was visually taken to her Higher Self. She was then asked to call out for her Spirit Guide. I suggested that she return to the cause of her irritable bowel syndrome, using the help of her Spirit Guide. The subject immediately began describing herself as an extremely ill twenty-year-old black female, living within an African tribe in the year 1903. Vicki appeared noticeably uncomfortable as she carried on with a detailed account of what was happening to her and to her tribe. It seemed that everyone in the tribe had been struck with a fulminating parasitic infestation that caused their intestines to be filled with worms. This parasitic disease caused a severe form of constipation, abdominal pain, nausea, and vomiting. This young woman died a horrible death, along with the entire tribe.

At this time I emphasized the importance of her understanding that this subconscious cell memory had somehow been reactivated and was now responsible for bringing back the pain, nausea, constipation, and other physical symptoms that had affected her and led to her death in a past life. I drilled home the fact that her conscious mind would now be able to recognize and fully comprehend the cause of her gastrointestinal problem. Such recognition and comprehension would then enable her to release the traumatic effect that this past life memory has had upon her physical body. Also, her conscious mind would view this memory with a definite distinction of time and be aware that her subconscious makes no such distinction.

How one dies during a past life leaves a rather indelible emotional imprint upon his cell memory, one which seems to enhance the ability of that memory to surface. When this occurs in one's present life it often appears as a phobia or an emotional or physical illness.

In a follow-up phone call three months later, Vicki exuberantly stated that she was very much improved.

7

VALIDATION

I carried out validation of specific events experienced during regression by comparing these events to recorded history. Many such cases are disbursed throughout this book, and any such documentation is noted at the end of each case. Uncovering historical validation of hypnotic past-life regression content is not only extremely rewarding, it is also incredibly exciting. But not all cases can be validated in this way. My thoughts on why this occurs are discussed on page 193.

The following five cases demonstrate how one or more incidents within a segment of the subject's previous lifetime have been verified by recorded history.

THE BATTLE OF HATTIN

Roger, a highly intelligent, middle-aged subject, wished to undergo regression to experience a past life. He was extremely fascinated with metaphysical topics, and regression was no exception. Following induction, he easily slipped into deep hypnosis and went back to the year 1187 A.D. In that lifetime the subject was a nobleman who had landed at Antioch to take part in the Crusades. He was 46.

It seems he was a knight delivering a message to other knights, all of whom wore cloaks to conceal their breastplates. These noblemen were in hiding in a remote mountainous area. The message was from the king of Jerusalem and carried his red and orange crown on the wax seal. Roger spoke to the group of men gathered there, "Jerusalem is lost... Edessa is being overrun by the Muslims. All the states are in peril." Roger had been present at the battle of Hattin, where Saladin surrounded and destroyed the Christian army. He again spoke, "When the states fall, Constantinople will fall. There is a terrible wave sweeping over the east. The Greeks will make their last stand there...too late for reinforcements."

On the following session, Roger was taken back to the battle of Hattin. He and another knight had occupied an observation point high above the field of battle. He was sickened by what he saw below and said, "Our solders are as chess pieces... all knocked down... so much smoke...must send message to Acre and Kerak and tell them attack is imminent. We need to get reinforcements before all positions are overrun. Such a great loss... prisoners will be shown no mercy. We were trapped, fooled by a treacherous forged message to bring our forces here, out in the open."

Roger explained how Saladin lured the many thousands of knights and foot soldiers out from where they were impregnable and well supplied with food and water. He told of how the water supply was soon exhausted and how the sun heated up the knights' mesh and armor as they searched aimlessly for the Muslim army.

The heavy armor of the Christian knights and their large horses made them defensively unbeatable, but in the open and on the offensive, this great contingent was easily overcome by heat, thirst, and exhaustion, making them easy prey for the Muslims. The slow mobility of their big, overheated horses, weighted down by armor, was no match for Saladin's lightweight cavalry. The Muslims had poisoned the closest water hole; and when this came into view by the Christian army, the thirst-crazed knights and foot soldiers broke ranks and ran for the water. With the ranks broken and in disarray, confusion reigned, and Saladin's hordes swept down upon the Crusaders and annihilated them.

Tearfully observing the aftermath of the devastating massacre, Roger murmured, "The smog hanging over the battlefield has a spiritual quality. Many thousands were killed; only a few hundred surrendered... they will be slaughtered. I saw very few escape... already the looters are there."

Historically: a fragile truce between the Muslims and Christians was shattered when Reginald of Chatillon attacked a Muslim caravan.

Saladin responded by proclaiming jihád against the Christian kingdom and bringing his army to a point south of the Sea of Galilee. The
Crusaders, some twenty thousand strong, including twelve hundred
heavily armed cavalry, waited in an area well-supplied with water and
provisions. Saladin, the nephew of the deceased Muslim ruler Nured-
din, had gained the reputation as a shrewd and cunning leader and
was able to unite the many Muslim factions and mold them into a
large and efficient fighting force.

Knowing that Count Raymond of Tripoli's wife was in the town
of Tiberias, Saladin dispatched a token force to take Tiberias, hoping
to lure the Crusaders out of their excellent defensive and well-supplied position. Raymond and others persuaded the king of Jerusalem
not to succumb to the trap and give the order to march; however, late
at night other leaders of the Crusade persuaded the king to change his
mind, and the message to march was given.

Within one day, the blistering heat of summer exhausted the
water supply, leaving the Crusaders to suffer a night of thirst and face
another day of stifling heat. Totally exhausted and dehydrated, the
Crusaders soon found themselves surrounded by the Muslims. Enduring heavy smoke from grass fires set by the Muslims, the Christian
foot soldiers broke ranks and ran, thus putting to ruin the vital coordi-
nation with the heavily armed knights in the cavalry. Following Saladin's last charge, most of the knights lay dead. Some averted the
carnage by surrendering, and only a few escaped. Saladin's overwhelming victory at Hattin had virtually left the kingdom of Jerusalem defenseless.

The historical version of what happened at Hattin is uncannily similar to what Roger recalled of the battle. The fact that the decision not to
march had been made and then rescinded late at night at the last moment
could easily account for the suspected forged message to march. Also, the
statement, "So much smoke" would be explained by the grass fires set by
the Muslims. The Crusading foot soldiers broke ranks as Roger had
described, although there was no mention of a poisoned water hole in the

historical rendition. The sight of water by thirst-crazed men would be more than a good reason for them to break ranks and run.

MAROONED ON AN ISLAND

Cindy was one of many subjects who, for one reason or another, had a nagging curiosity about being regressed to past times. She arrived on the morning of her first appointment with an air of expectancy. Easily slipping into a deep state of hypnosis, she soon found herself seeing large rocks by the ocean in the dim light of the moon. Advancing her in time to the light of the following day, it soon became evident that she was a man in his early thirties, lonely, dirty, and totally alone on a deserted island. His name was Robert Harden, and the story of how he came to be marooned on this God-forsaken island was about to unfold as I prodded him with questions and regressed him further back in time, so as to observe the circumstances that led to this unspeakable isolation and desperate attempts at survival.

I denoted pride in the way he spoke of himself as a young, 21-year-old Englishman, who was making a good living working for the East India Company. He was in charge of all cargo that went on or off the ships. Robert loved his work, but a burning desire to sail on one of the many ships he dealt with had become an obsession. He often dreamed of such an adventure and became ecstatic when his father contacted his friend, John Lars, a registered sea captain, who then made arrangements for Robert to accompany him on board his East India Company ship when it set sail for Madagascar. Robert described the day of his departure as a perfect day, being barely able to contain his excitement as the green and gold brig unfolded its rigging and was now under sail from Dover, England, in the year 1805. They were to pick up spices and plants from Madagascar and return to Dover, England. Robert thought it odd that Captain Lars' crew was French but did not let this observation detract from his much-dreamed-of adventure.

After two months at sea, they found themselves close to Madagascar. Captain Lars summoned Robert to his quarters and informed him that it had been decided that the ship will pick up the cargo but will not return to England as planned. Other arrangements had been made to dispose of the valuable cargo, and the crew will share in the spoils. The captain indicated that Robert's father was his friend, and so Robert will receive a share of this fortune. Robert was shocked by this revelation; his dream was crushed in this one, surreal moment in the captain's quarters. His moral values and loyalty to the East India Company could not be compromised, and so he swallowed deeply, gathered his composure, and informed the captain that he could not be part of this piracy. Captain Lars promptly confined Robert to his quarters.

While in confinement, a plethora of thoughts invaded Robert's mind. "I don't think he'll kill me, after all, he's my father's friend. They intend to steal the ship and the cargo. Captain Lars said I could be rich, but I could never do this... he's locked me in my quarters. He really doesn't want to hurt me, but he doesn't want me in the way, either." Engrossed in sadness and disappointment, Robert is soon taken to a small island and dropped off without food. Somewhat numb from the experience, Robert watched the ship as it sailed away into the horizon and thought, "Leaving me on an island was his better choice; I'm not very worried."

Robert survived on that island in the tradition of Robinson Crusoe. He was able to devise a shelter, make fire, save rainwater, and catch fish between the big rocks. The island was small, with very little vegetation and no animals. Robert was very low on energy and was only able to explore a small area of the island. The nights were getting colder, and his clothes were disintegrating along with his hopes, since there were no ships to be seen. He remained tired and weak and unbelievably lonely as the years passed.

Advancing him to the day of his death, he seemed to welcome his passing with a quiet resignation. He described his death experience as "quiet and beautiful and not a big deal." He said he just got too tired, as he saw himself with a long beard and fingernails, naked, with no hair remaining on his head. He felt happy and yearned for peacefulness, saying, "I see the light, the loving light… I don't feel as if I have to go anywhere."

Once securely in the afterlife, my subject began to review aspects of her life as Robert. "I trusted my instincts, but they were not always sound… I still trust people, in spite of what happened. I lived this life inside of myself. There were not a lot of people in my life, and I didn't pay much attention to those who were. I just wanted to sail. Friends were not important. People liked me, and I liked them, but I just wanted to sail. I was at peace with myself for long periods of time on that island. I was profoundly sad but not unhappy… for I had achieved my dream and experienced the joy of sailing."

Historically: Research indicated that an East India Company ship sailed out of Dover, England, in 1805, never to be heard from again.

SPORTS REPORTER

Several of my research subjects underwent scores of regressions. One such subject astounded me one day with a nub of information that proved to be true when placed under scrutiny. This intellectual and metaphysically-inclined female subject knew almost nothing about the history of baseball, yet she described a situation that occurred in a past life that turned out to be a diminutive factual nuance of baseball trivia that represented a hundred to one shot.

The subject recalled a life in the 1940s as Eddie Robert Johnson, a Pittsburgh newspaper reporter who wrote for the industrial and sports sections of the newspaper. As Eddie's life unfolded, it became obvious that reporting on baseball games had become a way of life for him. As I gradually advanced him in time from one significant event to another, he surprised me by saying that he was covering a very important game in New York City. It was a special game because the Brooklyn Dodgers had a new manager. The year was 1947.

Historically: My research into baseball history disappointed me initially when I discovered that Leo Durocher managed the Brooklyn Dodgers from 1939 to 1948. Digging further, however, I found that

Leo Durocher was accused of associating with known gamblers and was suspended for one year: 1947.

PERSPECTIVE OF A 19TH-CENTURY GERMAN SOLDIER

Curious about who she was in a past life, this subject went back to a life as a 35-year old man named Hans, who lived in Germany in the 1800s. Advanced one year in time, Hans was found to be in his home town in the eastern part of Germany, east of Berlin. Advanced one year further, Hans found himself crawling in a ditch, wearing a gray uniform and a bowl-like helmet, while he carried a rifle with a bayonet attached.

I asked Private Hans to go backward in time to when he had signed up for the German army. Hans saw himself signing up for service in the German army in July of 1812. He said, "I am writing down that I am thirty years old so they will take me in the service. I'm actually thirty-seven years old, but they don't know that."

Going forward in time in order to explore what happened to Hans in the ditch, Hans became very anxious and said that French soldiers were chasing him and his comrades. As Hans tried to escape Napoleon's troops, he felt a sharp pain in the back of his head as a bullet pierced his skull and killed him instantly. As his spirit separated and rose from his body, he recognized deceased family members coming to greet him. Hans felt great peace and contentment as he entered the light and felt very strongly that he had accomplished his lesson of duty and honor. He saw the date of his death on his gravestone as June 10, 1813. The subject awakened from this session with a headache in the left occiput and temple area, where the bullet would have entered Hans' head. The discomfort dissipated within minutes, and the subject commented that experiencing this lifetime was more real than she could ever have imagined.

Historically: the eastern part of Germany, namely Prussia, was the first region of Germany to declare war on France, well before the rest of Germany became involved. The declaration of war was formalized in February of 1813. Hans died in battle in June of 1813. His age progression was correct since he first observed this lifetime at 35 years old and was advanced two years hence, to a time when he volunteered for the army; at that time he said that he was 37 years old. Interestingly, he lied about his age so that he would be accepted into the German army, something that was often done by men entering the service, even into the 20th century.

LABOR FROM THE PERSPECTIVE OF THE FETUS

This young woman's first regression began as an age regression back to fetal life. Always interested in what labor is like for the infant, I then reversed the process and had the fetus progress in age up to the time of her mother's labor. The subject relayed how the squeezing sensation of the uterine contractions felt, when all of a sudden she became pale and said her body felt weird. Her pulse increased dramatically, and she claimed that she had difficulty breathing in this dark bubble. Attempts at removing her from the scene were not effective, so I took her back in time, once again, to when she was a young fetus and then woke her up. Upon awakening, the subject said that the experience was entirely too real. That particular regression took place early in my career, before I learned to reinforce my protective suggestions.

Historically: The subject called me sometime later and informed me that her mother confirmed she had had severe fetal distress in labor, requiring an immediate delivery. All I can say is, "It figures."

A form of validation can also be attained by comparing writing styles and personality traits of the subject with those that occurred during a particular past life. This is especially feasible when the past-life person was well-known or famous. Dramatic manifestations of inexplicable abilities under hypnosis, such as xenoglossy, or speaking languages unknown to the subject, as well as writing in such languages, also serves as proof of previous lives.

This chapter would not be complete without including an excerpt from McGill's *Hypnotherapy Encyclopedia*, by Ormond McGill,

Ph.D. This quote is from his chapter titled, "Evidence of Previous Lifetimes"[1]:

"The case of Alan Lee, a Caucasian man born in Philadelphia May 4, 1942, provides the best objective evidence of the fact of reincarnation. Alan Lee never completed school beyond the tenth grade and never had learned any other language besides English.

In research conducted at Maryland Psychiatric Research Center, 1974, Alan was regressed to sixteen previous lives by professional hypnotist Irvin Mordes. All of the sessions were witnessed and affirmed by the physicians and researchers who affixed their signatures: Walter Tauke, M.D., Jerome Rubins, M.D., Edward L. Reed, M.D., Ruth Martin, John H. Metzinger, Victor Schlector, M.D., Walter Panhnke, M.D.

With each previous life regression came an uncanny ability to speak and write in the language of whatever period of history he was reexperiencing. Half of the languages he expressed, not taught for centuries, were checked for accuracy. In the hypnotic state Alan spoke and wrote fluent American English, rural English, ancient English, Italian, Cherokee Indian (Tehalgic), Normal French, idiomatic Latin, classic Greek, Hebrew, Egyptian hieroglyphics, Egyptian demotic, Egyptian hieratic, Atlantean, and Lemurian. He was regressed back each time and requested to write a description of his memory in the manner of the writing of the time. The ancient scripts of his handwriting are persuasive, factual evidence of previous lives.

During this study, Alan's vital signs were carefully monitored. His blood pressure would suddenly drop from his normal 120 over 80 to 60 over 30 and his pulse decreased. Such a reaction may be normally associated with a state of shock, but no such thing occurred. He was fine in every way."

---

1. McGill, Ormand, Ph.D., *Hypnotherapy Encyclopedia*, Creativity Unlimited Press, 2001, Palos Verdes, CA p. 633

8

SOUL RECOGNITION

RECOGNITION DURING OTHER LIFETIMES

Of interest is how soul recognition occurs. I would like to
describe this process in detail; however, the best I can do is relate
the way in which most subjects describe it. I'm told that recognition
of familiar souls in another lifetime is primarily a matter of feelings
that the subject has about that soul. Thus, a past-life soul is identified by the emotions that it evokes from the subject. Once again, we
are reminded of the importance of emotions in the human condition. Our subconscious memory brings up individuals from the past
who look and sound quite different from those we know intimately
in our present life, yet we can only know who they are by how they
make us feel.

Emotions are powerful. They can kill us by allowing repetitive
damage to occur in our physical bodies, or they can keep us alive by
allowing the feelings of positive and joyful thoughts to enhance the
will to live. Awareness and intuitive analysis of our emotions can
help us integrate these feelings so as to bring about a greater understanding of our soul and its impact upon our personality. Thus, we
soon find that the qualities of the soul influence our all-important
intentions which then become more beneficial to others and lead to
a more harmonious karmic behavior and therefore a more peaceful,
joyous life.

RECOGNITION IN THE AFTERLIFE

From my observation of subjects who have died in past lives, I
have found that their recognition of souls in the afterlife is usually
visual. Subjects report that they carry over the same visual sense

into the afterlife as they have in incarnations; however, their recognition of another soul in the afterlife is based on this visual sense, not on emotional interpretations, as occurs during incarnations. It is what the subject sees with his mind's eye, and this is usually an etheric version of another soul's physical appearance when last seen on Earth, but often younger. Most subjects will describe familiar souls as being healthy, robust adults, in the prime of their life; however, occasionally these souls would appear to them just as they were the last time that they were seen by the subject, regardless of their age.

Subjects have told me that they can change how they appear to other souls in the afterlife, depending on how they would like that soul to see them, thus they would usually assume the appearance that is most recognizable to another soul. The subjects have also stated that regardless of the image portrayed, the soul's identity cannot be hidden from other souls. In addition, the telepathic communication that is carried on between the souls seems to complete the identification. Again, it is worth mentioning that my subjects' experiences are similar to those described in Michael Newton's book, *The Journey of Souls*. In my mind this only corroborates the fact that commonality in experience leans towards validity.

UNDERSTANDING UNEXPLAINED FEELINGS OF CONNECTION: THE LOVE OF HER LIVES

Evelyn Andreas was an attractive middle-aged woman who came to me in search of insights into her present life. She needed to explore the reasons for an unexplained feeling of connection with someone very special to her.

Easily falling into a deep hypnotic state, this subject went back to a 1700s life as a Native American in the Black Hills of South Dakota. In that life she was married to Running Bear. She had great love for him and their son and was extremely happy. During a battle with the Pawnees, Running Bear was killed, and her tribe had to keep moving to avert further battles. Eventually captured by white men, she and her son were "adopted" by a settler, and she lived a life of a farmer's wife until her death in her mid-50s. In the light, she became ecstatic, as she was reunited with Running Bear, recognizing him as Robert, her present fiancé.

Evelyn incarnated again as a woman, this time to Wickenburg, Virginia, in the mid-1800s. Her first husband died during the Civil War, and she remarried. I asked her to advance or go backwards in time to the happiest moment in that lifetime. She immediately recalled a very intimate moment of passion with a special person in that lifetime. I asked if there were many moments like this with her husband in that lifetime. She replied, "It was not with my husband; it was with Jack, a man who I fell deeply in love with. He was a sailor, and I only knew him for a brief time, since he had to leave. He said he would return, but he never did." Her life continued on in a mundane vein until her death in 1924. In the light she recognized Jack as Robert, her fiancé, aka Running Bear. Evelyn and Robert appeared very youthful to each other again as they embraced in the afterlife.

Following this session, the subject smiled broadly and said, "You have enabled me to understand why I feel so undeniably connected to Robert." Evelyn then proceeded to tell me a fascinating and heart-warming story that smacked of synchronicity. She had dated Robert exclusively while they were in their 20s. Then something occurred that made it necessary for him to move away. Evelyn knew that she missed him, for Robert had always treated her well, and she felt that he was very special. Many years passed. Evelyn married, had a child, and eventually divorced her husband. One day she heard from a mutual friend that Robert was coming to town for a friend's wedding. Circumstances were such that Evelyn and Robert missed seeing each other at this wedding. Two more years passed, and then synchronicity stepped into the picture. Evelyn was visiting a friend who also knew Robert. While she was there, a phone call came through from Robert, and Evelyn was invited to speak to him; they exchanged phone numbers, addresses, and small talk, and so it started. Evelyn had learned to listen to the voice of her soul when choosing the various paths of life that were presented to her. She had learned that she could not hide from her soul.

This session was to be Evelyn's one and only session, since she was moving to Wyoming within a few days to be with Robert on a permanent basis. I'm sure that these two souls had made a former agreement to cross paths again in this lifetime. They seemingly had made choices in this life which appeared to ensure that they would not be together; however, as it happened, synchronistic events gave them another opportunity to make these choices, only this time they followed their heart.

9

EXPLAINING DÉJÀ VU

Déjà vu is defined in Webster's Dictionary as "the illusion that one has previously had an experience that is actually new to one." When this phenomenon occurs, there is a feeling of intense familiarity with a person, place, thing, or activity, when there has in fact been no related experience to account for this. Most people have undergone déjà vu-type experiences sometime in their lifetime. My research has shown that, déjà vu, much like recurrent dreams, has its origin in a previous lifetime. Whenever I instruct my subjects to go back to the cause of this déjà vu, they routinely find themselves in a past life that fully explains the connection to their present experience.

VISION AT THE ALCAZAR

The following case is that of Natalie Torito, a middle-aged woman who experienced déjà vu on two occasions while visiting Segovia, Spain. Her first trip to Segovia was with her parents when she was ten years old. They toured the Alcazar, the castle of Ferdinand and Isabella; and it was in that courtyard that Natalie had a strong feeling that she had been there before. This same feeling was repeated with the same intensity thirteen years later, when she returned as a young adult. The fascinating and inspiring lifetime that I uncovered will follow, but not until I explain why this case presented as a bit of a challenge.

This subject is a shining example of why it is so important not to give up easily when attempting to hypnotize or regress an individual. The first session was an exercise in frustration, as the subject could not allow herself to relax or empty her mind of extraneous thoughts.

The second session was an improvement as the subject went into a light trance and was able to attain the beginnings of an age regression. I spent a full three hours breaking through the resistance that her conscious mind had put up. This was a true challenge, and I didn't mind using my usual three-hour session for this purpose, since she remained motivated and hopeful for success.

Natalie Torito was an avid pupil of Dr. Raymond Moody's Consciousness Studies program at UNLV and had become exceptionally metaphysical in her approach to life. The idea of experiencing past lifetimes had become an important aspiration, and she had made up her mind that she was not going to be one of the ten percent of subjects who are unable to accomplish this. I thought to myself, "Boy, have I changed." In the days of my practice, the use of three hours of time was so different. I could drive twenty miles to the hospital, deliver a baby, and return home in that time. I could also see a full morning of patients in the office or complete a major and several minor surgeries. In a way I was proving something to myself, that I indeed had developed a burning passion for this metaphysical work, and I was approaching it as I did my practice of medicine—tirelessly and full bore, with all stops removed.

The third session resulted in a state of deep hypnosis; however, when attempts at regression were made, Natalie stated that she felt that she was walking slowly, almost stumbling, with her arms outstretched in front of her. I asked her to describe what she saw.

She replied, "Nothing, everything is black... I'm wearing a hood over my head." She paused for a few seconds with a look of annoyance on her face and then spoke with great frustration, "I feel like I'm outside, but I'm walking blind... it's a cruel trick to deprive me of seeing and hearing my past life."

Having encountered no situation like this before, my mind metaphorically turned to thoughts of football games I've been in: "I could either punt or fake it and go for an end run." I went for the end run and simply said, "Then just take off the hood!" The subject displayed a rather broad smile as she began to excitedly relay a detailed account of what was around her and how she perceived herself. I thought to myself, "Well, I'll be damned… it worked." I smiled and continued with the session.

Natalie was impressed with the long red hair that flowed out from under the hood as she removed it. She was a young girl in her early twenties, walking along a dirt path in Segovia, Spain, in the early 16th century. Maricela Alvarez lived alone in a small stucco house surrounded by chickens in her yard and supported herself by selling eggs in town.

I directed the subject to go to the most significant event in her youth. She said that Maricela experienced a vision in her home when she was four years old. She described this vision as an angel; however, she thought the wings of the angel were actually a bright aura surrounding his body. She felt that the vision spoke to her in her mind and said, "I will be with you always… there is nothing to fear."

Shortly after this episode and many more visitations, Maricela became aware that she was gifted. Unfortunately, these psychic gifts were looked upon as the work of the devil by her family and the local townspeople. These feelings of mistrust led to rejection and resulted in her leading a lonely life. This however did not seem to bother Maricela; she felt that they did not understand and therefore remained fearful.

At thirteen years old, Maricela was in the courtyard of Ferdinand and Isabella's castle when she experienced a vision of the Blessed Virgin Mother. As her eyes transfixed upon this brilliant, shimmering, full-bodied figure, surrounded by a bright light several feet above the courtyard, Maricela heard Her speak telepathically, "You have chosen to proclaim the truth. Your faith and devotion have not gone unnoticed." People around Maricela thought she was crazy, for they saw and heard nothing.

The Blessed Mother continued, "Do not doubt yourself. Within each of us lies the same power that lies within Jesus. We have the power to heal, to resurrect, to forgive, to love all, to see good in all.

Listen to these intentions; they are accurate. Be not afraid of them...
you will not be alone... I will be with you. There is much work to be
done. Whenever you feel weak or afraid, come to the courtyard and
you will feel my presence." Then a shimmering vibration of energy in
the form of a golden aura surrounded Maricela. Unable to stand, she
remained kneeling and was enveloped by awe, humility, peace, and
strength. Her rational mind questioned this unbelievable vision but at
the same time was captivated by its reality.

Maricela felt humble that such a personification of authority and
peace should choose to communicate with her. She also felt great
peace and confidence, but not superiority, as she thought, "The Lord
will never let us down, as others will. Mary is the symbol of the
divine who is making me aware that I must address the needs of other
people and not judge them. I can sense my countenance and understand why my face feels like a diamond with many facets, many emotions all at once; at the same time, I am acutely aware of the
magnitude of this miraculous human experience. It is time for me to
touch other lives with my heart. Because of this vision I will be better
able to access and focus upon my inner strength."

By 20, Maricela often found herself at the courtyard of Ferdinand and Isabella when she felt weak or afraid. There she always
found strength, knowing that Mary was present. Maricela would
speak to Mary through prayer when she felt unloved and in turmoil.
Reassuring answers always came. Maricela could only speak of this
vision to the local priest, who said she was blessed by her awareness.
Maricela welcomed the blessing and strength that was imparted to her
by the priest, since the townspeople offered only ridicule and angry
statements. She did much healing with her hands but would always
put her finger to her lips, so people would not speak about it. People
were grateful but fearful. Maricela could break up lung congestion
with one treatment, stop bleeding, heal wounds, and perform many
other acts of compassionate healing for the people.

At age 25, Maricela began to bleed from her hands and feet. The townspeople who saw this did not trust or believe her. Only the local priest believed her. He told his congregation at church that Maricela's stigmata was truly occurring and that she was blessed. Still the people did not believe, and other priests were called in to observe this phenomenon, only to insist that she was tricking them by putting lamb's blood on her feet and hands.

Maricela never married, as men did not arouse passions in her; she did, however, befriend Fedrico, an old man who believed in her. The visions continued to occur every four or five years, until Maricela reached her mid-forties. During her last vision, the Blessed Virgin told her to be true to herself. Some of the people did believe that Maricela was blessed but would not acknowledge it. At one point, Queen Isabella summoned Maricela to question her about her visions and see if Maricela could help her mentally-ill daughter. Unfortunately, Isabella was unable to have faith in Maricela even though she wanted to.

When Maricela turned 56, she became ill with a kidney disease. The priest was present when she was near death. As she was dying, Maricela thought, "I'm ready to leave… I know I will see Mary again… I have no regrets leaving this Earth… I see Her!"

Maricela's spirit left her body as the Blessed Mother called to her and spoke words of comfort. "There, there, My child. Have no fear… we need you here."

In the light, Maricela saw Fedrico, her old friend, who turned young in front of her eyes; she then saw her parents and others who were unfamiliar to her. She now heard her name sung but did not see a choir. The song was welcoming her. She said, "This is where I'm supposed to be."

I asked what lessons she had learned as Maricela Alvarez.

She replied, "To listen to my heart; happiness comes from listening to one's own heart. Also, I learned to live love, and I did it well."

I then asked, "What was your happiest moment in that lifetime?"

"Seeing Mary for the first time. I had the most unbelievable feeling of awe, wonder, and value. I could live many thousands of lives and never experience that."

It's very typical of the reincarnation process for the soul to experience everything, including a variety of cultures, races, and religious beliefs. I thought it was very interesting that this subject was not Catholic.

This particular regression experience was very rich in detail and fully explained why the déjà vu had such a powerful impact upon this subject. I am sure that there are many readers out there who would be extremely eager to discover the source of their déjà vu experiences; however, there are also many individuals out there who are either disinterested or casually pass off such feelings of familiarity as a fluke. Rather than remaining numb and indifferent to the subtle and intuitive signs that appear in our life, such as déjà vu and synchronicity, people can enrich their lives by paying attention to these subtleties and pondering their meaning. In other words, if people follow their heart, it probably will get them back on their life's path.

10

SUBJECTS SHARING THE SAME LIFE

THE WORKPLACE

Occasionally and sometimes synchronistically I come across a regression situation that automatically validates a particular lifetime without the necessity of referring to events or dates. What I am speaking of here is a lifetime that two of my subjects shared. On two separate occasions I regressed a subject back to a lifetime whereupon she recognized an individual as a friend or relative currently living in her present life. Following this I was fortunate enough to be given the opportunity to regress the person who was recognized. In doing this I was careful to only instruct them to return to a life with the original subject if such a life truly occurred. In both cases, the details of the prior lifetime together were not made known to the second subject before that individual was regressed into that same life.

The first case involved Nicole, a restaurant owner, and her female employee, Doris. While elaborating upon her history, Nicole mentioned that she had one employee that she was very fond of; however, that employee for no apparent reason appeared to harbor resentment towards her. This confusing situation obviously remained prominent in her mind as I instructed her under deep hypnosis to return to a life that will help her understand her present relationships. She promptly found herself in Montana in the 1800s. She was a bearded man in that life, involved in a love affair with the woman she recognized as her present employee. In this lifetime he found it necessary to leave her, promising to return. He allowed himself to be blinded by the acquisition of material wealth and ignored his true feelings for her. He sent her money and often yearned to return to her but money was more important, so important that he never returned. She found someone else but never stopped loving him. He died lonely and miserable.

I saw Nicole's employee one week later and instructed her under deep hypnosis to return to a lifetime with her employer if such a lifetime existed. She found herself living in the same time frame as a 16-year-old girl. She described her employer as a man who took advantage of her innocence. She felt that their love affair was quite passionate, but also that this man was dishonest and "was all about money." He left her and never returned as promised. She continued to love him but found someone else.

The intimate and volatile love affair shared by these two individuals in that lifetime served to answer many questions for them regarding their present relationship as a business owner and employee.

THE CONVENT

The second case revolved around a subject who was regressed to a life as a nun living in a convent in Istanbul in the 1800s. The subject was an older nun who had taken a young nun under her wing. She was worried about this young nun, who she recognized as her present-life daughter. As this lifetime unfolded the young nun known as Sister Sarah fell in love with the young groundskeeper and, as a result, left the convent. She returned after several weeks in a sickened condition and endured many scalding sessions with Sister Superior. It soon became obvious that her illness was due to her being pregnant, and now Sister Sarah was forced to leave the convent permanently.

This subject had been encouraging her daughter to see me for regression. Within several days I was given the opportunity to carry out this regression. Instructing her subconscious to return to a life with her mother if she indeed had lived a life with her, the daughter relived the same life in the convent that the mother had described but through the eyes of the young nun. The details of the life were just as her mother had related, inclusive of the vow of silence that existed in the convent.

Dr. Brian Weiss and other pioneers in the regression field have written about similar such occurrences wherein two or more people living in the present day were found to have experienced a past life together and could describe events common to both of them in identical detail. Such cases add considerable credibility to the concept of reincarnation.

11

EXTRAORDINARY LIFETIMES

ROLANDO AND THE COLISEUM

This middle-aged woman was very motivated but extremely resistant to hypnosis for several sessions. However, once she broke through her resistance, she became an excellent subject. The following lifetime was the memory of Rolando, a Roman guard at the Coliseum during the reign of Nero. Rolando was in charge of all the Coliseum guards, and as such, was the one who determined which Christians would live or die on any given day. As time went on, it became increasingly difficult for him to carry out his duties. Pangs of conscience swept over him and caused him to feel wretched as he watched the Christians in their cells, awaiting their inevitable fate at the hands of the Romans. He knew that these people were engrossed in thoughts of an ineffably grisly death by being eaten alive by hungry lions. Rolando held a godlike power of life and death over the Christians and put it to use every day as he decided who would face the lions. He could see the momentary relief on the faces of those who were not chosen for a particular day. These growing feelings of compassion were in stark contrast to the insensitive feelings of the bloodthirsty crowd who were only interested in being entertained. As this cruel Roman citizenry worked themselves up into a heated anticipatory excitement, Rolando seriously pondered over whether they cared at all about the suffering of fellow human beings that was about to take place.

Annoyed with the wailing from the Christian cells, the guards prompted Rolando to choose the loudest Christian first in order to shut him up. Rolando complied to please his men but felt even worse as his men beat the old man while pushing him up the steps.

The old Christian, resigning himself to his fate, became quiet and prayed as the guards released his arm straps. He was then quickly led to the center of the arena, where he stood, trembling and frozen with fear. Four guards at the opposite end of the arena prodded a ferocious lion out of its gate. Deprived of food, the large beast snarled hungrily at the Roman guards, who quickly retreated to safety in a secure area. Standing motionless as the blood drained from his face and the noise from the crowd escalated into a deafening roar, the old Christian saw the crowd throwing their goblets at the lion in an attempt to rile him. He then closed his eyes as the excited beast ran around the arena looking for a way to escape. The lion panted heavily as he continued to try to get away from the noise, but the walls surrounding the arena were extremely high. Suddenly, the frenzied beast stopped and turned his head toward the old Christian. At that moment the sustained clamor ceased, and a veil of utter silence fell over the crowd. Hearing the noise stop, the old Christian opened his eyes, only to see the starving lion rushing toward him. The look of terror on that old man's face escalated into an inhuman sound as the lion lunged and bit into his left thigh. His screaming immediately ceased as the lion crushed his head, amidst loud sounds of cheering as the crowd voiced their pleasure and excitement. This had all become too much for Rolando, who now began to vomit. Many Christians, men and women alike, died horrible deaths that day.

Rolando was married to a woman who was pleased with his position in the Coliseum. Being a supervisor guard supplied him with a good income and his wife with the respect and admiration of her friends. Seeing and getting to know these prisoners in the dungeon and observing them as they awaited their fate slowly began to change Rolando's opinion about Christians. As his work became progressively more distasteful, Rolando discussed leaving his position with his family; however, his wife would not hear of this, nor was she interested in hearing about the suffering of the Christians.

Rolando's wife became ill and died. He now felt free to ask for a transfer and was soon sent to Jerusalem to seek out Christians and return them to Rome to be fed to the lions. Rolando went through the motions but did not turn over any Christians to the Romans. Instead, while living with them, he was won over and became a Christian himself. He now had to go into hiding, since he had failed to report to Rome. He experienced great joy and peace with the Christians, but now he feared for his life. While Rolando remained hidden for six months, he totally enveloped the Christian beliefs, culture, and customs. Unfortunately, he was soon found and sent back to Rome, where he now found himself in a familiar cell in the Coliseum, awaiting his turn. He was led to the arena by his former subordinates and heard the roar of the crowd for the last time as he bravely met his death.

The subject was noticeably disturbed following the session; however, her rational, conscious mind had witnessed the stark reality of many lifetimes by now and so she was able to view this experience from a 'big-picture' perspective and focus on its karmic value and not the graphically traumatic death.

THE EGO OF A WARRIOR

This session was extraordinary for several reasons. First, it survived two interruptions, after which I was able to pick up the same lifetime where we had left off. Secondly, the subject's conscious mind found it necessary to comment several times on how good she was at what she did in that lifetime. Thirdly, the mention of a rather unique technique used in battle was of interest to me, as I felt it would be rather effective during that time period.

The subject saw herself as Justino, a large and powerful young Roman warrior, chained to a stone wall within a cold, dark dungeon. His thick body hair protruded from his heavy armor, as his cold gray eyes stared aimlessly. Thoughts raced through his mind, "The barbarians have captured me, but they haven't killed me... I will survive." Just then, the subject's conscious mind interjected, "I'm a killing machine."

113

Taking the subject back in time to when the battle was raging, to see exactly what occurred, she spoke loudly, with an excited tone in her voice, "They're barbarians... I'm killing many of them." Again the conscious mind interrupted, "God, I'm good!" I then instructed her to advance to the moment of his capture. Justino is thinking to himself, "There are too many of them... they're ganging up on me and taking me down. They don't kill me!... They want me alive." After they subdued him, he was placed in heavy chains.

Advancing him to the moment that his enemy confronted him with the reason that they spared his life, he let out a yelp, "Ooh, my muscles are sore; the barbarians want me to soak in a warm bath. They want me to betray Rome and fight for them. They will reward me with much gold and many women. They want me to impregnate their women. This bath feels good. I told them I have no loyalty to Rome and to bring me wine and women to wash me." The subject's conscious mind interrupted for another reason; she had to use the restroom.

Quickly re-inducing her, I instructed the subject to return to the same life and the same moment. With his ego out of control, Justino laid out his demands to the leader of the barbarians. "I need ten good men, and I will be in command. We are to have the best horses and the best weapons, and I'm to have as many women as I want." Before he could continue, the barbarians were ordered to drag him back to the dungeon and again place him in chains. Justino laughed as he overheard others screaming in the dungeon. He then said to himself, "They will give in... I may have to kill them, too."

Within a few days, the barbarians again released Justino. This time they said, "We will give you the men you require, but they will be the weakest of our men." At that moment we were again interrupted by the subject's cell phone. She woke up, apologized, and shut her phone off. Becoming frustrated with myself for not checking on this detail prior to the session as I normally do, I again carried out a rapid induction and brought the subject back to where she left off in that lifetime.

Justino accepted the barbarian proposal but secretly had other plans. He pretended to train the weak barbarian warriors and when the opportunity arose, killed the barbarian leader, who controlled the warriors. Justino now picked his own men and trained them to kill efficiently. He was aware of Roman battle tactics and could use this knowledge to his advantage. The barbarians respected his power and looked to him for leadership. Justino enjoyed being a leader and was now very anxious to fight, even if it was against his Roman comrades.

The armies had gathered in great strength for the day of the battle. Justino liked charging the enemy on horseback; he galloped through the Roman ranks with his men behind him, killing all who got in the way and looking for Roman officers to kill. He and his men would go down the middle of the ranks at full speed, dart out of the ranks at a right angle, and back in at a 45-degree angle, killing two or three Roman soldiers at a time. Again the subject's conscious mind could not contain itself, as she blurted out, "Man! Am I good." Justino wanted his men to have the kind of power that he had when he raced through the ranks of Roman soldiers, killing many at a time, so he had his men double-up on one horse, both of them together wielding the same sword, for greater power. This was very effective, as they were able to slaughter two and three men at a time, just as Justino did. Winning the battle easily, the barbarians returned to their camp and gave great praise to Justino, who continued to win many battles for them and became a sharp thorn in Rome's side. Justino's ego remained inflated as he enjoyed the spoils of war, including his pick of women. One day he came upon a woman with an Asian look in her eyes. (The subject recognized this woman as a former lover in her present life.) This beautiful Asian woman could see into Justino's heart, and he returned to her following each battle. They married; and as the years passed, her love softened him and his desire to kill. They remained happy, grew old together and died together.

12

HIGH PROFILE INCARNATIONS

THE CASE OF JEFFREY MISHLOVE:
AKA WILLIAM JAMES

It was my good fortune to come to know and befriend Jeffrey
Mishlove, a well-known author who has written *The Roots of Consciousness* and *The PK Man*. He holds the only doctoral diploma in
parapsychology to be awarded by an accredited American university
and has hosted the national public television series, "Thinking
Allowed", for some fifteen years. Currently, he is president of the Intuition Network, an organization of recognized professional psychics
who have made it a priority to fine-tune their gifts and raise the consciousness of mankind by exchanging and integrating their thoughts.

In 1999, while hosting the Wisdom Radio program, Dr.
Mishlove conducted an interview with Dr. Walter Semkiw, a medical
doctor who was in the process of gathering research material for an
upcoming book on reincarnation, entitled, *Return of the Revolutionaries*. Soon after the interview, Dr. Semkiw observed that Jeffrey
Mishlove had created a website dedicated to William James, one of
America's most prominent psychologists and psychical researchers
of his time. This discernment, plus an uncanny likeness in similarity
of professional pursuits, led Dr. Semkiw to suspect that Jeffrey
Mishlove was the reincarnated embodiment of William James.

Following extensive research of the similarities that existed
between Jeffrey Mishlove and William James, Dr. Semkiw decided
to approach Dr. Mishlove about the strong possibility of this being a
valid past-life connection. Jeffrey remained skeptical at this time. In
Return of the Revolutionaries, Walter Semkiw was able to verify
past-life matches with individuals living in the present time by

making use of assistance from Ahtun Re, a spiritual guide who is channeled by Kevin Ryerson, a well-known and respected trance medium. Dr. Semkiw used rather stringent, objective criteria in developing the past-life matches, inclusive of the consistent presence of what he termed, 'forensic criteria.' Basically, this meant that he required certain conditions to be fulfilled in an objective fashion before a match would be considered. These requirements consisted of similar personality traits, writing style, and facial architecture, as well as the presence of soul groups, often with interrelating karmic agendas. The confirmation of these past-life matches occurred in a retrospective and prospective fashion, with regard to Ahtun Re, since he had revealed past-life matches that were then validated by objective criteria and had also confirmed matches that were already validated in this manner. In addition, all communication with Ahtun Re was carried out in the strictest fashion, with no hint of input from Dr. Semkiw that could be considered leading or suggestive.

Over a year and a half later, Walter Semkiw again approached Jeffrey Mishlove in regard to Jeffrey's supposed past-life match-up with William James, but this time he had a confirmation from Ahtun Re through the trance-medium Kevin Ryerson. Jeffrey knew and respected Kevin, who had served on the Board of Directors of the Intuition Network. Several months later, Jeffrey's skepticism softened enough so that he agreed to be in *Return of the Revolutionaries*. Thus Walter Semkiw made the convincing case that Jeffrey Mishlove was indeed William James reincarnated by applying his "forensic criteria", and obtaining confirmation from Ahtun Re. The parallels were formidable, and this direct quote from Semkiw points to the most glaring facet of similarity that connects these two extraordinary human beings. Semkiw stated, "As in the case of William James, two key words can be used to describe Jeffrey Mishlove's life work: pragmatism and consciousness. Like James, Mishlove is a psychologist and a parapsychologist who has dedicated his life to understanding spiritual phenomena in a scientific manner." [1]

117

The world of William James was indeed complicated. He was born into an affluent family with a loving but controlling father, who went to great lengths to keep William from affiliating with those who encouraged his love of painting. This was accomplished for the most part by careful monitoring and frequent changes in tutors and institutions of learning, in both America and Europe. William's father showed his love for his children in many ways, allowing them exceptional personal and social freedom, which he felt would stimulate their minds and further their educational experience. This freedom, however, did not allow for the expression of personal feelings regarding the choice of their life's work, especially in William's case. Here the situation became more acute, as William wrestled with a burning passion to paint, and at the same time tried to please his father, who had a different agenda laid out for his son. William could only watch helplessly as any encouragement of his gift would be methodically eliminated. He eventually caved in to the guilt and convinced himself that he was without talent. William's father not only disapproved of painting as a career for William, he did everything in his power to guide William into a career in philosophy or the sciences. This misguided paternal manipulation and control brought about an emotionally negative impact upon the exceptionally brilliant but extremely sensitive William. These conflicting emotional issues took their toll on William's health, as he reluctantly made the decision to enter Harvard medical school at age 19. At that time, he was fluent in five languages but already endured a fragile state of health, wherein he manifested repeated bouts of neurasthenia, a psychosomatic type of disorder resulting in fatigue, anxiety, and localized pain, without apparent physical causes. This ailment led to weakness and irritability, which contributed to the severe depression and gastrointestinal problems that plagued William James throughout his lifetime and prevented him from practicing medicine.

---

1. Semkiw, *Return of the Revolutionaries*, p. 97.

Three years after graduating from medical school, William was offered a teaching position at Harvard in the department of psychology. He accepted this position and remained a professor at Harvard for 35 years, teaching psychology, physiology, and eventually, philosophy. Often referred to as the "Father of American Psychology", William James' career was academically spectacular, laden with classic lectures and publications, most notably his two-volume, widely acclaimed work, *The Principles of Psychology.*

Throughout his life, Dr. James was intensely active in social and political causes and socialized in academic settings with the greatest thinkers and writers of the time. He operated the first laboratory of experimental psychology, experimented with hypnosis, and never wavered in his pursuit of answers to mysteries of the universe, especially as they related to the Self. Not being fully satisfied with the conventional, unilateral scientific pathway, he embraced an experiential approach, and as such, did not hesitate to delve into the psychical and supernatural arenas being somewhat derisive of his contemporary conservative critics.

As mentioned previously, the parallels between James and Mishlove were strikingly impressive. With this in mind, and with the knowledge that Jeffrey Mishlove has extensively researched William James' life, I decided that I would like to regress him for research purposes to see if I could somehow add to the validation of this match-up.

Jeffrey proved to be an excellent subject and was easily able to attain a deep state of hypnosis. When directed to go back to a life in the 1800s, if such a life existed, he immediately found himself in a lifetime as William James at age 42; however, when told to advance to the next significant event, he promptly awakened. Re-inducing him with instructions to return to that same lifetime, he regressed to a time when William James was in Europe, specifically, Florence, Italy, studying art and being torn from this pursuit by feelings of conflict, which he was somehow expressing in his charcoal sketches. He voiced his decision to give up being an artist. He then said, "I could go back to Germany, but it's lonely there. I had better go home." At that moment, Jeffrey began to manifest physical discomfort in his back and abdomen and woke up spontaneously.

During his second regression, no specific instructions were given. Jeffrey saw himself as a British infantryman in North Africa during WWII. In 1943 he was attached to the 303rd Airborne Group as part of a joint allied effort to be conducted against the Germans. He was to make contact with the underground forces behind enemy lines. Following a parachute drop somewhere in the Baltic area, his special mission came to an abrupt end as he was discovered and shot to death. As his spirit entered the light following his death, he described the light as "like taking a bath on the inside."

During this session, Jeffrey once again returned to William James' life in the 1800s when he was 42 years old. It was summertime, and he and his family were observing a Fourth of July parade. Asking the year, his response was 1884, the correct year for his age. His wife, Alice, and the three children were present. Alice referred to William as "Billiam" — an endearing nickname.

Regressing him further back in time to age 16, he again found himself in an art class and mentioned that some of his classmates called him "Billy". He would rather they refer to him as "William". At that moment I said, "What happens next, Billy?" I was immediately admonished as he became noticeably irritated and blurted out, "Call me William!"

Jeffrey continued, "I can draw people, but I can't know them. There's a sadness in me... I'm not comfortable anywhere. Father is very domineering... Mother's OK... My siblings are a strange lot, like Henry. He can't wait to get away. There's a world out there... he would like to imagine that he will live it up, but inside, he's lonelier than I am... It's about intimacy, relating, communicating, being real with people. We live in a world where manners and styles keep us distant from each other."

I found myself empathizing with William's depression and morbid attitude and asked him to return to the happiest moment in his adult life for a change of pace. "There isn't any. My main unmitigated moment of joy is a dream... I'm with angels who comfort me, give me consolation and life. My father limped... his suffering was manifested physically. It was always obvious. If it is not the body, then it is the spirit that suffers..." Jeffrey complained of abdominal pain and again awakened spontaneously.

During the third session I attempted to steer Jeffrey into a life with talents other than what he presently possesses. His subconscious immediately tuned into William James' life during his early years as a professor. James felt deep regret over not being able to practice medicine and agonized over the hypocrisy that he accused himself of. He lamented over his present state of affairs, gazing wistfully at his MD degree, saying, "Parchment, that's all it is. The whole MD thing is a sham. I'm not qualified... I've gone through the mechanics. I don't deserve it, nor do I want it. It reflects my hypocrisy."

As a husband he felt guilty, saying he should have provided for his family in a better fashion, both financially and morally and should have spent more time with them.

"My children feel pride at a distance; they don't even know me... I should have hugged more. My greatest weakness is my brittleness of character. Formality prevented much intimacy in our life."

As an adult he began writing about philosophy and said that this brought him a certain satisfaction so that he could overcome what he called, "the crippling attitude of a lifetime." His writings reflected the mastery that he gained over himself. His wife, Alice, was his only confidante and shared the depths of their souls.

Asking about his greatest contribution to society, he blurted out, "My crowning work was Radical Empiricism."

My last question received a typical William James answer. I asked him to relate the most impressive conversation he had had with an influential person of that time. His answer was that no man impresses him any more than himself, which didn't impress him. As he was slowly awakened, Jeffrey again said he felt various physical discomforts during the regression, and thus the session ended.

I opened the fourth session by instructing him to return to a life that would be beneficial to explore. He promptly returned once again to a life as William James in the year 1902. He spoke in a somber mood as he was departing from a funeral for one of his colleagues. Asking William his age at that time, he replied, "60 years old. I think I will die soon. I have a weak constitution. This is the way of all flesh; people usually die in their sixties. I don't believe this funeral is real. Burial is a formality, like taking out the garbage."

Remaining in a sullen vein, he then spoke of his family. "I feel distant from my family. My siblings irritate me… I'm only close to my wife, though not as much as my work. My wife is very understanding; she puts me at ease with other women."

In Jeffrey's fifth session, he recalled a life as Seneca, a statesman in ancient Rome; and following this, a life as a Druid teacher. Jeffrey would manifest various forms of physical discomfort when regressed to his life as William James; however, his robust demeanor was quite obvious in these other lifetimes.

The sixth session once again brought him back to the life of William James, while browsing in the library at Harvard. It was during this session that he expressed his inner thoughts regarding a book entitled, *Remnants from Ages Past*, and in the process, verbalized specific notations that he had placed in the margins of certain pages. It was also during this session that Jeffrey again woke up to pain, this time in his lower back area. Later, following the session, we discussed the problem of recurring pain, and I was surprised to learn that the low back discomfort began when Jeffrey had first arrived for the session and progressively became worse as he recounted events as William James. In my mind I recalled a few subjects who, for a short time, retained a slight discomfort in an area of the body affected from a death blow during a lifetime. Also, some subjects were so tuned in to the expectation of the hypnotic experience that they became overly relaxed to the point of being sleepy upon arrival. This, however, was a new wrinkle, an event I had not yet encountered; and as Jeffrey explained it, he felt that he most assuredly experienced the full gamut of emotions as well as the physical pain that William James endured during these episodes of James' life that were recalled by his subconscious, and he did this regardless of the protection that I had invoked.

In my mind, this phenomenon, although disconcerting and interruptive, was quite dazzling from the perspective that it adds another measure of credence to the reality of the regression experience. Jeffrey was not only in that lifetime emotionally but was experiencing the subtle, daily physical discomforts that William James believed he had. This is similar to subjects' experiencing chest pain with a heart attack or physical discomfort from a death blow in a past life, yet it differs in that the discomfort begins to appear expectantly before the regression takes place, and it does this after several regressions back to the same life as the physically-fragile human being that James was. It also differs in that William James' ailments were primarily psychosomatic. Did this mean that the residual illness that was carried over into Jeffrey Mishlove's present life would stay with him longer, much as a negative emotional feeling like sadness can?

Jeffrey was concerned that he would mimic William James' ailments more and more as he continued to live reality as William James during future regressions. Jeffrey Mishlove was healthy and robust physically and emotionally and desired to maintain the status quo. Neither Dr. Mishlove nor I had answers for what was occurring, placing this phenomenon neatly into a gray area called 'the paranormal'. As a physician, I would call the ideology of this phenomenon idiopathic, which is an impressive name for "I don't know what caused it." Due to the uncertainty of these unusual circumstances, Dr. Mishlove and I mutually decided that it would be better if we did not continue this series of regressions.

THE CASE OF HOWARD WILLIAMS:
AKA JIM THORPE

A most interesting case history involved a 50-year-old man referred to me with intractable pain in the right buttock for almost four years. The pain began spontaneously and was seemingly unrelated to trauma or other memorable circumstances. The diagnosis eluded all of the physicians consulted, and the pain was assumed to be of neurologic origin. Howard tried acupuncture but found it to be ineffective. He finally settled into a life of narcotics as both his neurologist and pain specialist prescribed heavy doses of oxycotin and neurontin for him, approximately seven hundred dollars worth per month.

Howard turned out to be an excellent subject during his first session, easily slipping into a deep hypnotic trance. Through visualization techniques I was able to elevate Howard from the subconscious to the super-conscious and thus work within the framework of his Higher Self. Once there I suggested he ask for his Spirit Guide's assistance. I then posed a question to his subconscious mind regarding the origin of his pain problem. I received no response. Using imagery techniques I was able to substantially lessen his pain. These suggestions were effective and allowed him much pain relief until the second session, when he again went into deep trance. Once again I brought him up to Higher Mind/Higher Self and once more had him summon his Spirit Guide. This time I directly asked the Spirit Guide to take us back to the cause of this pain so that we may resolve Howard's problem.

Howard found himself playing in a college football game. He had just been tackled and was in great pain. His right leg was folded under the left leg in such a fashion that it sustained a painful sprain injury that spread up to his right buttock.

Dr. T: "What year is this?"

Subject: "1911"

Dr. T. "What is your name?"

Subject: "Jim... "

Dr. T.: "Jim what?"

124

Subject: "Jim Thorpe."

I couldn't believe what I was hearing. Could this really be Jim Thorpe in that lifetime? I swallowed hard and asked Howard, "Who's playing?" Howard said his school was playing against Le High, and his school is an all-Indian school. He then focused on the pain, which he said even bothered him later when he participated in the Olympics. I advanced him to the Olympics and asked him to describe the various events that he participated in. He then blurted out his entire Olympic schedule.

Advancing him in time to the next significant event, he became visibly upset, saying loudly, "They want to take my medals away!" When I asked him to explain, he responded, "… because I played baseball for money, and that means I wasn't an amateur when I was in the Olympics."

Continuing the questioning regarding the events in his life and finally taking him through the death experience, he read the inscription on the gravestone as "Greatest Athlete Ever." My research revealed the inscription to be as follows: "Sir, you are the most wonderful athlete in the world," a quote from King Gustav of Sweden, following JimThorpe's feats during the 1912 Olympics in Stockholm.

All in all, Howard's recollection of the events in Jim Thorpe's life were accurate approximately 75% of the time. Howard loved sports but knew only that Jim Thorpe played football and baseball. I was able to validate entirely too many dates and events for the information recalled by his subconscious to be a coincidence. The emotional response and disappointment following the loss of his gold Olympic medals, along with his explanation for this loss, was uncannily real and accurate.

Howard continued to improve, and at his third session, I again asked his Spirit Guide to uncover any further causes of the pain in his right buttock. Once again Howard returned to a past-life experience, this time in 1872. It was one in which he had been a farmer and had fallen from a horse and was subsequently trampled, breaking his right hip. He then spent the remainder of that life as a bitter cripple, enduring much pain. No further cause or source of pain could be elicited from the subconscious.

During these last two sessions I addressed Howard's conscious mind and reinforced the observation that these injuries occurred a long time ago in another lifetime and have no relationship to his present life, a conclusion that is not made by his subconscious mind, since it is not analytical but rather a storage house of memories that makes no distinction of time. Often a present-day event, or even a thought or vast array of occurrences can allow a subconscious memory to surface, with all its consequences, even to the point of becoming permanently disabling. A subconscious cell memory that has been buried for centuries can thus respond to such present-day stimuli and rise up to the 'forefront' of the subconscious mind. When this happens, the rejuvenated subconscious memory is now able to affect the conscious state in a very real way. In Howard's case, the cell memory was related to a specific area of his physical body, namely, his right buttock, the area that was traumatized in the two previous lives. In addition, his subconscious mind allowed such negative programming to overwhelm his conscious mind with the same disturbing level of physical and emotional discomfort that first affected him in the lifetime that originally filed the memory away.

Under deep hypnosis, an individual whose life is burdened by such physical and emotional handicaps is now able to see through this veil of apparent reality and come to understand that he is creating this reality for himself. Within the framework of this more-than-realistic drama, which the subconscious mind is reliving, the conscious mind is able to review this sequence of past events from a present-day perspective. The vantage point is now far above the strikingly realistic moments that had enveloped all of one's senses and were responsible for bringing on the intense emotions experienced in that past life. One is now able to understand the connection of this vivid past-life traumatic memory to present-life circumstances. The analytic conscious mind immediately perceives this past-life relationship to one's present life to be false. It understands that this event occurred a long time ago and logically should have no effect on one's present life. Thus the individual's conscious mind observes, analyzes, and now deletes this negative programming from the subconscious. This entire process appears to be energized by conducting it within the realm of the super-conscious mind (Higher Mind or Higher Self) that is within the confines of one's ultimate wisdom, knowing, and spirituality. The individual is now free to release the cell memory along with its physical and emotional components, providing there are no secondary gains or emotional needs requiring its presence. If such is the case, one must deal with them. One may also need to release spurious feelings of guilt that are carried from lifetime to lifetime due to misperceptions and misinterpretations of misperceptions regarding events that have occurred. This often requires the recognition of the guilt as being false or may require forgiveness of oneself and others involved.

Howard's improvement remained at approximately 90%, spectacular to say the least. The next step was to have him undergo detoxification and get him off of Oxycotin and Neurontin to which he had been addicted for three years. I was able to locate a suitable local rehabilitation program that would accept his insurance. Unfortunately Howard's pain specialist, with whom he had an appointment, promptly talked him into staying on his narcotics, saying that this is the only effective long-term treatment he should be considering. (An easy sell for someone who was now addicted to the stuff.)

As synchronicity has it, within an eighteen-day period three of my subjects recalled lives of individuals who made history in one of the greatest publications of mankind, the Bible. Following the last session involving these subjects, all I could say was, "What are the chances of that occurring?" The following three cases clearly show these Biblical characters giving an account of well-known Biblical events from their own perspective. The subjects involved were three middle-aged women with entirely different professional backgrounds, including the travel and insurance industries, as well as one in the healing profession with known psychic talent.

THE CASE OF NATALIE TORITO: AKA GOLIATH

When I suggested that this subject recall a life with a talent of which she was unaware, she bounced into a rather startling lifetime. She sensed that she was a man of great size and strength, by the name of Goliath. He was trained as a warrior by his people, the Philistines. Goliath could lift the largest and heaviest rocks, nearly three cubits high. He did not need to work for money, as the Philistine people brought him food and clothes because of his popularity. They came in droves to be entertained as spectators and watched with baited breath as Goliath engaged in hand-to-hand combat with volunteers from surrounding villages. Goliath loved challenges and was always triumphant in defeating his opponents but never killed anyone unless it was in battle. Believing that a woman would sap his strength, he remained celibate.

Just then, something very unusual occurred. The subject's subconscious began to voice Goliath's subconscious thoughts, which included the precognition of his impending death. "The purpose of my life is to be slain, so mankind will learn that size matters not. The small and weak can also be powerful. A small boy, David, will bring me down with a stone."

As the Philistines stood poised for battle against the army of Saul, Goliath came forth and issued a challenge to any warrior to engage in single combat with him, and thus determine the outcome of the battle. There was no response for days, until a small boy by the name of David, armed with a sling and several small stones, stepped forward to accept the challenge. The stone found its target and Goliath fell dead. The Philistines, disheartened by the loss of their champion, fled from the battle.

Goliath's spirit rose but hesitated long enough to see his enormous body placed on a horse-drawn cart. His subconscious mind had been well-aware of the noble purpose that he had to serve, and now, even in spirit, he basked in the glorious pride of having fulfilled this purpose. When in the light, he was asked by his Spirit Guide whether he felt he had accomplished his lesson of humility. Goliath knew that he had not, for he manifested entirely too much pride in his lifetime and will need to learn humility in his next life. At this point, the Spirit Guide informed my subject that this lifetime was very important for the growth of her soul, since God's focus, and therefore our focus, is to bring more consciousness to a higher level. The guide told her that her task of raising the consciousness of those people who witnessed this history-making incident and of all those who would eventually hear of the death of Goliath was accomplished. Goliath's death in this way served a noble purpose by introducing humanity to the notion that the small and the weak can overcome the big and the strong by using the talents given to them by their Creator, namely, belief in themselves, cleverness of action, and the courage that resides in one's heart from the knowledge that he is an eternal being and cannot be harmed. Goliath had indeed been instrumental in elevating man's belief in himself and in what he can accomplish by allowing David, a symbol of the small and weak, to triumph.

THE CASE OF CATHY HAYES:
AKA MARK THE APOSTLE

The second subject saw herself as Mark, a disciple of Christ, who, at fourteen years old, had a job that was very distasteful to him, that of slaughtering sheep. Upon advancement to the next significant event, Mark talked about being a friend of Jesus and the fact that he knew of the plot against Jesus but could not do anything about it. He saw Jesus carrying the cross and knew he would die soon. As Mark comforted Jesus' mother, she told him that Jesus will be OK in death, but it is so difficult to watch his suffering.

Advancing to the next significant moment in that lifetime, Mark found himself in a room with Mary and the disciples except for Thomas. A green light filled the room. Jesus appeared and showed the wounds on his hands and feet. At that moment, many thoughts filled Mark's mind. "We don't have to be sad any more… we can be at peace now… Jesus has shown us what He has done… suffered, died, and buried, and now He forgives all. I can do the same."

I asked Mark to tell me what he considered to be the most important statement that Jesus made. Mark replied, "I love you." He continued, "We celebrate that Jesus resurrected… He's alive again… we will tell His story over and over."

The subject's Spirit Guide then spoke and related these Biblical events to the eternal life of the soul by saying, "We live hundreds or even thousands of years on Earth but never really die. We have choices to return. Some Masters are higher than others, but they all continue to teach. The more we love, in whatever way, the easier it becomes, and the lighter we feel, because of our higher vibration. This allows us to move up to higher dimensions or levels of energy fields."

THE CASE OF SHELLY STEINER:
AKA THE APOSTLE SIMON, THE ZEALOT

The third Biblical case involved a woman who saw herself as a man who became known as Simon, the Zealot. When he was very young, Jesus told him that someday he would help Him; Simon did not believe Him. When Simon became a young man, he went fishing with Peter and Jesus. The wind increased as a storm suddenly came upon them, frightening Simon and Peter. Jesus told them to have faith and not to be afraid. He then stood up in the boat and raised His hands, causing the disciples to worry about the boat capsizing. At that moment, Simon and Peter could see a bright light shining through the dark sky. The wind then became calm and the water very still. The disciples were amazed at how Jesus could have such power and love for them. Later Jesus came to Simon in a dream, telling him, "Lead my people."

Jesus fished with the disciples many times. One morning, after praying, Jesus was seen to walk across the water to where Simon, John, and Peter were fishing. Once again the disciples couldn't believe their eyes.

Advancing to the next significant moment, Simon talked about the Last Supper and the sadness that permeated the group of disciples. Simon was not present for the crucifixion but saw Jesus' tomb two days later and embraced Jesus' mother. Advancing further, Simon witnessed Jesus' wounds following His resurrection. At that meeting, Jesus asked His disciples to lead His children. Advanced to the day of his death, Simon died at the hands of the Romans by being stoned to death.

THE CASE OF SAMANTHA JAMES: AKA JOAN OF ARC

This life is extraordinary for many reasons. This subject is not only an extremely advanced soul but is psychically gifted and claims she has had contact with extraterrestrials since she was three years old. The past life involved is a so-called 'high profile' life that clearly demonstrates the phenomenon of 'walk throughs', which is discussed in Chapter 22. This past lifetime also involves the use of out-of-body astral projection, which she has mastered in her present life.

Under deep hypnosis, I instructed the subject to go to a life that would represent her first experience with extraterrestrials. She went back in time to a life as Joan of Arc, describing herself as an instrument of God in a pure state of being, with no malicious intent in her heart towards anyone. She had no agenda other than to make things right. As she knelt in prayer she saw herself working in other dimensions to accomplish the work. This included beings representative of many dimensions, galaxies, and universes. She saw herself receiving energy and guidance through prayer and felt it deeply in her heart, knowing if one is open to receive, prayers are answered quickly. She felt that she was an aspect, one of several consciousnesses present in the body of Joan of Arc. They had come in to perform certain feats in order to accomplish specific purposes. These merged consciousnesses and advanced spirits, including extraterrestrials, were all present at the burning at the stake. All were present in a respectful conscious agreement with the permission of Joan of Arc's primary soul. The people's fear manifested as a pain in Joan of Arc's heart as she left her body prior to the burning. The feat of astral-projecting herself away from the physical pain did not spare her from the pain in her heart, which she felt was balanced by her great love of God.

While still under hypnosis, the subject was returned to the present time to reflect on her life as Joan of Arc. She responded by saying, "Speaking to spirits is one of my gifts in my present lifetime. Knowing this was my reality, I have shut people out. I knew I was different, but I couldn't share this wisdom with those who did not understand. Therefore, I have shared this information with only a few. To deny feeling this way would be to deny who I am. I closed down to the general public when I was young; however, now that I am older, I have opened back up to the public but don't want to be persecuted for this. It all goes back to Joan of Arc's life. People just aren't open; it's not a natural state for them to be so. They can accept good things, but bad things, like predictions, frighten them. Some people are fascinated, some are shocked, others terrified.

"I am proficient at leaving my body at will, especially during physical pain, much like Joan of Arc did. After I surround myself in a protective white light, I work myself into an energy frequency which feels as if my body were paralyzed; I then hear a buzzing sound as pressure builds up, and my spirit then leaves my body through my crown chakra at the top of my head. The same polarity of life exists for me as it did for Joan of Arc, when her great love of God was balanced by the fear of the people."

This subject is in a healing profession, and in addition, practices healing in non-conventional ways as she sees fit, in spite of the prejudice of mainstream society.

In my experience the most prevalent comment made about high-profile incarnations is, "How can several people be the reincarnation of the same high-profile person, such as Cleopatra or Joan of Arc?" Some will say these individuals tapped into the same life within the Akashic Records. Others say the soul intuitively knows if it truly lived that life. Still other rely on the knowledge of spiritual beings who are channeled by gifted mediums.

My experience defines my reality, and my experience centers around my own channeling to the many Spirit Guides of my subjects. When I posed a question to a Spirit Guide whom I considered quite advanced, the answer was directed to me personally and was as profound as it was astonishing. The question was, "When a person is regressed to a past life, is that past life his, or has that individual somehow tapped into the Akashic Records and relived another's lifetime as if it were his own?"

I was told that a soul may choose to temporarily incarnate into a high-profile person's body to learn specific lessons and then carry out a more permanent incarnation in another body following this visitation. The Spirit Guide called this type of temporary incarnation, which was for a limited period of Earth time, a "walk-through" phenomenon. Once again I was being handed another important piece of the complex reincarnation puzzle. Almost immediately I intuitively felt that with this piece of the puzzle we will be able to connect and click into place many other pieces that didn't seem to fit. (See Chapter 22, Spirit Guide explains "walk-through" phenomenon)

I feel that my subject who saw herself as Joan of Arc is a classic example of the "walk-through" phenomenon, in that she described several consciousnesses present in her body at the time of her death. These souls were present with the permission of Joan of Arc's primary soul.

Of note is the fact that other very advanced Spirit Guides have confirmed that such a phenomenon exists and is commonplace; also, subjects who regressed to high-profile incarnations felt in their hearts that they truly experienced life as that person. More importantly, the results of my research comprise my experience; and as I said before, my experience is my reality, and it compels me to embrace the "walk-through" phenomenon, especially when it involves incarnations of a high-profile nature.

This phenomenon not only explains how several people could have been the incarnation of the same high-profile person, it also provides an explanation as to why some of these people are able to be regressed to the high-profile person and be aware of verifiable details of that lifetime, but only up to a certain period of time during that life. After the specific time period, the subject relates experiences that cannot be validated. It occurs to me that having multiple souls present within a high-profile person may also contribute to his extraordinary success and fame by infusing a larger measure of what it takes to achieve eminence, namely courage, proficiency, wisdom, strength, daring, creativity, compassion, and so on. Keep in mind that until we find ourselves in these other dimensions we will not have a clear understanding of the laws that govern these realms, including those pertaining to reincarnation.

13

PARALLEL LIVES

Parallel lives are believed to occur when the soul divides and occupies two or more bodies so as to learn lessons from different perspectives. According to my subjects and their Spirit Guides, the same soul can occupy more than one body during an incarnation or in overlapping incarnations. Parallel lives are not rare. I have come across them many times; however, a current parallel life is not often seen. When a current parallel life is discovered, it presents a wonderful opportunity for validation. Such was the case with Vanessa Jackson.

Vanessa was a very outgoing young woman who was exceptionally open-minded. Guiding her up to her Higher Self under deep hypnosis, I asked her to make contact with her Spirit Guide and made several inquiries, including whether Vanessa had any parallel lives. Receiving an affirmative answer, I followed with, "Currently?" And again the answer was yes. I then suggested that Vanessa find this individual who was sharing her soul.

Vanessa spoke after several minutes, "It's a man, and he's presently in the United States."

"Can you connect with his mind?" I blurted out.

Vanessa began to speak again. "He's in his late thirties... I'm with him now. I see a beach, ocean, and palm trees... he's in a house by the ocean. He's very sad and lonely."

I was amazed that Vanessa was able to find him and somehow blend into his mind and experience his feelings, but then I thought, well why not? They're the same soul. I became bolder and said, "Can you sense his thoughts? Why is he lonely?"

Vanessa spoke again. "He used to have a family... He's alone now... There is a great sense of loss. He has lost everyone close to

135

him." As Vanessa continued to assimilate the thoughts within this man's mind, she discovered that she was also able to delve into his memory as well, and piece together the complete story of what has happened to him. Vanessa continued, "It seems that his home by the ocean is in Oceanside, California. His name is A. J. M.,[1] born in June of 1959. His wife, W. G., and he were married August of 1979. They had no children and divorced after 20 years of marriage. His parents, P. and A. J. M, died in 1983 in a private plane crash in northern California. J. goes by his middle name, as he did in high school in Alameda, California. He graduated from U.S.C. with a degree in law. He is presently an attorney specializing in corporate law." The subject named the firm and its location.

My boldness took on an element of creativity and I decided to try something I had never tried before. I now suggested to Vanessa to have him go back in time to when he received his phone bill in the mail. As he went through his mail, I had Vanessa read me his address, and as he opened his phone bill, his phone number. Vanessa had a difficult time making out his license plate numbers, however the colors were correct for the state of California.

The address in Oceanside, California, was a legitimate address on a street that overlooked the ocean. The zip and area codes matched; however, the phone was currently out of service. The law firm is located within thirty miles of his home. Vanessa had no previous knowledge of Oceanside, or, for that matter, southern California.

---

1. Author has all complete names and dates, which are hidden here to protect privacy.

14

LIFE PATTERNS

PATTERNS IN RELATIONSHIPS

Reincarnation into lifetimes with a group of souls, each with karmic agendas, lends itself to observing patterns of behavior that repeat themselves, especially in regard to the individual souls that make up the group. Souls within groups often make agreements with each other that will benefit each of them karmically. When born into an Earth life, the memory of the life script soon fades, and the individual begins to exercise his free will. As a result, the lesson or lessons that are needed for a soul to advance may or may not be learned, and so he may find himself repeating these lessons over and over if he continues to exhibit the same negative patterns of behavior.

The regression experience is the most effective means by which a person can spot these repetitive patterns and clearly see the futility in continuing them. The conscious mind does this most effectively as the subconscious brings up the long-forgotten memory and exposes the pattern for what it truly is: negativity based on one's personality with no thought of the attributes of the soul. Once these negative patterns are brought to one's attention they can be easily changed.

Voluminous examples of these negative recurring patterns were encountered in many subjects and were seen to occur most often in close family relationships. The subject would recognize the same soul presenting a similar karmic challenge but in different roles within the family. In observing this scenario being played out, the subject's conscious mind often saw the necessity of interrupting the recurring negative subconscious programming which placed unnecessary stress on relationships. In this way subjects were able to rise above current daily relationship problems and handle them in a loving, compassionate way.

PATTERNS IN CIRCUMSTANCES

Another form of pattern that can occur in several lifetimes may have nothing to do with relationships with other souls. It may strictly involve events or circumstances that are imprinted upon a person's subconscious cell memory, which may be reactivated for some reason and affect his attitude and how he approaches the situation surrounding an event or circumstance. A case in point was a 35-year-old woman who could not rise above her money problems. Every time she thought she was about to be financially successful, some unforeseen situation would surface and torpedo her efforts to climb out of financial crisis. Under deep hypnosis the subject was taken to her Higher Self and her Spirit Guide summoned. When directed to go back to the cause of this consistent money deficit, the subject immediately regressed back in time to a life as a nun in the 16th century, where she was obligated to take an oath of poverty.

When asked about other causes, the Spirit Guide indicated that two other lives contributed to this lack of money problem. One of those lives took place in the thirteenth century, where she was treated as a lowly female servant by a rich Italian family. She was actually a cousin to the family but was never fully accepted and was forced to work in the kitchen for her room and board. She felt that she was permanently stuck in the throes of poverty and could never rise above it. She died in a fire which started in the kitchen.

The last life that contributed to her problem was spent as a boy who grew up in Argentina as the son of rich seventeenth-century parents. The parents were unloving and neglected him a great deal, being more interested in traveling. The boy was raised by the caretakers until, as a young man, he ran off to join the army. He often voiced the sentiment that the lack of love and caring by his parents made him feel extremely poor in spite of the family's wealth. He died in a battle when he was 23 years old.

Following the session, the subject clearly understood why she felt as she did about never being able to be financially successful. Having made this connection and having understood how this negative programming was holding her back and blocking her progress, the subject excitedly declared that she felt as if a heavy weight had been removed from her.

15

THE EVOLUTION OF AWARENESS

A STUDY OF FIRST EXISTENCES ON EARTH

When I decided to return subjects to their very first existence on Earth, I was not sure of what I would find. In a single three-hour session I would be able to carry this out by regressing a subject back to his first existence on Earth and then to several successive lifetimes while observing how the evolution of awareness developed for that particular subject. Many subjects envisioned their initial life on Earth as early man in varying degrees of a primitive state; however, a good number of them recalled seeing the succession of their lives on this planet commence as a being which was not human.

The sequence of incarnations will often be found in chronological order; however, in my experience, this is not always the case. Occasionally, the sequence of lifetimes will be intermixed with the past, present, and future. I believe this is due to a distinctive and peculiar characteristic of the subconscious mind, namely, timelessness. I say 'peculiar', since the conscious mind functions in a time-oriented physical world and expects the same temporal laws to apply in regard to the chronological placement of lifetimes.

SUBJECT ONE

The first time that I regressed a subject to her earliest existence on Earth, I stumbled upon a lifetime that was hard to fathom. The subject looked somewhat confused, saying, "I am not aware of what I am." Then it all became clear to her as she continued to speak.

> Subject: "I am a bird, a large bird... I see rocks below. I feel no fear... I am ruled by instinct. I'm not worried about the

future, just now. I feed on small animals... sometimes what others kill. I don't think; I just feel. I'm a male, and I copulate with females to reproduce."

Dr. T: "How long do you live?"

Subject: "About twenty years..."

I advanced the subject to a time when she is soaring very high in the air; I did this on purpose, to allow her to experience the exhilarating feeling of this life as a high-flying creature. I then took her to her death experience.

Subject: "I was preoccupied by looking down at something that caught my attention and slammed into the side of a mountain."

What followed was very interesting.

Subject: "I sensed that my 'soul' was not complete, that it was only an essence of my nature, and I was returning to a special place in the afterlife, a sort of primordial soup, lower than the human realms. It was here that I felt my essence blend in with lesser-evolved essences of souls, like mine. It was as if I was part of a plasma of feeble consciousness, joining others like me who have died, so as to move toward what eventually may become a soul. I had experienced Earth from instinct only and was not advanced enough to remember my life. I am to come back as another animal, another essence of a soul."

Dr. T: "Please give me an overview of that process."

Subject: "I sense that we are to return to Earth as a more complex animal with each incarnation, until we come back as one of the most advanced animals, such as a cat, dog, or horse. Such more-evolved animals are able to communicate with humans and would be ready to incarnate as humans following their death."

Dr. T: "Are insects included?"

Subject: "The evolutionary process could start as a fish or even as a one-celled animal, such as an amoeba. Insects could be included. I don't see minerals or plants."

Dr. T: "I want you to advance in time to your incarnation as the last animal before you incarnate as a human."

Subject: "One of the Master Spirits plucked me out of a group of essences, held me up and smiled… I soon found myself in the belly of a bitch. I was born and grew into a large yellow dog. I knew I was higher in this progression of soul development since I communicated and worked with people. I first became conscious of being; then I became aware of my needs and the effort required to fulfill them. Finally, I learned to sense the needs of others and the fact that there are many more around besides just dogs. My job in this life was to hunt with my master and learn about humans and their needs. I did…"

Dr. T: "I now want you to advance in time to the day of your death."

Subject: "I felt closer to the light than I have ever been. I was being told where to go by people spirits. I could understand commands but I could not comprehend where I was going. Things happened rapidly, and I found myself growing up in a cave somewhere in Central America, as a very hairy, primitive, human female. We could not stand up straight. Sex was indiscriminate; the strong ruled, and love was not known. I died as a young woman and went to the light to a special place, where there were no animals or other human spirits, except for souls who, like me, were not very aware. There were Masters there, who looked at us with love and understanding and told us when and where to incarnate."

I advanced the subject to her next incarnation, which was as a less hirsute primitive Asian man who could stand upright. His tribe had learned to belong but not to love. When he died, he went to a special area in the afterlife for the less aware. Again the subject was given instructions from the Masters regarding when and where to incarnate. She was told her lesson would be to learn to love herself and others.

The next incarnation was to somewhere in the northern hemisphere. This time she was a female, still primitive, but starting to learn the meaning of love. The beginnings of this can be seen in her love for

142

her parents. Family love followed, as partners stayed together for life. She recognized her partner as someone in her present life. As a young woman she began to experience a heightened awareness of divine light. She marveled at the sun and felt a primordial spark of spirituality stir within her. She was killed by a bear while gathering nuts.

As her spirit rose toward the light, she was greeted by those she loved and who had died before her. She arrived in the light at the lowest level, where human souls go. As her soul rested, she reflected on these primitive incarnations and understood that it was all about evolving in awareness and in the ability to love. She felt there are many levels within the spirit plane. Four of those levels had to do with human love. The lowest level had to do with parental love; and next, family love; then, love of many; and finally, love of all. She also was aware that other planes existed above and below these levels. Upon awakening from this regression, the subject appeared to be quite exhilarated and informed me that she considered this regression experience a spiritual revelation.

SUBJECT TWO

Taken back to her first existence on Earth, this subject sensed that she was a minuscule ocean creature, most likely composed of just a few cells. She felt herself floating and moving with the undulations of the deep, cold water. She could see seaweed floating around her and barely perceived light penetrating the dark water near the ocean floor. Large, dark, ugly creatures moved about on the ocean floor, causing the water to be cloudy. Advanced to the last day of life, this tiny, simple form of sea life was devoured by one of these bottom creatures. The subject now seemed to move upward toward a bright light that seemed to be far away. As the light became brighter, she felt as if she were in the presence of someone who was trying to communicate with her. Then she felt the sensation of being scooped up and almost immediately sensed that she was a shiny, salmon-like fish, swimming upstream, only to once again see the bright light. She kept moving upwards into the whiteness and this time saw figures moving about, as she felt herself again being picked up by one of these figures. He was a large spirit with a white beard and hair. He stroked her and told her telepathically that she was going back. She now felt darkness all around her and then saw a valley by a river. She felt quite different. Responding to my request to describe what she looked like, she replied, "I'm a human female, a young human female, with dark skin and lots of hair. I can stand erect, but I'm slightly hunched over. I live in a cave, where we have drawn pictures of animals on the walls."

When advanced to being a young woman she described the very primitive life of a tribe living by a river, subsisting on fish and vegetation. Nights were cold, but they were able to build fires in their caves. There were no families within the tribe; sex was indiscriminate. She became pregnant four times but never was sure who the father was. Being the obstetrician that I am, I inquired as to how the umbilical cord was severed. The subject replied, "One of the women would wrap it around a stick until it broke." (I thought to myself, they either wrapped the umbilical cord around the stick after delivery of the baby, or more likely, following delivery of the afterbirth. The latter situation would allow the umbilical vessels to clot, and this way, bleeding would be minimal. If it was accomplished right after delivery of the infant, the tension on the cord would aid the delivery of the placenta, or afterbirth, but would put the infant and mother at great risk of excessive bleeding if the cord ruptured.)

Infants were breast-fed for at least two years; however, older children often died of starvation if food was scarce. Men were fed first, women second, and children last. Another tribe attacked her people when the men were hunting and took many of the women away, including her. She described her remaining life as a virtual sex slave, being raped many times a day. Each pregnancy weakened her; and when she delivered her sixth child, her strength was so depleted from the bleeding that she could barely stand. She soon died, and as she did, she sensed that she was floating toward a beautiful light and could feel the presence of others nearby and recognized the tall white-haired Master Spirit, who now placed his hand on her head, causing her spirit body to become warm and light. "Is this love I'm feeling?", she thought. She then said, "He's smiling and telling me something. I can't understand what it is... now I can! He is asking me what I learned in that lifetime. I felt that I had not learned any lesson. He's now telling me through his mind that I must remain here for a while, until I heal. Then I will be sent back, clean and free of fear. In this next life I must learn to love and be loved. There are other less-aware souls where I am, and there are also much more aware souls; they treat us gently and lift us up; some even wrap around us. The Masters are now giving me instructions and I must go... I have no choice."

The subject entered darkness again and found herself in a new lifetime on Earth, where she was living in a mud hut in a desolate, desert country. She saw herself as a young woman wearing sheets wrapped around her. She had a husband and children, and they were one of many families in her tribe. Later in that lifetime their tribe was attacked by their enemies, and she was killed. This time, as she entered the light, she immediately felt healing energy and knew intuitively that she was a complete soul. She had indeed learned to love and be loved in that past lifetime.

An interesting aspect of this case is that the same subject had been regressed to her first human life on Earth several months earlier. During that session she recalled the same first human life that she had experienced in this session. The lives were identical in every detail. In my experience, I have found that when a subject is asked to return to a life that has already been previously recalled in a former session, the details of both lifetimes are identical, regardless of the time that has passed between recollections. I have seen this happen when years have passed between recollections of the same lifetime, and have always been rather impressed when I compare the details of these lives.

SUBJECT THREE

When asked to recall a life that was her first existence on Earth, this subject sensed that she was a small, female, furry creature, about the size of a hamster. She felt that she had a soul but was very much unaware. Upon death, she entered what she described as a bright light, feeling that she learned what it is like to be an animal. She soon reincarnated on Earth as a primitive female, where she learned how to share with others. This primitive life was followed by several sequential lives in Egypt.

SUBJECT FOUR

Following an instruction to recall her first existence on Earth, this subject was surprised to find herself floating on water with no arms. She felt she had a strong midsection and could be fast if she wanted to be; she could even jump over the water. As her impressions became clearer, she determined that she was a small, young male dolphin, who was beginning to become independent of his mother. He could communicate with other dolphins who were watching over him by making a clicking noise. I advanced the subject to when he had a mate. "I'm on top of her, trying to impregnate her. We eat small fish and confuse the sharks by all of us swimming in different directions; we work as a team. We can think and consider choices consciously."

I asked for an overview of this lifetime. The subject responded, "I lived about seven years, until I was speared. As I died, I remember seeing below me as I floated upside down." (A large fish normally sees what's above him but upon dying is belly-up, his eyes directed downward.) "I then began to feel good... I had no pain and no fear, as I now felt myself rising. It became brighter as I rose higher, until I was totally surrounded by light. I then heard a familiar clicking sound in my mind and found myself in front of a semicircle of heads. They were the heads of dolphins; their bodies seemed to fade into the light. I saw other entities, human spirits, and then I understood that the Master Spirits were appearing as dolphins so as to make me feel comfortable. They welcomed me, said I was a good dolphin and needed to experience life again in another form."

I advanced the subject to the next incarnation. "I'm a young boy; I am bent over, but I walk on two feet." I now advanced him to when he was a young man. "I have sex with different females… those who smell good. The women have many children, who are cared for by all of the women; there are no families. Many children die in childbirth. We are extremely hairy, however, women have much less hair on their chest, face, and belly. We wear no covering."

I asked about drawings in the cave and fire. "There are no drawings. We do not have fire; we sleep together if it's cold. We eat small furry animals, like rats. Men are fed first, then women, then children." (This comment had been made by many subjects.) "The old ones starve first, then the children. There are other creatures like us, but they are bigger and more upright; they are also smarter and not as hairy. They scare us because they win battles and steal our food and women. They communicate better among themselves than we do; they think more. We only grunt. The other tribe has a better spear. It will go farther when thrown."

As these words were spoken and registered in my mind, I immediately could envision the far-reaching implications regarding a tribe of early humans existing simultaneously with one that is much more advanced. Information like this regarding regression experiences of individuals taken back to primitive lives would be quite interesting to paleoanthropologists in that it could either support or refute their claims in regard to man's primordial beginnings.

After being advanced to the death experience, the subject again spoke. "One night I died in my sleep; I was a young man. I saw a very bright light… it felt good. I sensed a lot of activity going on, but I heard no sounds. I then saw trees and birds; these were familiar and made me comfortable." (My experience shows that Masters will often create a familiar environment for newly-arriving souls, especially if they are less aware.) "I was greeted by spirits who seemed to open themselves up to me, releasing love and bathing me in its embrace. I was being told in my mind that I am ready for challenges that are more physical; I will learn to feel, but it will be more difficult. This will be where life truly begins. I could hear the Masters speaking in my mind… they are saying that they need to see what they are working with… the foundation of my soul; all souls don't start out the same." At that moment the subject took on a defiant tone and a facial expression to match. "I don't know what a soul is… they do… but they don't know me! I have not had a chance to manifest."

The Masters again spoke to the subject telepathically, saying that her uniqueness, her spiritual being, and her feelings for others will be tested. The subject replied, "I'm ready, but until now I have not been able to manifest. As a dolphin I was an 'egg of a soul', and as a hairy human, an 'unaware soul'."

The Masters interrupted, saying that this breaking-in period was needed to get the soul accustomed to the physical world and that a soul needs to experience all feelings; it needs more choices that are beyond instinct and survival, choices that have to do with interactions with other souls and a comprehension of the future.

The subject commented, "There are three Masters; I'm only able to see their faces… white beards… kind eyes. I have no choice now; I will incarnate as they instruct me to. They don't want to warn or coach me; they just want to see the reality of my soul."

The subject was then advanced to the next incarnation and led a less primitive life. As a woman in that lifetime, she received love but did not give it. She was only able to show gratitude. In the light, she was told by the same three Masters that she had a beautiful spirit but will still need to receive instructions from them regarding her next incarnation, since her assessment will take more lifetimes.

The following incarnation proved to be one in which she learned to love and be loved. In that early medieval lifetime she suffered greatly as a black man, a slave for the rich, who was horribly mistreated and who loved a disfigured peasant girl who returned his love.

148

Following a public whipping and an agonizing death, the subject entered the light, knowing she had found more happiness than she could ever have imagined. By loving and being loved, she had been able to find beauty in a difficult life, in spite of intolerable circumstances. She had found strength in her spirit and would now make her own choices about reincarnating again.

16

LIFE ON LOST CONTINENTS

My research through the years has yielded rather fascinating results, allowing me to identify several common denominators that surfaced during many of my regression sessions. When I detected that a common thread of experience was running through several regressions of my subjects who found themselves in certain time periods or specific geographic locations, I conducted further inquiry into the details but in a general way, so as not to lead the subject. Such was the case during several lifetimes in Atlantis and Lemuria. My excitement was difficult to contain as I became more and more captivated by the consistencies of these lifetimes.

Lemuria was thought to be an ancient civilization existing well before and during the time of Atlantis. It is believed both civilizations existed as large islands, possibly the size of continents, which occupied the Pacific and Atlantic oceans, respectively, the occupants of which were thought to be highly evolved and possibly included inhabitants from other planets. Atlantis, on the other hand, was seen as more technologically advanced. Both so-called continents were supposedly destroyed by cataclysmic geophysical occurrences, the initiation of which makes for very interesting conjecture. Theories advanced have suggested that Lemuria existed anywhere from 2 million B.C. to 14,000 B.C.; Atlantis, from 25,000 B.C. to 8,000 B.C. First mention of Atlantis can be found in Plato's writings in about 380 B.C. Many individuals presently feel that they have a connection to these ancient civilizations.

LEMURIA

What follows is a synopsis of life in Lemuria as described by several subjects under deep hypnosis. In regard to Lemuria: the dates revealed by my subjects ranged from 60,000 B.C. to 30,000 B.C. They described Lemuria as having multiple dimensions and no physical location. The inhabitants, many of whom were originally from other galaxies, existed in spirit form, and their etheric appearance took on the color of their energy. The Lemurians communicated telepathically and would be tuned into frequencies originating from human beings on Earth who are experiencing disharmony in their lives. With the intention of helping those Earthlings in trouble, individual Lemurians would instantly travel to specific locations by just thinking themselves there. They would then accomplish their task by appearing on Earth in either spiritual or physical form. If they chose physical form, they would either be born into a lifetime or enter as a walk-in, which would require an agreement with a particular soul who is leaving. (A walk-in is thought to be a spiritual entity who makes an agreement with an existing soul which is occupying a physical body for the purpose of exchanging places.) A Lemurian's physical life on Earth would only differ in that he had a purpose to accomplish for someone else; and in doing that, he would not experience physical death. Rather, he would return directly to Lemuria in spirit form, leaving no physical remains.

Further descriptions of Lemuria, such as "Masters are present", and "Time does not exist", led me to believe that Lemuria eventually existed as a type of afterlife dimension whose inhabitants remained in spirit form and were tasked with assignments to help people on Earth. I was told that each time a spirit from Lemuria took on a physical body, he increased the density of his energy, and with each successive "incarnation" it became progressively more difficult for him to return to Lemuria. This eventually resulted in Lemurians remaining in physical bodies and no longer remembering where they came from, thus making it necessary for them to experience true physical death as other

Earthly human beings did.[1] Following death, the dimension of afterlife that they would return to would be determined by the level of spirituality or vibration that they had achieved in their lifetime on Earth.

If the above scenario sounds like science fiction, consider this: these spiritual and physical depictions of life are coming from the subconscious minds of several subjects, all of whom are extremely unlikely to be contriving the same fantasy.

ATLANTIS

In regard to Atlantis: several subjects stated that Earth and star people settled Atlantis, using the technology of other galaxies and Lemuria. The dates ranged from 23,000 B.C. to 11,000 B.C. Two subjects lived a life as a priestess and described their respective living quarters as white apartments that were linked together with walls enclosing a garden adjacent to the living area. The living quarters were located in a specific compound separated from other residents of Atlantis.

Several subjects spoke of the "rejuvenation chambers", where certain higher-class Atlanteans would go to heal and increase their longevity, including the removal of signs of aging. The chambers were located inside a special pyramid that contained a uniquely-designed crystal platform or bed, below which was encased a rather large crystal that served as a generator. The power of this crystal generator was modulated and shielded by the design of the pyramid, which acted as another energy source as these privileged Atlanteans reclined on the platform. Other crystals inside the pyramid were placed in precise locations for the purpose of capturing sunlight and focusing this light on the person's body, in conjunction with the use of specific sound wave energy. These crystals were aligned in such a way so as to activate other crystals to gain the maximum amount of energy needed to effect healing or longevity.

---

1. An example of this can be found in "The Case of Jean Collins: Depression and Feelings of Abandonment" on page 75.

The pyramids were built from the technology of sound and magnetic wave energy which was brought to Atlantis by extraterrestrials. These pyramids were used to concentrate crystal energy for several specialized purposes, such as water purification, interdimensional travel, and rejuvenation chambers, as previously described. Several subjects corroborated this information regarding Atlantis, and, in addition, came up with identical lists of other uses for crystal energy:

- in local healing
- as a generator
- to alter genetic codes by splitting DNA
- as weapons
- in heating and cooling
- in lighting
- in cooking
- in projection
- in cutting
- to make music

The energy of smaller crystals could be activated easily by touch. Most people of Atlantis, those of lesser birth (according to several subjects), were required to wear a special crystal around their necks or have it implanted in their bodies. This crystal contained the individual's training and life path program encoded upon it by the High Council of Atlantis. This Council utilized that crystal implant or necklace to telepathically control the lower masses.

THE DESTRUCTION OF ATLANTIS WAS DESCRIBED IN SIMILAR WAYS BY DIFFERENT SUBJECTS:

Subject One: Egos and weapons were out of control, leading to the overloading of two generator plants which ultimately exploded. The imbalance of the crystal power caused a huge storm and Earthquake, resulting in a shift in the Earth's alignment. The energy mindset of the people was thought to have somehow influenced this catastrophe, since their mass consciousness could easily be manipulated by their programmed crystals, which were controlled telepathically by the ruling Council. It was believed that the ruling Council at that time was infiltrated by Earth people and extraterrestrials, with evil intentions, who were thought to be responsible for destroying the two pyramid generator plants by either using weapons or by just allowing them to overload.

Subject Two: Atlantis was destroyed by too much power being released from several pyramid power stations. This resulted in a huge storm and earthquake, which caused a shift in the Earth's alignment.

Subject Three: Atlantis was a physical place that was destroyed by energy which was transmuted.

Subject Four: The ego of Atlanteans exceeded their spiritual state. Atlantis was destroyed by an earthquake which was caused by their technology failures.

Subject Five: Some Atlanteans had more power than others. They had learned how to use this power but were not particular who they shared these secrets with. This created much conflict in the High Council, which became corrupt. The Council became divided, and this was followed by much violence and killing. For some reason, three of the pyramid generators were thrown out of balance, as a result of a domino effect. This affected other pyramid generators throughout Atlantis, causing explosions and earthquakes, which in turn brought on tsunamis in different areas at different times. (In this subject's past life in Atlantis, he was one of the scientists who worked feverishly in an attempt to put a stop to the impending destruction.) Eventually, over a period of time, the entire continent sank into the ocean, except for several mountaintops, which have remained as islands. Some of the ruins of these huge crystal generator plants are submerged in the area of the Bermuda Triangle and have caused an inordinate amount of electromagnetic interference with the compasses and navigational equipment of ships and planes for many years.

17

FUTURE-LIFE PROGRESSION

Progressing subjects into the future made me feel rather seren-dipitous as I continued to uncover information about the future that remained quite consistent among my subjects. Eight subjects were progressed to future lifetimes, the dates of which ranged from 2061 to well within the 31st century. Six of these subjects were asked the same questions regarding progress in the future. These questions were about illness, longevity, politics, and land vehicles, such as automobiles. Improvement in all these areas occurred chronologi-cally as time passed, except for world peace, due to faulty politics.

Other rather interesting futuristic information from the subjects is presented in chronological order and is followed by a more in-depth summary of what the seventh and eighth subjects had to say.

CONSISTENT OBSERVATIONS OF THE FUTURE BY SIX SUBJECTS

• All stated that there was much less illness; and five of the six subjects claimed that illness was controlled with the mind. Two of the subjects surprised me when they volunteered that birth control was effected by mind-control; men could choose whether or not to produce sperm.

• All of the subjects felt that longevity was increased.

• All of the subjects described smaller vehicles that replaced automobiles. By 2061, these vehicles could hover. By 2080, these same vehicles could not only hover, they could fly at higher alti-tudes and were automatically programmed with a set course and destination. These vehicles utilized electromagnetic energy fields to prevent collision. Two of these subjects described in detail how they could park their vehicles directly outside their high-rise apartment.

• In regard to government and politics, all of the subjects who lived prior to 2700 AD felt that war was a rarity. Those living in the latter part of that century and later tell of increasing world tension, war, and destruction. Five of the six subjects spoke of a world government of federations headed by a Supreme Council of men and women.

LIFE CHANGES AS TIME MARCHES ON

• By 2061, the atmosphere was less polluted; however, clean water was a problem in the oceans and lakes, so the water supply was now coming from the glaciers. Interplanetary travel was possible. Contact with extraterrestrials had become commonplace.

• By 2234, some homes were made of a special plastic material that could be suspended in the air by an energy source, up to 60 stories high. Education was carried out by computer connection, since schools had become too violent by 2100. Earthquakes had caused much destruction. Cloning was for animals only and was illegal for humans.

• By 2310, communication was mostly telepathic, and humans could travel with or without the physical body.

• By 2406, wormhole technology was being used for space vehicles. People were taller and had larger brains. Communication was both verbal and telepathic. Since extraterrestrials were acclimated to space travel, they were very useful on long trips throughout the cosmos, while humans remained in suspended animation. When asked about extraterrestrials among us, I was told that the list included Ben Franklin, Albert Einstein, Thomas Jefferson, Gandhi, and several of the Kennedy's. These individuals suspected that they had a calling; however, they had full knowledge of their origin upon dying.

• By 3012, some cities found it necessary to be enclosed in a 'protective bubble', for protection and because of the harsh environmental conditions. Nuclear weapons were still present and as ominous as ever. Terrorist activity and the resultant destruction had begun to worsen by 2785. People wore light-restrictive clothing and numbers were often used for names.

COLONIZATION ON CENTAURI

This increasing threat of nuclear war was consistent with the lifetime envisioned by the seventh subject who was progressed to "sometime in the 31st century." She and a contingent of survivors boarded a spaceship and left Earth, which was virtually destroyed by nuclear war and disease. They eventually arrived on another planet to colonize and survive. The planet had an atmosphere and sun with a dark blue sky. It possessed oceans and mountains but no vegetation. It was larger than Earth, but like Earth, it had a single moon. The colony expanded as other ships arrived from Earth. Food was grown, water purified, and the colony survived and grew on this planet called Centauri.

EXTRATERRESTRIALS ADAPT TO A WOUNDED PLANET

The eighth subject progressed to a life in 3020. She was from another planet that was aware of the devastation occurring on Earth. She spoke of a genetic engineering experiment to produce a species that would be able to live on the planet Earth as it was. Her people carried out this experiment and successfully lived on Earth for five generations. This is her story.

Dr. T: "Where are you?"

Subject: "I'm in a city on Earth, with short, bright yellow-looking buildings."

Dr. T: "What year is it?"

Subject: "3020".

Dr. T: "Describe yourself and what you are wearing."

Subject: "I'm a male, in my 20s, and I'm wearing a white and silver reflective covering over my entire body and a panel over my eyes, to see through. The light is bright, there is too much sun... everything has to be reflective."

Dr. T: "What are you doing?"

Subject: "I'm in an enclosed vehicle, which is moving people
and running close to the ground. I'm surveying the area and
doing standard maintenance on our energy power source, a
combination of solar and magnetic energy from the Earth's
core."

Dr. T: "How do you communicate?"

Subject: "Ours is a number language, the numbers have meaning. [1] We speak rapidly in a high-pitched, monotone voice."
(At this time, the subject began speaking in a very unusual
way, and her facial expression indicated an obvious conscious
repulsiveness to the high-pitched, rapid sounds that were coming out of her mouth.) "We communicate from a distance with
a box that we wear. The box contains buttons with numbers
that we push to send messages to each other. The messages are
coded and come out on a screen on the box. There is no sound,
we just read the screen and punch in our own message. Central
Command has all of our numbers and keeps things running
smoothly."

I advanced the subject to that evening.

Subject: "I rode home in a transporter that hovers and flies, and
now I'm home. We live in cubicles that are close together. The
door opens fast, and my wife and children are there. She is
spraying something on the surfaces that smells like sulfur; it
cleans the soot that comes from the air."

Dr. T: "Describe what you and your wife look like."

Subject: "Everyone is very thin with exaggerated arms and
hands. Our faces are flat and wide, and we have big eyes, with
a small mouth. We're about five feet tall... our legs are about
half of our body size, and our feet are wide and short. My
wife's face and essence make her a female; our nipples and
breasts are alike."

Dr. T: "Can you take showers?"

---

1. The concept of number language, although bizarre, was mentioned by
two other subjects experiencing life on other plane.

Subject: "Our shower is like a steam pressure which keeps excretory stuff off our skin. We must do this three times a day."

Dr. T: "Can you now take a shower and describe the rest of your body to me?"

Subject: "I have no hair; my skin is hard and smooth, with some give to it… there is no fat. I have no genitals or anus."

Dr. T: "Can you explain what happens to food when it's taken in, and how you excrete waste?"

Subject: "When we cook, we eat by breathing it in; we blow toxins out our mouth into a pipe or chute, once for every time we eat."

Dr. T: "You are obviously not a human being; so can you explain how you came to be on Earth?"

Subject: "People on Earth were being poisoned slowly from black particles, a contamination in the Earth's atmosphere, which filtered down to the air. We watched it from where we were, a different universe. We saw it in our minds. Also, travelers reported back from spaceships and beamed back visual records of what was happening on Earth to our Central Command. Our planet created us, the new species. They considered us an experiment, and thus we were genetically engineered by combining the cells from our planetary beings with those from human beings from Earth. The inhabitants from our planet were mostly all head, with very minimal body, to propel the head. They exchanged energy with the Earthlings in order to reproduce. Babies were a by-product of that energy exchange, an asexual, pseudopodal type of growth. The corporeal shell of Earthlings was used for this energy; the children are therefore made from the harvest of cells from people that lived before. The children are pre-made, so we order them when we desire to have them. The problem is that we are running out of a harvest, and there is no other way for us to reproduce here. We are an experiment. We have been here for several generations, and our longevity is well over 140 years old. But now we don't want to think about the future."

Dr. T: "Can you tell me if your Earth species is devoid of emotion?"

Subject: "We have inherited romantic emotions from the humans and jerky movements from those on our planet."

Dr. T: "Can you describe the romantic emotions in detail?"

Subject: "We use our fingers to make love; we place our fingers close to each other and bend them. There is an energy exchange… it feels good, better than a human orgasm, because it's more than a physical sensation, it's totally energizing. This feeling begins instantly and lasts for a long time."

Dr. T: "How long?"

Subject: "Until it is depleted; if we give it 100%, it can last well over an Earth hour. It can also be done from a few feet away, and waves of energy can be seen beaming off of our fingers."

Dr. T: "Is this done indiscriminately?"

Subject: "I think you can only do this with someone you love. Everyone needs a partner to live. Energy finds its own compatibility very quickly, and so we meet and bond as children. In the early years of our life, we stood close to each other and used our whole hand to implement this process. As we became older, we were able to exchange energy with our fingers and accomplish this from a greater distance. It could only be done while standing or lying down. Actually, we don't sit down unless we're in transports. We have no use for chairs."

As this regression session came to an end, I thought to myself, 'How could anyone make up such an intricately detailed story, with rapid-fire answers to my questions, in so short a time?' I rest my case.

18

AN EXTRAORDINARY FUTURE LIFE

PART MACHINE

When the subject was asked to go to a life with her two children, she found herself in the future in the year 4586 AD. She described the three of them as clones emerging together from a large white egg. "I see us as hybrids… part human, part machine. Our heads resemble that of an insect, light green and expressionless; our bodies remind me of cartoon figures with large belts. We share consciousness. We presently are on a spaceship with many who look like us. There is one named Chloe, who is in charge and delegates. We are low on the evolution totem pole and are without emotion.

"A human has turned us off… I'm back on again. It feels strange to be alive without a physical body. I have no lungs… there is no breathing. I can think but I am not encouraged to do so. I'm telepathic and adaptable. We were created to see if such a combination of human and machine were possible, another phase of the soul."

I asked for an overview of this life. The subject replied, "I sense our goal is to explore the expanding universe and determine how far out it goes. We will fly out as far as we can go for half of our projected lifetime and then return to report our findings. We travel at great speeds. Our home base measures and studies the effects on our own bodies as we report the findings. Nobody leaves the spaceship; we are self-contained. We have five hundred humans and one hundred of us aboard. We are more efficient because we perform without emotions. Humans are more creative and do the thinking. They have emotions with each other but treat us like machines. Most of the time they remain in suspended animation, like human sleep.

"We are part machine and will wear out at a predictable time; we live on emotional energy that is harvested from humans. The emotional energy expended during their interaction is absorbed by us. Strong emotions help us the most. This process does not cause them harm and actually is a relief for them.

"We are now out there 250 years. Many humans are born aboard ship. Their number will double by the time we return."

I advanced the subject in time to when they returned to home base. "We are worn out; we are buried like pets." Their spirits arise and they go to the light. "All three of us are laughing; we have a feeling of great joy, superiority, and accomplishment. It's liberating to be free from the confines of those machinelike bodies."

Asking about their lesson, she replied, "All of us have learned humility and cooperation and have submitted to the good of the whole group. Our personal goals were considered more discordant and therefore ignored."

19

LIFE ON OTHER PLANETS

IN THE PINK

This recently postpartum young female subject experienced a succession of traumatic past lives, including one in which she was beheaded. For a change of pace, I instructed her to recall her happiest lifetime. She promptly found herself on another planet in an extraterrestrial life that was totally without stress.

"Everything is pink... our skin and the atmosphere. It's like pink gas. We are small, about 4' tall and have a soft body with arms and legs, but we are not heavy, so we don't make marks in the soft ground. We have no hair and wear no clothes, since the temperature is constant and perfect. We have no breasts and no buttocks, just a small anus and a flat area; our genitals are different, and we breathe through our belly-button. We have very few bones, but we have a hard head. Our face is pretty, with big cheekbones and large eyes. There are no teeth or ears, and only holes for the nose. Language is like a vibration from our small mouth.

"We eat rarely; and when we do, we eat a kind of grain mush. Our excretion is white and is used to grow things. Reproduction is by a spiritual union between two people; when one chooses to have a child, it is by energy contact... by spirit only. I have had a child with my identical twin sister; she had the child by contributing with her being. We made love spiritually, and there is no physical feeling, even when we hold each other. My sister and I study a lot about other planets and cultures.

"There is no day or night. Everything is pink all the time, like a sunset. Our planet is smaller than Earth, and there are oceans. Water is sacred; it makes the pink gas. There are no tides and no boats in the ocean. We walk or fly with our bodies.

"We feel we are close to the Creator, as we receive spiritual teachings from our religious people. Our planet is peaceful and happy and without war. There are different types of beings here, some taller, and some with a blue or green color. Some of us study, and others build things. Homes are high and white, with windows; however, shelter is not really needed, for there is occasional rain and never any storms. We have no entertainment or music; therefore, it's boring, but peaceful.

"Some people are born with deformities and die. Most of us live a long life and die from old age, since there is no disease. We remain young for a long time, but our mental state changes, and we eventually die. Our energy tells how old we are. When we feel the time has come, we make a decision to die. Our body is left in the house until it deteriorates and evaporates, leaving only the head, which is then placed in the ocean."

This subject explained her soul's lesson in the afterlife thusly, "Life was a blessing and a spiritual training ground before my first existence on Earth."

THE WATCHERS

This female subject was regressed to being a male on a warm planet, very close to the sun. He is a "watcher" of a path leading to a fortress. He has a long metal rod with a crystal at the top, which reflects the sun, and is used to signal others that it is safe to cross the path. He watches for large carnivorous birds of prey that are attracted to the wristbands and necklaces worn by all the inhabitants. The color of these bands represents their status. His is red and amber, the status of a "watcher." The inhabitants are described as tall, around 7', with burgundy eyes, pointed noses, and long faces and chins. Their skin is gray, and they have large, flat feet, since they travel only by walking. They have very flat teeth, since they subsist on fruits and vegetables. No one eats meat, other than the birds. The inhabitants thrive on light reflected in crystals. They whisper, touch, and understand through this light. The crystals are also used for light and heat.

The fortress is a sanctuary for these people, so they may see the young birds that eventually get bigger than them and will eat them if they get knocked off the path into the valley. The birds are more aggressive when people are on the path. This is because the birds are very protective of their young. Most of the time, they will not bother people and will eat only other animals. The people must always be aware of the birds and must never be careless. They must listen to the watchers. No weapons are ever used against the birds.

Offspring come about through sexual reproduction. There are no schools; the young must learn from the older ones. There is not much disease; however some inhabitants can become sick from the mountain air. The oceans are far away, but there are many streams to nourish the plants, animals, and insects that reside there.

When the inhabitants get old, they lose their body hair and eventually die but are not buried since they immediately turn into dust. The subject was taken through the death experience and went to the light. Of interest is the fact that their light was of a purple color. In his book, Saving Lost Souls, William Baldwin states that the afterlife light that aliens return to following death varies in color from the human experience and from other types of extraterrestrials.

CITY BENEATH THE SEA

Following a suggestion to return to a life on another planet, this well-traveled middle-aged male subject regressed to a life as Rolo on a planet called Ur. Rolo began by stating that he was under water in an enclosed transparent vehicle heading towards a city lying at the bottom of an ocean. He was dressed in a thick, shiny, pressurized suit with a clear helmet. As Rolo approached the city, he described it as enormous and enclosed within a gigantic 'bubble'. The 'bubble' appeared as an undulating, shiny, soft atmosphere of energy surrounding the city. As his tiny vehicle passed through this thick, shimmering wall of energy, he could see the tall buildings and the vast multitude of inhabitants flying about as they held on to saucer-shaped discs which he said are automatically programmed to go to a destination by telepathically tapping in to the passenger's thoughts.

Asking Rolo to describe himself and the appearance of other inhabitants, he excitedly stated that his skin was covered with soft scales that appeared iridescent, reflecting multiple colors. He and other inhabitants looked extremely similar, being approximately five to six feet tall, with proportionately long arms and legs and a long face, with very wide ears. Their eyes were large; the nose appeared as two openings above rather full lips. Male genitalia were tucked into the body and would protrude only when necessary. Sex was indiscriminate. Everybody, males and females, had multiple partners; there was no such thing as marriage or family. Males controlled the production of their sperm with their mind and were only allowed to produce children with permission of the government. Children were cared for by the government or by those inhabitants who volunteered to care for them.

The city was full of apartment-type rooms. There were no jobs, as it was unnecessary to make a living since everyone had everything they needed through the power of their minds. When it came to meals, they created the color and taste of their food as they desired it, and it appeared immediately in the form of a gelatinous consistency.

Illness was unheard of, and these inhabitants could literally live forever, or at least until they tired of this life; however, there were many accidents, some of which were fatal. Those who decided to no longer live were allowed to die, and as such, were placed on a large platform from which they were seen to soon disappear. This scenario would occur following a ceremony which was celebrated by others, so these individual souls could move on. Injuries occurred quite often, and those affected were seen by a 'mechanic', who then 'fixed' the individual by attaching living cells to them to regenerate the injured part. These living cells were being continually harvested within the city.

Interested in the unusual physiology of these extraterrestrial beings, I asked about the genitourinary and gastrointestinal body systems. I was told that these genitals were similar to humans'; however, there was no anus, and excrement was allowed to exit from slits on the side of the body in the form of a steam-like consistency.

Asking sociologic questions, I was made to understand that there was no crime and religion was not practiced, as everyone thought life was perfect. Individuals communicated telepathically and created their own entertainment in the same fashion; this occurred in the form of colorful holograms which were also used for their ongoing education, since there were no formal schools. The government was structured as a pyramid, whereupon the leaders at the top served in that capacity for a short time but soon left that position by rotating and starting again at the bottom of the pyramid. Rolo called this a 'monarchy in transition.'

Asking about the source of power to supply the energy needed to run everything within the city, Rolo replied that very large machines used an energy source that reached very high temperatures as it moved through these machines. This energy source was organic and was grown within the city. In regard to other cities being present, Rolo commented that he was not aware of any others. He and others from the city would on occasion venture outside the protective bubble to explore the ocean. It was common knowledge that no one is to travel to the surface of the water, for those who had done this in the past were never seen again.

UTOPIAN INCARNATION FOR AN UNMOTIVATED SOUL

Patrick was a young man in his early thirties with many personal problems, especially those that were related to his relationships with women. His Spirit Guide was extremely helpful in assisting me to tailor-make his therapy; however, it became clear to me that this Guide was somewhat frustrated with Patrick's attitude while in the afterlife. Having been told by the Spirit Guide that Patrick had lived only nine lives on Earth, I found that I also was unable to uncover any more lives as Patrick would continue to return to those same lifetimes. According to his Spirit Guide, Patrick was quite unusual in that he was rather resistant to the idea of reincarnating over and over into an Earth life. Patrick actually felt much happier and quite comfortable just 'hanging out' in the afterlife, with no real motivation to incarnate to a place that presented great challenges that would accelerate the growth of his soul. On the contrary, he was quite content with growing in awareness at the slower pace that exists in the afterlife.

Thinking that returning to a segment of a lifetime that was happy and content would help Patrick's attitude regarding reincarnating to the Earth plane, I instructed him to do just that. In response Patrick did not return to a lifetime on Earth but rather recalled a life on a planet called Quasar.

He described Quasar as a large Jupiter-sized planet that was located in another galaxy. It was surrounded by three suns and five moons and was populated by five billion inhabitants that closely resemble humans. One exception to this resemblance was the presence of different internal organs, namely having three stomachs and two hearts. There were no separate nationalities or countries; however, facial differences were unmistakable. Male and female inhabitants carried out reproduction and cared for their families much as humans did. Longevity exceeded one hundred and fifty years, as disease did not exist on the planet. Inhabitants died of accidents or old age. Everyone was trained in helping with injuries, and the injured either healed by themselves or through the use of a healing energy compartment which they were placed in. When individuals died their spirit went to an afterlife that was described as a soft, white light.

Oceans were present, allowing the inhabitants to travel by boats; however, land vehicles were unknown since everyone had the availability of special mechanical devices that could immediately transport one's molecular structure to another location. Travel by aircraft was quite common, and spaceships often traveled from Quasar to other planets, including Earth for purposes of observation. Animals were present on Quasar but did not serve as a food source; food was mostly grown. The entire planet was ruled by a governing council who was elected by the populace. War was unknown.

The lifetime that Patrick returned to was obviously a utopia of sorts and could only exist on a planet other than Earth, since the challenges here are undeniable but necessary for giving the soul a wide spectrum of experience so it may grow spiritually and advance in awareness. I found it extremely remarkable and unusual that Patrick manifested this rather 'lazy' attitude in regard to his advancing spiritually from the comfort of the afterlife. Addressing this particular attitude, and knowing that personality traits often remain with the individual through each incarnation, I would like to repeat a phrase that he would often utter in several of his very few past lives. He would say, "Too much work... too much work."

20

IS THERE A DOWNSIDE TO PAST-LIFE REGRESSION?

Is there a downside to past-life regression? I can only speak from experience. In order to avoid negative influences or the illusion of such influences, I routinely initiate certain practices under hypnosis. Thus I have the subject visualize his mind and body being surrounded by a protective spiritual light which will only allow helpful or positive influences to affect the subject during the hypnotic session. In addition I instruct the subject to not feel physical pain or experience emotional discomfort, including extreme sadness. When life situations occur that have the likelihood of bringing on such emotional or physical trauma, I immediately utilize various techniques to remove the subject from being emotionally present at that scene.

I have found that a small percent of subjects appeared to break through their protective barriers emotionally during the session; however, techniques, as mentioned before, to raise them above or remove them from the scene, were always effective in these situations.

Following a death scene, wherein the subject had been shot in the head, the subject exhibited no signs of discomfort; however, upon awakening, the individual experienced a slight headache which soon dissipated. This carryover of a physical discomfort into present waking consciousness from a death blow in a past life has occurred rarely and is mild and fleeting when it does. Another example of residual physical discomfort that was conveyed from a previous life was the unusual case of Dr. Jeffrey Mishlove. This case stood out in my mind, as his tenacious adherence to William James's psychogenic illnesses was very much out of the ordinary boundaries of my experience. When I questioned Carol Ann Dryer, a well-known psychic, regarding this unique series of events, her response was that such occurrences served as a form of validation of Jeffrey Mishlove's past life as William James.

Another disturbing but rare situation is the temporary retention of negative emotions which were relived during an unusually traumatic life experience. Two such past-life regressions come to mind that were carried out prior to my routine use of protective instructions. The first case involves a physician who was regressed to a life as a loner who died very much alone, engulfed in his isolation and loneliness. A feeling of depression and loneliness lingered within him for several days.

The second case had to do with a woman who lived a life as a Native American Indian chief who led his warriors into battle against hopeless odds in the name of honor. The entire war party and most of the tribe was annihilated during this battle. The sadness that permeated the chief's very being as he died remained on as a heavy veil of sadness for this subject for several days following the session.

These few cases illustrate the realistic quality of the regression experience. The emotions that are experienced appear to be extremely genuine, wherein all five senses are totally involved, and the subject absolutely swears that he is there. Of note is the fact that many of the residual negative effects that occurred in these subjects occurred following their first session, wherein the subject had been regressed to one or more emotionally-charged lifetimes, which impressed the subject's conscious mind in a negative way. This initial impression was brought about without the benefit of a balance which comes from experiencing other lifetimes that encompass joy, peace, and love.

It's one thing to tell someone that the soul must experience everything. It's quite another to have that individual actually relive the full breadth of life's experiences through several regressions. I am convinced that one's present perspective must be expanded in this way so that he need not identify with an often restrictive and less positive attitude that he may have engendered from a particularly negative life-time in which he manifested extreme emotional trauma. Thus, experiencing more lifetimes gives the subject a broader, more well-rounded perspective and a more complete understanding of the fact that the soul must experience human life from every vantage point in order to grow and advance in perfection. The negative and sometimes traumatic events of other lifetimes should be looked upon in this way, so as to not allow negative emotions from that lifetime to be carried into the wakeful state. The understanding and acceptance of this greater purpose, namely, that the soul learns from experience, gives one the ability to assimilate and integrate these lessons for the betterment of his present life. One must always remember that karma is a learning process. Its function is to teach, not punish.

One always dies in every past lifetime. Interpreted in the proper context, this is seen as part of the normal cycle of life, death, and rebirth into another body for the purpose of learning lessons, and in doing so, advancing the eternal soul on its evolutionary journey. Such an outlook is not only positive and relieves one of the fear of death, it also hammers home the truism that we are indestructible beings; nothing can harm us! This is a very positive thought indeed — one that can fully empower an individual and profoundly change his life for the better.

21

Contact with Extraterrestrials

Material Channeled from Adari

When asked about experiences with extraterrestrials, the subject placed her head in an erect position and began to speak in a deep, masculine voice. "I am a leader... I am in a position of authority. Those of us who have learned are here to teach others. The world belongs to us as a group, not as individuals. I feel at peace because I know this. I am no longer seeking... I have found. People on the planet Earth are too busy. I am from somewhere else. I have come to Earth to tell them to slow down... to stop plundering the Earth.

"I am an essence that has taken on a bodily form. My mission is to promote peace. Some countries have agreed to peace, and some have not." At this moment there was a pause; the subject became more erect and again began to speak. "I am a leader but I don't demand obedience. I want people on Earth to cooperate with one another. They are not subservient to me." I then asked him to describe himself. He replied, "I stay in bodily form for a lifetime, but I can go everywhere on Earth and beyond the stars that we can see. My name is Adari."

Feeling as if I were channeling directly to an extraterrestrial entity, I continued the dialogue and questioned him about his world. "It is peaceful. Everyone there is very kind to everyone else. My people there are different; they all look alike and are of the same sex so that there is no jealousy. We scare humans because we look different. We are smaller and have more physical senses. We have two eyes, no hair... and we use a lot more of our brain but with much less emotional sensitivity."

The channeling stopped as mysteriously as it began, and the subject remained very quiet. I woke her up slowly. What she had to say confirmed my suspicions of this being a true channeled conversation with an extraterrestrial. She said that the words spoken had 'originated beyond her' and felt the most genuine of any material that had yet come through to her during her exceptionally numerous hypnotic sessions.

ALIEN INFLUENCE

Doris Reicher came to me because of steadily increasing negativity which was affecting her life in many ways. She felt agitated and was frequently impatient with others. Her sleep patterns were becoming progressively disrupted, and she was developing an attitude of hopelessness, engendering thoughts such as, "Why bother?"... or, "What's the point?" Even more disturbing was her feeling that she had a deep allegiance to the forces of darkness in a past time. She was identifying with the bad guys but somehow felt a need to free the dark forces from the darkness. She said that she had an overwhelming sense of not wanting to let the hierarchy of the spirit world down but didn't know if she could accomplish this. During meditation she found that she was able to converse with Michael the Archangel, who told her to pray for the dark forces.

In a dream state, she had seen herself in a dome-shaped area, being programmed and forced to remember symbols; and at a recent seminar, she had felt a connection to a woman who had undergone an alien abduction. With this history and her unusual statements well in hand, I swallowed deeply and plunged into the session.

Under deep hypnosis, I was able to bring this twenty-nine-year-old subject up to her Higher Self and had her call forth her Spirit Guide. Once the Guide was present, I asked about the presence of a foreign energy or attachment. Surprised at receiving a negative response, I then questioned the Spirit Guide further about the statement the subject had made earlier, namely, having an allegiance to the forces of darkness in a past time. The Guide replied that the statement had to do with an alien culture.

"A culture other than on Earth?" I shot back.

"Yes," the Guide retaliated.

"On the count of three, please help Doris go back to an alien culture that she lived in prior to living on Earth."

Doris began to speak, "I'm looking at a power plant. I'm a man living on the planet Moldec; it's close to Mars and is in the same galaxy as Earth, but larger than Earth. We look very much like humans. I and many other inhabitants have been abusing Moldec's resources, and as a result, have destroyed much of its culture. I'm trying desperately to stabilize this power plant's system. It's overheating, and I'm afraid it will explode and set off a series of explosions which will destroy our planet. I fear that our fate is sealed."

I advanced the subject to a point in time after the destruction had occurred. She was now in the afterlife in spirit form. "I did not accomplish my lesson of peace. I will next incarnate on Earth."

Somehow, I felt that I must not have given the right instruction initially to the subject, so I said, "On three, return to the original source of the negative thoughts, especially the thoughts relating to the forces of darkness."

The subject began, "I am in a group of reptilians… I am with them, or I am one of them." She started to look at and touch her body, "I am one of them; I hear their voices telepathically. They are making guttural, hissing, and gurgling sounds." The subject then tried to imitate their voice. She continued, "This is where I was created from, but I chose something different for all my lifetimes." The subject now spoke from her present conscious mind, but with the knowledge of her alien origin. "They can control people's minds here on Earth… they can affect me here. This is a separate lifetime, but I am still connected to them. They make contact with me through my mind and physically through my dreams when they take me out of body to their ship." I then asked for details of her visit to their spaceship. "They

175

want to know what's going on with me... why I want to be on Earth and not with them. They're curious about the outcome of our world situation and how I will evolve. They think differently from Earth people. They have fear but don't embrace the God connection. They have their place... they are very advanced."

"Tell me about people who claim to have been abducted."

"They are mostly monitoring, not experimenting. They are reading the Earthlings' energy and thoughts... they're tracking. Aliens come from many places; there are some who do sexual experimentation."

I asked again, "Is this the cause of your negative thoughts?"

"Indirectly."

"On three, I would like you to go back to the cause of your allegiance to the forces of darkness."

"Reptilians are part of the dark force, but I am not supposed to pray for them or send love and light to help them heal and complete their journey. But I do have an allegiance to showing them the way home. I am holding the portal open for the reptilians so they may go back to God. Some are receptive; some are not. There are those who are opportunistic and are watching to see what happens on Earth and around Earth, to see if it affects them. They create the duality of light and dark."

I asked the subject to define "dark force."

"That which does not work with light. Some humans are also part of the dark force."

Noticing that the subject appeared fatigued, I decided to end the session. Also, I felt somewhat numb from this experience. This material was bizarre and frighteningly realistic in the sense that this subject felt that she had a mission to rescue those of her previous extraterrestrial clan who were receptive to going back to God, thus abandoning the dark forces.

Documented testimonials from alien abductees often refer to a reptilian clan in addition to other alien entities. My research involving the regression of several individuals who were convinced that they have been abducted by aliens bears this out and adds support to the existence of these reptilian entities. Here we have a multitude of sub-conscious minds from subjects of all walks of life coming up with descriptions of entities assumed to be extraterrestrial which are iden-tical in all respects. I say, once again, that such a large number and variety of subjects cannot possibly all be contriving such similar and intricately-detailed stories strictly from their imagination. We must not forget to be open-minded and multisensory (including the sixth sense) in our thinking when we consider the plausibility of such accounts, even though the material offered is so disparate from our previously held beliefs.

Communication with extraterrestrials who have attached to liv-ing human beings will be discussed in Chapter 24, "Releasing Attach-ments" on page 206, which also deals with disembodied spirit attachments and mind fragments.

22

COMMUNICATION WITH ADVANCED SPIRITUAL BEINGS

SPIRIT GUIDE EXPERIMENT

As a physician I feel obligated to be scientific in my approach to almost everything, including the paranormal; however, as a physician, I also believe in doing what works. I am certainly not a medium, nor do I claim to have psychic gifts; nevertheless, I found myself embarking on a fascinating path that allowed me to carry out a channeling of sorts with a subject's Spirit Guide during hypnosis. After taking subjects to their Higher Self hypnotically, I would ask them to silently call for their Spirit Guide or Guides and inform me of their presence when they would see, hear, or otherwise sense the presence or the energy of these spiritual beings.

The subjects would report their presence approximately 80% of the time and would often relay a vivid description of their Guide, along with his name. I would then ask their Spirit Guide if he or she would answer questions for me. The many Spirit Guides that I communicated with appeared to have very specific personalities; some were humorous, others were all business, most were very cooperative and answered all my questions. The spiritual entity would telepathically communicate the answers to my subject who would then impart this information to me verbally. Some Spirit Guides were evasive when asked certain questions about particular lives. Others made it clear that specific topics or certain lives were not to be brought up at this time, for it would not be in the best interest of the subject. What the Spirit Guides had to say was often profound, illuminating, and laden with wisdom. My questions would often refer to the subjects: where and when they had lived; who in their present life shared those lives; and whether they, the Spirit Guides, lived a life with them. Eventually I began asking about the presence of a foreign energy or attachment (see "Releasing Attachments" on page 206).

These Guides were wise, but they still maintained human personality traits, such as humor and irritability, even in the spirit realm. I have also been admonished for continuing extensive questioning, being told that I am "diverting energy from its proper place". When I have a very cooperative Guide I touch upon their explanations of parallel lives, pyramids, Atlantis, other dimensions, and an array of other esoteric topics.

Out of curiosity I decided to ask the Guides if they could see and describe my Spirit Guide. The more I thought about this, the more intrigued I became. Certainly the Guides that were being channeled were more than cooperative; and, if in fact they could identify my Spirit Guide as a specific personality, I could then look for a common denominator in future descriptions given by other subjects' Guides. Satisfied with this model for my experiment and being careful not to lead the subject, I began to embark on a journey into the hypnotically altered state of consciousness, rendezvous with Spirit Guides, and check out their credibility.

I decided to use this technique with my next two subjects. So, having no idea about the kind of answers I would receive, I thrust myself into the spiritual arena with a full heart and an open mind.

What followed was something I was not prepared for. The responses were not only consistent in identifying the same Spirit Guide dressed in medieval fashions, but they also indicated that my Spirit Guide had lived a life with me during a certain medieval period. The clarity and accuracy of the information that came through literally raised the hair on the back of my neck. The medieval life referred to was one that I had been aware of several months following my retirement from medical practice.

In order for you, the reader, to understand why this incident had such a powerful impact on me, it is necessary that I relate some background information that will make it very clear:

While still in practice, I often found it useful to utilize past-life regression to relieve patients of their fears and phobias. The regression sessions on one such patient were carried out so as to determine the cause of frequent nightmares and phobias (See Chapter Four, Early Cases, Case One). Her regressions under deep hypnosis were rather vivid in their descriptions and emotional content. She fully took on the previous personalities of the lives that were explored and was able to clearly see dates in her mind. Follow-up research revealed an uncanny accuracy in matching historical events with dates. As if this were not impressive enough, the patient also exhibited a phenomenon known as xenoglossy, the ability to speak a language not learned. This feat was accomplished during two past life regressions. The languages that she spoke included ancient Gaelic, one that has been long since forgotten. Following several regression sessions, the patient ceased having nightmares and was cured of her phobias.

Several months after I had retired from practice and moved out west, I received a phone call from this same patient. It seems that she was consciously having flashback memories of a medieval life with me. In that lifetime she was my half-sister from a village on the coast of France and knew me as a Count who afforded protection for the entire village. My chateau overlooked the village on the ocean. Since I was unable to discuss this in more detail at the time of the phone call, the patient promised to call me the following day with specifics. That evening I informed my wife of this unusual phone conversation, and in her usual psychic manner, she then proceeded to tell me that in her mind's eye she could see my coat of arms on a flag. It was made up of four alternating red and black quadrants separated by a white cross with ornate lions in the upper quadrants. I laughed and reminded her that red and black had always been my favorite color combination, citing my current sports car and my first bicycle, which

I painted red and black. I also had a large pair of brass rampant lions overlooking my desk and lying just above a large medieval shield.

Filled with more than a small measure of curiosity, I anxiously awaited the patient's phone call on the following day. What she had to say was like a bomb going off in my mind. She described the heraldry on my shield as a white cross with a red and black section above and a black and red section below. A gold lion appeared in the middle of the upper quadrants in rampant position. She related two visions which had come to her: first, she saw me assembling my knights and leaving for the crusades; secondly, she envisioned me not returning and the village being overrun by a rival power.

Having validated the historical accuracy of all of her past lives that we had uncovered through hypnotic regression, I tended to believe that we indeed shared this medieval life. This revelation also shed light on why I have always had an affinity for medieval weapons. My home and office have been decorated with such weaponry and depictions of knighthood for many years.

As I continued my Spirit Guide channeling, I designed a form of questioning that would further convince me that I was truly communicating with these spiritual entities. I also would follow the Spirit Guide's lead with further questions if I saw that would enhance the interview. I did not have any idea where this pursuit would take me; however, I was open and eager to observe the results of this experiment. The following paragraphs contain excerpts of dialogue from the first two Spirit Guides with whom I had made contact. The only question asked initially was, "Can you see my Spirit Guide? And if so, please describe his or her appearance."

SPIRIT GUIDE ONE

"Your Spirit Guide has a masculine energy… very strong. I sense leather… horses and riders… dark medieval clothing… headdress. There is a sense of battle and urgency… seems to be trouble… a need to protect. There is a gathering of many behind… like an army. You are there... you are a leader and carry a warrior energy... wearing a metal helmet... large, masculine... wearing padding with protective metal mesh. I see pointed weapons, daggers and swords. There's a crest on your chest, an ornate white cross. I see red and black..." I then asked her to describe the design of the crest in more detail. "A lion comes to mind, but I cannot see it. Your Spirit Guide was with you in that lifetime. He saved your life by getting in front of you and taking a blow for you. He gave his life for you. He did whatever it took to keep you safe. His shield was red, black, and gold, and shaped like a diamond."

Continuing my experiment, a second subject's Spirit Guide responded in the following way to my two questions regarding my Spirit Guide: Can you see him or her? If so, what does he or she look like?

SPIRIT GUIDE TWO

"I see your Spirit Guide in medieval armor. His shield is of a red, black, and gold metal design and is diamond-shaped. He is in his forties, very strong... and has much wisdom. He was in a life with you... says 'brother' and 'friend'. He was a fellow knight and fought in the same war. He stood in front of you and died for you in battle. He is always with you until the end, no matter what. He has a French accent... his name is long and French."

The information acquired from the two preceding Spirit Guide encounters was undeniably similar and appeared quite compatible with the medieval life I had been told that I lived. For the remainder of the experiment, I would initially ask these questions: Can you see my Spirit Guide? If so, describe him or her, and has my Spirit Guide ever lived in a lifetime with me? Some Guides volunteered much information after the first question, others, very little. Armed with an eerie confidence, I continued my channeling.

SPIRIT GUIDE THREE

"Your Spirit Guide is very strong, like a warrior, and is stoic. He is dressed in medieval garb and wears a chest shield. He saved your life in a medieval battle and in other lives with you. He took a death blow for you. He was French."

SPIRIT GUIDE FOUR

"Your Spirit Guide is powerful and a protector. His appearance is medieval. He carries a shield, which is mostly red. He has been with you a long time and is very dedicated to you. He was in a lifetime with you. You were a knight with a strong energy. Your colors were red with black, and your castle was in France, by a mountain, over-looking the ocean."

SPIRIT GUIDE FIVE

"Your Spirit Guide is in a white robe. He lived a life with you; you were like brothers. He saved your life in a King Arthur-kind of battle. He protected you and gave his life for you by putting his arms around you, falling on you, and taking the blow, sacrificing himself. Your heraldry involved orange and red colors, with a silver cross and a lion. Your castle is on the coast of France. Your Spirit Guide gave his life for you in a previous lifetime in the same way. He has always pro-tected you and has great love for you."

SPIRIT GUIDE SIX

"I see someone in armor waving."

SPIRIT GUIDE SEVEN

"I see your Spirit Guide as someone in armor. He is very bright, like an angel, but I see scars on him." I then inquired about the source of the scarring. "From a battle... you were in that battle, and he saved your life." I asked what country we fought for: "France." Asking about my heraldry and colors, she replied, "I see a silver cross on black with red. I then inquired as to whether there was a design present. "I see a cat with no hair and an open mouth."

SPIRIT GUIDE EIGHT

"I see an image of a man. He's wearing something shiny and red; he's wearing protective armor."

SPIRIT GUIDE NINE

"Your Spirit Guide is a well-built male, with very dense energy. He took many blows for you in several lives and in spirit form."

In order to reaffirm my original facts, I decided to communicate with my former patient who had flashback memories of our medieval life together. She informed me that several months after the flashbacks had occurred, she had experienced a lucid dream, during which she was visited by my Spirit Guide. She was completely unaware of my research involving the channeling of various subjects' Spirit Guides while under hypnosis, and hence had no knowledge of the experiment. As she relayed the events of the dream, I once again felt the hair on the back of my neck rise up. She told me that my Spirit Guide had appeared to her in medieval clothes and spoke to her regarding me. He stated that he was also present in the life that she and I shared in medieval France. He said that he was a French nobleman who joined forces with me during a long march to the Crusades. We became close friends and made a mutual pact to protect each other in the Holy War. This pact became a reality as he later took a death blow in battle meant for me.

Having once more heard this familiar scenario, I now began to feel a certain confidence that this lifetime with my patient and my Spirit Guide indeed occurred just as it was described to me, and that the several Spirit Guides that I had communicated with were truly authentic. In my mind this experiment under hypnosis not only strengthened the case for credibility of these spiritual entities, described by nine different subjects, but also served as a form of validation of the lifetime that I had shared with both my Spirit Guide and my former patient.

INSIGHTS FROM SPIRIT GUIDES

Spirit Guides have proven to be very useful in offering answers to many questions I have asked of them. The inquiries were often of an esoteric nature that dealt with metaphysical or paranormal topics that had ethical and philosophical overtones. Hoping to attain a more objective perspective that is detached from the human condition, I posed the following questions to various Spirit Guides.

Dr. T: "Tell me about parallel lives."

Subject One: "The soul or consciousness splits; there is a desire of the soul to learn at twice the speed. It suffers twice as hard, to learn faster. There are many souls that split... they attain a different perspective of the same situation. The process is speeded up so the soul may advance toward its source. Our Creator also split... God could not take action without man; that's why God had to manifest. The whole soul has the potential to be of more benefit to mankind than a split soul. The whole soul gets a greater picture of perception of the whole life experience of Man, the manifestation of God. The split soul gives this up and does not remember the whole picture of evolution."

Dr. T: "Tell me about pyramids."

Subject One: "They are found on other planets as well as Earth. The great mass at the bottom, moving from a large base to a smaller point, acts as a form of energy for movement and can be used for the transfer of consciousness from one planet to another. Extraterrestrials built the pyramids... they chose the stones used in the construction for their resonating ability. The secret of the pyramids' energy lies in the position of the whole configuration of the pyramid. Souls that incarnate as walk-ins on Earth use them for transfer of consciousness into a physical human being. This occurs for certain "chosen ones" who are on Earth to enlighten others."

Dr. T: "Tell me about cryogenics."

Subject One: "The soul is suspended in its development and is in pain. This goes against the laws of nature. The body is designed to have a finite time on Earth. In this state, the soul cannot learn and evolve, it can't go to the light; it is isolated and tied to the body."

Dr. T: "Tell me about when a person is in a coma."

Subject One: "The body is breathing and nourished. The soul receives energy from the breath."

Dr. T: "Tell me about cloning."

Subject One: "It is good; it multiplies the possibility of perception. If a soul splits and this is combined with cloning, it increases such perception."

* * * *

Subject Two claimed that she had contact with extraterrestrials since she was three years old.)

Dr. T: "Tell me about pyramids."

Subject Two: "They are used for healing and longevity as a rejuvenation area, with crystals amplifying the healing patterns. Essences and sounds assist the spirit in leaving the body so the body can be worked on; later the spirit returns. This is available for those who are of the higher order." (This sounds like the pyramid rejuvenation centers that were described in Atlantis.) "Pyramids can also be used for harnessing energy for many different purposes, such as gaining easy access to other dimensions and states of consciousness. The pyramids would be aligned with portals to allow intergalactic and interdimensional travel." (The latter part of this description is consistent with that of the previous subject's.)

Dr. T: "How are other realms accessed?"

Subject Two: "Extraterrestrials have no physical limitations, as humans do. They travel faster than thought, which is an expression of energy. If you focus on a thought enough, it will manifest as a reality. You're adding energy to it by focusing on it."

Dr. T: "What qualities must humans possess in order to access other realms?"

Subject Two: "Pure intention."

Dr. T: "Are extraterrestrials from many different realms?'

Subject Two: "Yes, they have a much higher vibrational frequency and use many portals to travel to many galaxies. They travel with an intention before the thought is even formed. There is no time or space in these realms. It's instantaneous."

Dr. T: "Can extraterrestrials walk through walls?"

Subject Two: "Yes, but not because they manipulate matter or mentally overcome limitations. It is because they know they are the wall; there is no separation."

Dr. T: "What do extraterrestrials perceive our relationship with them to be? Do they want something from the Earth or humanity?"

Subject Two: "Extraterrestrials feel that it is a symbiotic relationship. Extraterrestrials and humans each have things to learn and to teach."

Dr. T: "Are there intelligent beings residing deep inside the Earth?"

Subject Two: "Yes, they are a different life form with the same powers as extraterrestrials but with a different vibrational frequency. They are now working with core magnetics and magnetic energy of the universe. There is no contact with humans at this time."

* * * *

Dr. T: "How many souls are there?"

Subject Three: "There are as many souls as stars in the sky, and there always will be."

Dr. T: "Is the consciousness of the people on Earth being raised?"

Subject Three: "You can incarnate to many different places; but only Earth is a learning place, and presently, it is going through a speeding-up process, an opening up. Now is a great vibrational time for growth. More people are becoming aware. Even though you're only here for a short time, the blink of an eye, you are learning. People who have been coming back and forth are growing with each incarnation. The many millions of people who have been killed in the big wars are returning. This is truly a time of challenge."

Dr. T: "Are Spirit Guides different from angels?"

Subject Three: "Spirit Guides are assigned to specific souls to render them help in many ways. They help in dreams or in the waking state. Angels have a much higher vibration and carry out a different mission."

Dr. T: "How does the impact of religion increase our awareness?"

Subject Three: "We have become too materialistic, too religious, too lost… religion and moral conduct have their place but are warped by people seeking power. More and more people are becoming spiritual in the correct sense… we are in the midst of great learning. Great revelations are being given on the good and evil of righteousness. Step back and take a world view and see the stupidity of religious conquering instead of spiritual understanding. Masters have come to Earth with one point of view… with no desire to have an army of followers. They come only with love for one another. They all are saying the same thing… the message never varies."

Dr. T: "Please explain parallel lives."

Subject Three: "If there is a need to learn a variation of the same lesson or learn the lesson from a different perspective, the soul splits and occupies two bodies. The soul can split more and occupy more bodies, but this can scatter the thoughts and therefore the soul often limits itself to two bodies at the same time, or at overlapping times in one's life. Both parts of the soul contain the Higher Self. This splitting of the soul allows it to see both sides of a situation at the same time or within a period of time; thus information is exchanged between Higher Selves and enhances the learning process. This information can also be transferred to others in those lifetimes who are receptive. Many lessons can be involved but do not hold as much importance as the key lesson."

* * * *

Dr. T: "Can you tell me about the gap between thoughts?"

Subject Four: "It's peace and love; it's where we are complete and create. It's where we connect with God and feel bliss. It's where we find our true self and know who we are."

Dr. T: "When does the soul join the fetus?"

Subject Four: "The soul determines the time, which can be anywhere, from conception to just before delivery."

Dr. T: "Is God still creating new souls?"

Subject Four: "There are no young or old souls, just souls who are advanced or more aware, because they have learned much, and there are those who are less aware. All souls were created at the same time."

Dr. T: "How many lives can one have on Earth?"

Subject Four: "As many lives as it takes to learn the lessons."

Dr. T: "Are there evil souls?"

Subject Four: "There are no such things as evil souls, just dark souls who don't go to the light. There are no lost souls, just confused souls. Darkness surrounds these dark souls, and it is necessary for them to shed the darkness before they can see the light. Until they do this, they will not be able to see the light and they will have to incarnate again, without going to the light. Eventually all discarnate souls go to the light, even the dark discarnate souls. Fortunately, there are not many of these very dark souls. Examples would be Adolph Hitler, Saddam Hussein, Bin Laden, serial killers, and others. They refuse help for a long time but eventually will want to listen to the Masters and accept their help."

Dr. T: "Does the soul retain the energy field after the death of the body?"

Subject Four: "No. The soul is pure energy."

Dr. T: "Tell me about cryogenics."

Subject Four: "The soul is dormant and stays with the body. It is stifled and stagnated… it suffers."

Dr. T: "How is the soul affected when a person is in a coma?"

Subject Four: "A coma is not completely detrimental; it is not a choice of free will. The soul can grow and travel and learn."

Dr. T: "Tell me about pyramids."

Subject Four: "They were made by extraterrestrials. They were used as laboratories for experiments on humans and as beacons for interdimensional travel."

SPIRIT GUIDE ADMONISHMENT

Following fourteen very beneficial sessions, this particular subject (Subject Five) informed me that she's resistant to a particular life that we were about to regress her back to. She had the feeling that she should not know about this lifetime; it may disproportionately affect her thinking. She said she was being told this by a higher power. Lives in Atlantis and Mexico were not to be recalled until she was ready. Certain things had to transpire first. The session continued, and I now had the subject recall a different life, a medieval life in 1227 AD. Midway through the regression, the subject's female Spirit Guide interrupted by telling the subject that this is what she doesn't want, and if the subject keeps going back and reacquainting herself with a particular situation, she will carry it forward to the present. The Spirit Guide explained to her that she is trying to ease the subject to where she needs her to go… this way is too forceful. According to her

Guide, it was all about timing, and the subject was not finished with what she needed to do in her present lifetime. "There is order in these seemingly random lifetimes; it's like trying to make a baby run." She further stated to me that she feels more responsible now that the subject knows about her; and because of that, she could now exercise a greater amount of influence over her (the subject), who is presently more empowered. The Spirit Guide made it clear to me that she wanted more time to work with the subject before we accessed more lives and expanded her awareness any further. She then repeated, "The subject must learn to walk before I get her running."

Making it known to the Spirit Guide that I would be most happy to comply with her wishes, she then replied, "You're pretty humble for a physician." I returned the subject to the present time and gave her ample time to communicate further with her Spirit Guide, who followed with, "Please be patient and trust me. You are benevolent and compassionate. Everything in its own time; every baby in its own way."

That particular session with this longtime subject was rather memorable from another standpoint. Her Spirit Guide exhibited very human qualities as she (the Spirit Guide) complimented me in one breath (so to speak) and admonished me in the other. Having peppered the Spirit Guide with questions regarding when a Spirit Guide is assigned to a fetus, she said she was touched and commended me on my awareness. One statement later, she then said that the subject has one mission, to prepare for the future, and I'm diverting energy from its proper place. I scratched my head and continued the session. The subject took a three-month breather and then returned for another regression. At that time, the Spirit Guide informed me that she was grateful and gave me permission to regress the subject to lives in Atlantis and Mexico.

* * * *

In an attempt to take Subject Six back to a parallel life with her Spirit Guide, I encountered a rather aggressive behavior on the part of the Spirit Guide. Before the subject could recount that lifetime, the Spirit Guide opened the dialogue with, "We know nothing of negative forces. The time came when she left me. There are things she must experience… don't disturb her! Let her go, she has to find her own way. I am with her but now I am in spirit and cannot help. We were happy then, but there was a thirst for knowledge, and we both decided that she should leave. I was in many lives with her, but that is not my reality now that I am in spirit."

The Spirit Guide's tone turned ominous as he then said, "You are interfering with some lifetimes. Parallel lives are usually in a different reality… I warn you… leave her alone!" I was taken back by this sudden, unwarranted outburst by the subject's Spirit Guide. After a few moments of silence, his tone became authoritative as he now spoke on a less personal basis. "Most people are not open to these realities. Be open and meditate if it's your path… it will come. It is the journey that matters, the evolution of our soul. Revelations that come into our soul open our spirit and our mind. We can have many parallel lives at one time. Every choice creates a different universe for us. When we have a multiplicity of lives, we can travel from one to the other. Those who are aware of their psychic gifts and have the proper intention can do this." The Spirit Guide's next statement surprised me, as he once more resumed a more personal attitude towards the subject. "There are some that you are not to do this cell memory healing on. My beloved always makes her own choice."

The rhetoric then continued on in a general vein and ended with, "You are on the right path, and you are gifted, but I can't help you any more than I have. You are here because you are following your passion. You are being guided."

SPIRIT GUIDE EXPLAINS "WALK-THROUGH" PHENOMENON (SUBJECT SEVEN)

Indirectly channeling through a subject's Spirit Guide, I decided to pose this question: When a person is regressed to a past life, is that past life his, or has that individual somehow tapped into the akashic records and relived another's lifetime as if it were his own?

The spiritual entity responded authoritatively, but in a personal way by saying I have a gift for you. He continued "A soul living in a physical body will intuitively know if that lifetime is truly his incarnation. He will know in his heart whether or not he experienced that lifetime from birth to death."

The Spirit Guide spoke of things I had heard of previously, such as, the soul incarnates on Earth because of the great challenges that exist here and because there is an expansion of consciousness with every hurdle we overcome. He went on, "The akashic records are very orderly. Every incarnation has been tracked and everyone has access to it collectively, so that each soul can access any portion of other lifetimes before he incarnates. Thus a soul may make an agreement with another soul to temporarily occupy the same body, and with this permission, physically visit that lifetime. Remember, a soul has many lessons to learn, and attention goes where it will fulfill a need. Consider this a visitation. It is similar to a 'walk-in', wherein a bodiless soul makes an agreement with the host soul that resides within a person with the express purpose of exchanging places permanently. The visitation is similar in that it requires permission of the occupying soul, but it is different in that it is temporary, requiring a specific amount of Earth-time for the visiting soul to complete its lesson. Think of the visitation as a 'walk-through'; the soul in charge is allowing another soul to 'walk through', so that this other soul may also experience that being."

I then asked if this set of circumstances would apply more to a so-called 'high-profile' life, namely one with excessive challenges and great accomplishments in spite of insurmountable obstacles. The answer came quickly, "Yes, there is no need to visit a life which is spiritually stagnant and without challenge. The goal of enlightenment, of experience, of actualization, is to be where the action is. It's where the energy is, it's where the focus is, it's where the soul needs to be."

It immediately dawned on me that this so-called "walk-through" phenomenon could explain why in some cases I have only been able to validate a portion of certain past lifetimes and not the entire life-time. This partial-validation problem had haunted me for years, and now I was being handed an important piece of the puzzle. This pearl of information from the spiritual realm was indeed a gift, just what I needed to encourage and shore up my belief system about the entire process of reincarnation and to present my investigative mind with ammunition to quell insidious self-doubt.

Thinking this through further, I wondered if this so-called "walk-through" could also be considered a form of a parallel life, a situation that occurs when a soul splits so it may occupy two bodies at the same time for the purpose of learning lessons from different perspectives. At this moment, words I had heard from this Spirit Guide several years ago began to ring loudly in my mind: "A shared aspect of a soul is for more opportunity to learn." This statement now took on a deeper meaning, which was all-encompassing. It could easily be referring to both a soul dividing so as to occupy two physical beings (a parallel life) or to two souls sharing the physical experience of a particular human being (a walk-through). Both scenarios offer a soul the choice to increase its learning opportunity.

Then I remembered another quote by this Spirit Guide, made at the same time: "All lives are parallel." This was true, I thought, even though this was a more expansive way of looking at parallel lives, since the past, present, and future all occur at the same time. This expanded definition of parallel lives could also possibly include the existence of many different versions of any given moment of a life-time that occur simultaneously in a reality that we are unaware of, the so-called 'multiverse theory' of the renowned theoretical physicist,

David Deutsch.[1] Deutsch felt that the quantum theory should be applied to every level of reality, just as it is to the subatomic world. Since man is composed of subatomic particles, he too would exist in many universes at once. If this were true, the lives existing in multiple universes would possibly be another version of parallel lives with shared aspects of one's soul. However, if these universes are truly holographic, such a parallel life would still have all aspects of the soul present and available to undertake the life experience.

SPEAKING TO THE MASTERS (AKA 'ELDERS')

This subject (Subject Five) had one particular Master, by the name of Roholoman, who would communicate with her from the spirit plane. During one of her early sessions, I asked if this Master would please speak to me. He did so, saying, "We are proud of you because you are helping others… a lot of good things will happen for you."

A few days later, while working with another subject who was aware of several Masters being present, I asked if I could communicate directly with a Master Spirit by the name of Roholoman. I was told no. Within a few weeks, I again saw Subject Five, during whose session I had originally spoken to the Master Roholoman. Once again I communicated with him, and he started off the conversation by saying, "You're crafty. You asked to speak to me through another." This statement flabbergasted me because there was no way for this subject to know what had transpired during my sessions with other subjects. This Master, Roholoman, was obviously well tuned-in. During that same session, Roholoman volunteered information about Spirit Guides in general. "Of the Guides' many responsibilities, helping individuals know themselves and protecting them are primary. Knowing thyself is knowing thy soul. The choices not pertaining to the soul are not important. Have faith…"

---

1. David Deutsch, "The Structure of the Multiverse," *Proceedings of the Royal Society* A458 2028 2911-23 (2002).

Having completed her tenth regression and gone through the death experience, Subject Five found herself in the afterlife, listening intently to what Roholoman, her favorite Master spirit, was saying to her. The Master was telling her to really absorb and apply what she is learning from the regression experience. "The first steps are easy, but don't miss the last crucial step of learning. You can make a big jump in enlightenment or learning in this lifetime, since you now have much more knowledge than ever before. If you can apply this knowledge, there will be great rewards."

The Master thanked me and said that the subject was very close to making that leap. The subject then asked Roholoman what else she could do. The Master replied, "Stop asking questions and do what you need to do. Don't be selfish… don't take anything for granted, deserve it by earning it, and do the best you can do."

* * * *

Following a death experience, this 23-year-old female subject (Subject Eight) regressed into the afterlife and carried out a dialogue with an entity she described as an Elder. I requested that she ask him if he would please speak to me. I was surprised when the subject's conscious mind responded with a flippant comment. "This is cheesy…"

The words of the Elder immediately followed, with the subject's voice changing to a rather eloquent and authoritative tone, saying, "The meaning of existence is to learn to be open; and in doing so, you will be free." I was reminded of John 8:32, "And you will know the truth, and the truth will make you free."

* * * *

This particular session with an advanced female subject (Subject Nine) yielded a rather unique situation. Attempting to progress her into a future life, I found that I was not being successful. This subject was literally drawing a blank as she described seeing nothing but blackness. This confused me, since this is what I would usually hear

196

from a subject when I am unaware of his impending death and attempt to advance him beyond the time of his death. I felt that something was blocking this lifetime and decided to ask her Spirit Guide for help. Her Guide informed me that the subject was in spirit form. I then asked where.

The Spirit Guide said, "She just is."

I then asked if the subject was going to incarnate soon.

"No. She is waiting. She doesn't want to incarnate… she doesn't need to… she is a Master Spirit and has something to say to you." I noticed a slower, deeper voice, as the Master spoke to me.

"You and others are doing a great service. It will take many more like you. Your work is acknowledged."

The subject appeared fatigued, so I decided to end this session with the thought that, as usual with regressions, I will continue to always expect the unexpected.

23

LIFE AS A DISCARNATE SPIRIT

CASE ONE:
REMAINING IN THE ASTRAL PLANE BECAUSE OF GUILT

Deborah was a young woman of 27, who possessed several psychic abilities, one of which had to do with seeing spirits of deceased individuals. She had this psychic gift since childhood and had the support of family members, several of whom also possessed psychic powers. Deborah was one of many college students wishing to participate in my research in past-life regression. Her first regression helped her to understand why a small boy-spirit wanted to physically cling to her during her early years in school. She recognized him in a former life as her son, who died in his youth in the early 1800s.

During a subsequent session, she lived a life in the 1970s and had an untimely death from an accident in 1978. As she died in the arms of a close girlfriend, it occurred to me that this friend of hers is probably living in the present time and is currently in her late forties. As this subject was nearing the end of her death experience, I decided to ask her if she could astral project herself to where her friend is. Not knowing what would happen next, I waited patiently for approximately fifteen minutes. I had never suggested this to a subject before; however, Deborah appeared to possess rather remarkable psychic abilities. At the end of this time span I inquired as to what was happening. She replied,

"I'm looking at a map." I once again remained silent and several minutes later, she howled, "Boy is she fat!" She went on to describe her friend's appearance in the office she was working in. I now asked the subject to go through her friend's papers at the desk she was sitting at. I can only speculate at what happened while she was doing this, since her friend became quite frightened and ran from the room. I then asked Deborah to see if she could find a business card and read it to me. Unfortunately, she had extremely poor vision and very thick glasses in this lifetime and could not make out the blurry words and numbers on the business card.

Following the session the subject described what occurred when I had requested that she attempt astral projection in order to locate her friend. She said she called out her friend's name and felt a response. Following this, she saw herself hovering over a globe of the world and received a picture of Florida in her mind. She then seemed to know that her friend was located in a state close to Florida as an image of a coastline appeared in her mind. Within seconds of seeing this image, she was there with her friend. Deborah later confessed that she has voluntarily had previous out-of-body experiences in order to help friends in trouble.

Deborah's third regression was a most memorable experience for it was within this lifetime that the stage was set for an individual soul to allow itself to remain on Earth following death. A soul such as this is more often than not confused and wracked by emotion and usually left to aimlessly wander within the confines of the physical place in which it died. The term discarnate spirit is often used to describe a soul in these emotionally traumatic circumstances.

Unlike most death experiences, this soul resisted being drawn to the light of the afterlife. Such hesitations are often related to not wanting to leave the presence of loved ones who are in mourning and emotionally distraught. Such was not the case here. The subject lived this lifetime as a woman who today would have been diagnosed as having a severe bipolar disorder. Thus this lifetime was overshadowed by this affliction, resulting in dramatic mood swings, wherein she would be pleasant one moment and vile the next.

She gave birth to a daughter whom she disliked, even as an infant, causing her to make statements such as, "I don't want to deal with caring for this baby."

Following her death in that lifetime, she began to exhibit exceptional signs of fear and torment as she approached the light. She recounted in great detail the daunting feelings and agonizing thoughts that weighed heavily on her soul, particularly the smoldering guilt of the unnatural state of dislike for her own daughter, which now haunted her spirit at the crossroads of her departure from this Earth. These emotionally packed circumstances caused her to hesitate at the entrance to the light and not cross into it. As this subject tearfully relayed these events, I found myself engulfed in empathy and overwhelmed with the emotions that she was projecting. I was beginning to understand how the circumstances of one's life can lead to such desperate thoughts and the abandonment of a soul to the Earth plane. In my mind I could only compare this picture of despair to the thoughts of one who is marooned and isolated on a barren island and missed his only opportunity to be saved. This truly was an unprecedented glimpse into the very private but confused consciousness of a tortured soul who was about to make a momentous decision that would clearly affect its evolutionary growth in this timeless realm.

As Deborah continued to recall this sad and emotionally volatile tale of subconscious memory, I felt myself identifying with the feelings of confusion, isolation, and loneliness that seemed to permeate her very being. The following account of her death experience and what followed gives us a strikingly real picture of the thought processes that pervaded this soul, leading to an engrossing mental conflict. More importantly, I was being allowed to view this entire scenario from the perspective of a discarnate spirit.

"I have pneumonia; my chest hurts." I rose her above this scene. "Everything is white. I do love my daughter; she reminds me of me in other lives." She then stepped past the light, saying "Everything is understood... I don't want to go there. There's a spirit observing me;

they are waiting for me to pass through the light. I'm afraid I will lose who I am if I cross through. I'm being pulled by a bubble… I can't see what's on the other side… I'd rather stay in the room with the people, but I know I cannot return to the same body, and I know I must go through the light before incarnating again. I'm still in the room with the other souls and the people who are mourning. The light is leaving. I missed my chance to move on. The spirit observing me is leaving. Everything in the room has stopped… it's now moving again. There is a large bed against the wall. The room is dark... the drapes are closed. I see only a light in front of the bed." At this moment, the subject appeared to focus on her lifeless body, saying, "My body is dead… my daughter won't let go of the arm. I want to tell her I'm sorry." Deborah was crying uncontrollably during this time; following calming techniques, she again spoke. "I can walk inside the room, but when I'm outside, I can only float above the people. I am unable to ground myself and stay in one spot. I even pass through some people. Ooh! Something burned me!" She continued, "I have no further pain, and my hip doesn't hurt any more… my hair is down… it was always up. Outside the room I have no form. I can see through walls… it hurts to be outside the room. I am content in the room. Others can't see me, but in the room I have a form like my body. I have no desire to ever leave this room… I've watched it change."

Deborah's discarnate spirit never left this room; rather, she remained content, looking out the window to observe an occasional horse and carriage. She fondly recalled two children who entered the room and were able to see her.

Life as a discarnate spirit continued for her for an indefinite period of time, only as it could in a timeless state until, as she described it, "All of a sudden, everything became light, and I became engulfed in it…like a fog, which settled on everything… I became part of it. I found myself immediately released, and now I was on the other side of the light, with full understanding, with the ability to incarnate again. I felt that the lesson I needed to learn had to do with just being happy being me. In that lifetime I prevented myself from accomplishing this lesson by being upset most of the time about everything and by being aggressive with everyone until the end."

CASE TWO:
REMAINING IN THE ASTRAL PLANE BECAUSE OF COMPASSION

Another case involving a spirit who chose to remain in the astral plane for an entirely different reason is dramatically represented by a thirty-year-old female subject who was easily regressed on her first visit and recalled a life as a young French knight during the Crusades. During a battle for Constantinople his courage and fear collided in his mind as he once more raced his horse toward the enemy. "I'm on a horse rushing the infidels. I'm focused and praying hard... they are evil vermin... I've killed several while they were on their horses. They are dark-skinned, evil, and bald with mustaches. They are out to destroy us and take over the city. It's God's will for us to win."

The siege settled into a stalemate for two months, and the city remained in anarchy. "I go to brothels, where beautiful women dance for us and serve us wine. My friend Pierre and I refuse to have sex with the women. On the day the battle resumed, I felt angry and drank too much mead. I was foolish to fight this way; I was not at my best."

The subject became anxious and tearfully continued, "I was hit from the side... my head was cut off... I see my body still on the horse... the infidel laughed as my body slid off the horse. I looked at my head on the ground... I could see my curly brown hair, beard, and moustache, my blue eyes staring lifelessly." Silence permeated the room as the subject quietly wept. Speaking softly once again, "I stayed there until the battle was over. I then prayed and thought the Lord was going to take me. I looked around and saw other spirits on the battlefield. We all looked at each other and knew that war was a waste... there is so much more to life. I became terrified when I realized that I would not see my family again. As I looked around, I could see that some of the infidels had more of a connection to the light than

I did. How wrong it is to kill each other... I felt tricked... I was prepared to fight Satan."

The remorse was overwhelming as a veil of silence once again fell upon the room. Acting as if she had made an important decision, the subject spoke firmly, "I went to see my wife and children...," and then, tenderly, "...she's doing chores, soaking clothes in a large tub with other women... now she's baking bread, round loaves with seeds, and staples from the cows. I felt pure love as I decided to watch over them." A broad smile lit up the subject's face as she became comfortable with her decision not to go to the light. "I've communicated with them, the children are receptive... my boy would talk to me in his mind. I always told him to pray to God and not to me."

I advanced her to the next significant event. "I stayed there... time collapses there. Hubert, my son, grew up and became a soldier. I was with him in battle when he was killed. We went to the light together. It was beautiful there... beings of all levels, planning out their lives." Asking what was learned in that lifetime, the subject answered, "War is wrong. We are all alike. I even felt love and compassion for the Moslems."

CASE THREE:
DISCARNATE BUT NOT DESOLATE

Alice was an extremely pleasant middle-aged subject who wanted to experience a past life strictly out of curiosity. Her first session scanned four lifetimes, three of which I will briefly mention so that the motivations of the souls involved will be more clearly understood.

Alice first experienced a life in the 17th century, which came to an end during a storm at sea. Following a drowning death, her spirit was greeted and led to the light by Peter, her Spirit Guide, who she immediately recognized and lovingly described as an "old friend". Once in the afterlife, I began to ask my usual questions of the Spirit Guide and discovered that he and the subject had shared a life together.

Taking Alice back to that life with her Guide as primitive natives of the fifteenth-century Amazon jungle, I soon discovered that they were lovers, and Alice bore him many children. Unfortunately, she also bore witness to her mate's grizzly death as he made a futile attempt to fight off a tiger's attack. Alice escaped into the jungle as the tiger feasted on her beloved mate. The subject, now in tears, went on to describe the remainder of her long but lonely life.

The third life took place in late 19th century Barcelona, Spain, where the subject was a young woman attending college. Following the death of her wealthy parents in a train accident, she met and married a man who she recognized as her present brother-in-law. She had two sons, one of whom she knew to be her present son. Her life remained uneventful until 1933, when, at age 42, she was killed in an automobile accident. As her spirit separated from her lifeless body, she once again was greeted by Peter, the love of her 15th century life, who had been watching over her as her Spirit Guide. As Alice rose toward the light, the remorse over leaving her family grew unbearable. Still consumed with Earthly concerns, she worried about the fate of her children. She needed to watch over them and help them in whatever way that she could. The turmoil that churned within her came to a tumultuous head as she was about to enter the light. Her Spirit Guide sensed her overwhelming concern and tried in vain to soothe the scathing terror that enveloped her soul. She was not about to take off her coat of Earthly cares and enter the light. Thus the decision to remain in the astral plane was made. She would now be able to watch over her sons; her husband was already with another woman.

Alice felt that she could at least know that they are okay as they grew up. Knowing that Alice had chosen to remain as a discarnate spirit in the astral plane for quite a while, I asked if she had attached to anyone, such as her children. Her answer came as a shock as she replied, "I attached to Peter, my oldest friend." This was definitely not what I expected, a discarnate spirit "attaching" to her Spirit Guide. Obviously Peter, her Guide, did not enter the light as he normally would have. He remained in the astral plane with Alice, his former mate. Being extremely curious over this touching gesture by Alice's Spirit Guide, I asked when it was that he was assigned to watch over Alice.

He answered, "The Masters assigned me to be her Spirit Guide after my death in the life we shared."

I chuckled as I then heard Alice exclaim, "Peter has been very pushy about going to the light."

I asked, "How long, how many Earth years, has he been pushy?"

Alice replied, "Many Earth years. When my children were grown, Peter and I entered the light together."

When Spirit Guides are assigned to watch over an individual soul, they show their unconditional love for that soul in many ways. Alice's Guide never missed an opportunity to show the magnitude of his love for her. He did this on Earth by sacrificing his life for her and again in the afterlife by remaining with her in the astral plane and encouraging her to go to the light. If there is such a thing as love more powerful than unconditional love, it was manifested by this Spirit Guide.

The session was coming to an end, and my brain was becoming sore from being thrown another curve. As always, the comic relief lobe in my brain began to fire, and all I could think of was, "Heck! If you're going to hang out in the astral plane, you might as well hang with your Spirit Guide; he'll keep you straight and get you back to the light."

24

RELEASING ATTACHMENTS

MY BAPTISM OF FIRE

One of my most surprising and challenging cases was one for which I was totally unprepared. It involved a young man named Jason, who began to have vivid, conscious memories of himself, but as different people in other times and in other places. These disturbing memories had been occurring since he moved to Los Angeles three years earlier to begin a writing career. One memory portrayed him as a sailor of the 1800s, perched on a crow's nest during a violent storm at sea. This memory appeared to surface during the somewhat altered state of consciousness that was induced while working out or jogging.

The second memory took on a more ominous tone in that it only seemed to occur during times of stress, causing his thoughts to be dominated and beleaguered by negative emotions of anger and regret. He described this recollection as "loud and wanting attention." The memory was of a young farmer's son in feudal Japan, who became a foot soldier in the Emperor's army and was killed with a spear during his first skirmish. The spear penetrated his left upper abdomen and caused Jason to experience pain in this same area during this emotional recall. The subject claimed to have always had a vague interest in Japanese culture; however, this interest had mushroomed into a burning obsession since arriving in Los Angeles.

Jason proved to be a good subject and was easily guided into a deep state of hypnosis, whereupon he was regressed to a lifetime that would explain the recurring memory he experienced while jogging. In this lifetime he was a red-bearded 45-year-old alcoholic third-mate on a slave ship bound for North America. The ship encountered a powerful storm, causing him to be swept overboard and lost at sea. In the afterlife he easily determined that he did not accomplish his lesson of compassion for others and must again incarnate to learn this lesson.

Jason was now taken back to the origin of his memory of feudal Japan. Under deep hypnosis he began to relive the life of "Ishi", the 16-year-old son of a farmer who joined the Emperor's army. His parents could only afford to give him armor made of bamboo, but this did not dampen his pride and enthusiasm. The Emperor's army of many thousands approached a narrow gorge. Through the thick morning fog he was able to make out several fierce-looking men on horses, cutting into the ranks of the Emperor's men. In the confusion that followed, he felt a spear pierce his belly. As he removed the spear from his left abdomen, he felt himself dying. Lying in the mud, he uttered," They surprised us." Then, angrily, he shouted, "I've been cheated! Where is the glory? I marched … never fought … how unfair is this universe? I feel only pain and numbness. I want a second chance. I want glory and prestige, a name, not a farm boy!" As he died and entered the spirit plane, I asked about the lesson his soul needed to learn in that lifetime. His answer was full of anger and not at all compatible with what I had been hearing from souls once they had entered the light. He said, "Don't be a foot soldier; be a general! Next time, I want to be the warlord. Nothing was accomplished. I hoped for good but it didn't happen."

I began to suspect that he had not entered the light. My suspicion was confirmed when he was greeted by his grandmother from that lifetime. She told him, "Don't be angry… don't be a little boy."

He responded in a bitter tone, "I am angry… and Jason doesn't do what I tell him! I tell him to train and learn Tendo to get him honor."

This statement took me completely by surprise. I almost blurted out, "Excuse me!" as my mind accelerated into high gear. "So that's what's going on," I thought to myself. "I'm dealing with a spirit possession, a discarnate spirit who has attached to Jason." At this point I

felt immersed in a quagmire of conflicting emotions, a truly inextrica-
ble position as I attempted to maintain an air of confidence. Hoping I
was misdiagnosing the situation, I threw out another question, "How
long have you been with Jason?"

His response was chilling, "I've been with him a long time. I've
been waiting patiently. He let me in, and I'm here now. He let me in
when he was five years old. He is not aware of my presence."

This was now blowing my mind! Here I was, carrying on a form of
channeling with an attached spirit, and an angry one at that. I had heard
of such entities not going to the light because of a variety of reasons,
including the presence of very strong emotions, such as fear, anger, and
guilt. Other reasons would include the spirit's refusal to believe he is
dead or possibly his confusion regarding the awareness of his death.
These discarnate spirits are reportedly opportunistic and attach to
unsuspecting people when they least expect it, often in their youth.

The pieces of the puzzle were now starting to fall into place. I
remembered that such attachments were very much like a parasite and
host relationship, affecting a person in all aspects of mind and body.
Shaking off my feelings of vulnerability, a barrage of thoughts
exploded in my mind. I felt a sort of comic relief as I once again
remembered my timeworn saying from my days in surgery: "When
things turn to shit, just calmly turn around, rinse your hands, and
think like hell." Well, the rinse pan wasn't there, but I was thinking
like hell! I plunged ahead, asking, "Why must you fulfill your wishes
through Jason?"

The spirit attachment responded angrily, "I live off of him. Following his arrival in Los Angeles, things became more difficult. Jason
was more adventuresome before; now he writes all the time. I've been
waiting for someone to hear me for a long time. I don't want to leave
and give up this anger. I've survived on it."

Having no experience in these situations and vowing to myself to
read extensively on this subject, I decided to use common sense and
my gut feelings. I knew this discarnate entity needed to go to the light,

so I appealed to him with the idea that he is not doing himself or Jason any good by remaining in this attached state. I then called for Spirit Guide and Master spirit assistance to help release this discarnate spirit's anger and other negative emotions and help him seek the light, where he will be elevated in awareness, find true peace and be propelled on the evolutionary journey his soul must travel.

Jason felt a sense of relief and freedom, even under hypnosis, as he felt the attached entity leave. I then explained to Jason that the memory of the Japanese feudal life was really the memory of the discarnate spirit and not his, and therefore should not affect him, leaving him free to carry on with his passion of writing without interference. Also, he should no longer be plagued with the abdominal pain that was retained in the subconscious cell memory of the attached spirit. I then surrounded Jason with a visualization of protective light that encompassed his mind, body, and spirit. I suggested that this protective light would render him impervious to further possessions or intrusions in the future by spiritual entities with their own agenda.

Following the session I reflected on the experience. This was to be my baptism of fire with regard to attached entities. It then dawned on me that the regression back to the feudal Japanese life had actually been performed on the attached discarnate spirit, not on the subject. Making good on the vow I made to myself, I immediately purchased *Spirit Releasement Therapy and Healing Lost Souls* by William Baldwin, DDS, Ph.D., and further educated myself on this most captivating topic. I soon came to the realization that being able to discover and safely release these entities from subjects was a requirement for anyone who intends to heal individuals with past-life regression therapy. Dr. Baldwin discussed releasement of attached entities in great detail. This included the attachments of discarnate spirits or Earthbound souls, extraterrestrial beings, soul fragments, and dark entities. Since I had already made it a routine to take subjects up to their Higher Self and have them call forth their Spirit Guides, I would now in addition ask the Spirit Guide about foreign energy or attached entities being present in the subject. If I receive an affirmative answer I would inquire as to what kind and how many are present. Following this, I would then carry on a dialogue with the entity or entities and proceed with the appropriate releasement therapy for that type of entity. Once I have been given confirmation from the Spirit Guide or the subject that the entity or entities are no longer attached and have left, I utilize Dr. Baldwin's Sealing Light Meditation, a guided imagery of light which fills in the void that is left and protects the subject from future intrusions.

CLOSE ENCOUNTERS OF A NEW KIND

In the next few months I came upon several more cases of possession. Two of them involved extraterrestrial attachments, there for the purpose of experimentation. As Dr. Baldwin's experience dictated, these entities were reasonable and agreed to leave once they understood that being discovered negated the validity of their experiments. This releasement was carried out through specific steps, requiring a dialogue with the extraterrestrial beings.

RELEASING MORE UNINVITED "GUESTS"

A rather large number of my subjects had attached Earthbound entities, so I will briefly discuss the highlights of just three of the more challenging cases. The first case involved a man with several undesirable personality traits, including the frequent use of obscenities and an addiction to pornography. Six Earthbound entities were discovered, and two of them admitted to being responsible for these particular problems. Dr. Baldwin's terminology regarding this number of attached entities is the "pancaking effect." In this particular case, I released all of the entities into the light as a group. Following confirmation of their releasement, the subject blurted out, "I feel three hundred pounds lighter!" Noticeable improvement became obvious to the subject over the next few weeks.

* * * *

The second case involved a discarnate spirit who was attached to a 24-year-old woman with sexual intimacy problems with her husband. The discarnate spirit identified himself as 'Peter', and claimed that he was the subject's lover in a previous life and has been Earthbound since he was killed by a wartime explosion in that lifetime. Responding to my further questioning, he said that he had been attached to the subject since her childhood. As the dialogue continued with this Earthbound discarnate spirit, it became clear that he loved the subject and was not about to leave her. At this point the source of the subject's intimacy problem with her husband became evident, since this attached entity was obviously acting out of jealousy and interfering during the couple's intimate moments. The discarnate spirit became progressively belligerent, insisting that he did not want to leave this woman. The subject now reported that three spirits had arrived to help guide this emotionally distraught Earthbound being to the light. Peter, however, held his ground and refused to depart. Having exhausted what I had recalled of Dr. Baldwin's releasement techniques, I then decided that I needed some big guns to convince Peter to head for the light. Not knowing or having the time to investigate the subject's belief system, I blurted out in a very firm voice, "I invoke the help of Michael the Archangel to please guide Peter to the light."

After several minutes the subject said softly, "He's gone."

The subject underwent further therapy under hypnosis for a range of other problems, and when contacted over a week later said that her attitude was much improved and she looked forward to a better relationship with her husband.

* * * *

The third case started out as a simple task, namely eliminating a smoking habit in a young woman. It, however, turned complex in a rather unexpected way during this otherwise routine hypnotic session.

Camille had been smoking for four years, ever since the traumatic suicide of her mother. The subject was rather metaphysical in her thinking; and since I expected more problems to surface because of the emotional baggage she carried, I decided to work within the vestibule of her spirituality, namely, the Higher Mind. While there, I had her summon her Spirit Guide to help with what we needed to accomplish. I then proceeded with the typical suggestions to stop smoking. Within a short period of time, Camille became noticeably emotional and blurted out, "My mother doesn't want me to stop smoking!" As a large piece of the puzzle fell into place, I immediately asked to speak to her Spirit Guide and inquired about the presence of foreign energies or attachments.

The answer I received was, "There are many." I then asked if her mother's spirit was among them and was told, "Yes". I now asked to communicate with her mother's spirit directly. As the dialogue commenced, it became obvious that the discarnate spirit of the subject's mother did not want to leave her daughter for many reasons, one of which I assumed was a need for nicotine which she would be able to continue to satisfy by staying attached to her daughter's body. I was sure this was the reason Camille took up smoking in the first place; thus negating my first impression which was that she began smoking because of extreme anxiety due to the unusually traumatic circumstances of her mother's death.

While conducting this dialogue with the deceased's mother's Earthbound spirit in an effort to convince her to leave her daughter's body and go to the light, the subject's voice again rang out with an emotional plea, "I don't want my mother to leave. I'll be all alone!"

At this moment, I thought to myself, "Boy, do I have my hands full." I then directed my dialogue to both the subject and her discarnate mother, attempting to convince Camille to release her mother's spirit into the light so her mother may return home to the afterlife and continue to evolve on her spiritual journey as she should. Also, it was evidently comforting for both of them to know that the mother's spirit could not only love but help her daughter from the light, as opposed to causing her harm as an attached Earthbound spirit. I was told that guiding spirits appeared. I then decided to wait quietly.

The subject, who had been crying hysterically, suddenly ceased and appeared to have a glow about her face, as she smiled and said, "She's leaving."

Following this episode wherein Camille bid her mother good-bye, I once again filled in the void with the Sealing Light meditation and continued with nonsmoking suggestions. I'm sure this subject subconsciously wanted her mother to stay with her; however, her conscious mind understood the consequences. Unfortunately, I was unable to follow-up on this subject, but I have a feeling that she is doing okay without her mother's interference and addictions.

ADDRESSING ISSUES OF KARMIC RESPONSIBILITY

My experience with attachments, limited as it may be at this time, indicated to me that Dr. William Baldwin's ideas and techniques regarding attached entities and their releasement were right on target and certainly reflected his massive experience during the past two decades. In my estimation the entire idea of entity attachment has opened many new doors leading to the successful completion of past-life therapy; however, there is a negative aspect involved as doors are also opened to unsettling questions regarding free will and the creation of our own reality and karma.

In his book *Healing Lost Souls*, Dr. Baldwin expresses his ideas as follows:

"Following death, the Earthbound soul maintains its personality structure, with all the idiosyncrasies, emotions, character traits, and attitudes it had when living, as well as physical needs such as for food, alcohol, and drugs.

"The attached entity (or entities - rarely is there just one) uses the energy of the host.

"The host is usually unaware of the presence of attached Earthbounds.

"Thoughts, desires, and behavior of an attached entity are experienced as a person's own thoughts, desires, and behaviors.

"Many drug users are controlled by the attached spirit of a deceased drug addict.

"In some cases, such an entity can attach to someone who is drug free and influence them to begin drug usage.

"An attached Earthbound can influence the choice of marriage partners or the desire to have an extramarital affair.

"A newly-attached entity who dislikes the partner can drive the couple to divorce, even when there was no problem prior to attachment.

"The mental, emotional, and physical influence of an attached Earthbound can alter the path of karmic options and learning opportunities for the host.

"Except in rare cases, entity attachment is not part of a planned life script.

"Although it seems to be a violation of free will, spirit attachment does not require the permission of the host. This appears to refute the popular belief that each person is responsible for creating his or her reality; there are no victims. The apparent conflict stems from the definitions of permission and free will choice.

"Few people refuse permission to these nonphysical intruders. They simply pay no attention. Individuals have the right to deny intrusion by another being. With limited knowledge and distorted perceptions of the spirit world, many people leave themselves open, creating their own vulnerability as part of creating their own reality." [1]

My thoughts on this rather controversial monkey-wrench which has now been thrown into the basic precepts of reincarnation and karma will refer primarily to attached, Earthbound spirits. They are as follows:

---

1. Dr. William Baldwin, *Healing Lost Souls,* Hampton Roads, Charlottesville, VA 2003, pp. 16-22.

First of all, I believe that karma represents justice in the truest
sense. A human being creates karma primarily by free will, leading to
intention and then choice, which may or may not lead to action. However, when a spirit attachment is 'calling the shots' by overprinting its
thoughts and desires upon an individual soul host, that individual soul
cannot be held totally accountable for the karmic outcome. The
responsibility for the intent, and therefore the effect, of such influence
upon the host falls squarely upon the shoulders of the intruding
attached entity. This rather unique situation is initiated by an unwarranted invasion of a living person by the Earthbound soul of a
deceased person. Once that intruder has somehow attached to the living human host, the most fundamental justification and requirement
for incarnation on this Earth, the ability to exercise free will, becomes
compromised. Thus the living human host is unable to create his own
reality and becomes something he should never be, a victim. This
unusual circumstance appears to stand as a lone exception to the
rationale of reincarnation.

Those in the mainstream majority may not be interested in or
take seriously the basics of increased awareness, including an understanding of the spirit world. This lack of interest in spiritual matters
may affect the day-to-day reality that they are creating for themselves
and produce a vulnerability to attached entities. This vulnerability is
not to be misconstrued as being synonymous with culpability. What
makes one culpable is a choice to be vulnerable to a spiritual intrusion. Such a choice could only occur if someone were completely
enlightened in regards to these matters. Without such enlightenment,
the choice would be spurious and completely invalid. One must not
falsely assume that this lack of enlightenment and misperception of
the spiritual dimension somehow causes an uninformed soul to be
culpable or karmically responsible for the negative karma that is pro-
duced due to the influence of such an intrusion.

Those individuals who are exceptionally enlightened and totally
aware of the possibility of spirit attachments would have limited cul-

pability at best, since most of the time the host is completely unaware of the presence of the spirit intruder. If an individual soul gave permission for a spirit to attach or is somehow aware of its presence or suspects such an intrusion, he or she is much more responsible for karma created and should seek appropriate therapy. In such circumstances, the individual soul would most likely have an ongoing mental conflict, as the attached entity would constantly challenge such thoughts in an effort to maintain the status quo.

It must be remembered that the attached spirits do not require permission to intrude and that a great number of attachments occur when an individual is a child, well before the age of reason. Thus the opportunity to become aware of such intrusions is minuscule, unless one is made aware through the help of a skillful past-life therapist.

25

DISSERTATION ON DEATH

Because death has reeked of mystery for many millennia, it has invoked fear, and therefore, anxiety in all mankind. We are fortunate to be living in present times and to be able to witness the disrobing of the unknown. What better way to accomplish this than to make use of deep hypnosis to throw open the floodgates of the subconscious mind and allow the sparkling liquidity of memory of all of one's existence to pour forth. By doing this in conjunction with taking the subject to his Higher Self, I find that the conscious mind steps aside and assumes the role of a silent, impartial observer as it allows the subconscious mind to carry out the retrieval of these memories under the orchestration of the propitiously candid Higher Self. When regressions to past lives and especially the afterlife are carried out in this manner, wisdom and spirituality abound and enrich the experience.

I have found that during many regression experiences the subject will often expound on extremely esoteric themes which are totally excluded from conscious memory following the regression, regardless of suggestions to remember everything that has occurred. I am convinced that some of the profound information that comes through the subject is originating in his Superconscious or Higher Mind and is bypassing the subconscious and conscious mind. It is my hope that I will be able to offer a good deal of evidence to support this hypothesis by working with a subject who transcribed in detail what she remembered of each regression experience following the sessions. If the evidence is as copious as I suspect, we will publish our findings.

Through the years I find that I have grown progressively impatient with skeptics. There will always be those who must criticize, comfortably camouflaging themselves with banners of scientific approach and proofs, and spewing out fanciful terms, such as 'fantasy' and 'imagination'. I say once again that the many hundreds of thousands of regression subjects throughout the last twenty-five years cannot all possibly be creating the same mental images and imagining the same scenarios about death and the hereafter. Add to this the millions of personal accounts[1] of those who have survived near-death experiences and you now have a vast multitude of people all saying the same thing about their experiences in the afterlife, speaking in one very loud voice about a place we are all going to but know nothing about. Are we to ignore this massive body of evidence? Yes, I call it evidence; for is it not true that a person may be put to death in our legal system based on another's testimony? This evidence is the collective testimony of a vast number of individuals who have affirmed their very personal experiences with death, through recall of past lives and near-death experiences. These countless occurrences are not just similar, they are practically identical. We are being handed, on a silver platter, a rare, but exceptional glimpse of what lies beyond death.

Our perception of finality to our physical existence on this planet has, and perhaps always will, be associated with an emotional void in our minds and hearts. This emptiness is a reflection of sadness, leaving behind those we care for, and of fearful uncertainty of what lies ahead. Moments before death find the conscious mind being pummeled by rampant emotions, brought on by fleeting but piercing thoughts, such as, "I have more to do… I need to make up for… I should have apologized… I never said, 'I love you'… I am so afraid…"

The experiences of many who have been regressed to the afterlife or who have nearly died tell us that the emotions embroiled within one who is dying can carry over through the death experience and

---

1. Gallup, George, *Adventures in Immortality,* McGraw-Hill, New York, 1982.

continue to smolder during and following the transition into spirit, especially when a soul finds itself procrastinating on its journey to the light because of concern for loved ones or because of confusion. I personally have witnessed many such scenarios during regressions.

Those who think the moments before death are not difficult need to realign their God-given thinking process and truly contemplate the meaning of this conclusive event and all it entails. Death is the final period at the end of the book of life on this Earth. It means saying farewell to those you deeply care for, knowing how much you will miss them and worrying about what will happen to them. It means no longer smelling the air or enjoying the beauty of a day or an evening on this Earth.

This place where we all go at the end of physical life, this realm where spirits dwell and time does not exist, is a dimension that is completely foreign to most people; however, even the most closed-minded are forced to open their minds to come up with a possible explanation and description of what lies ahead for peace of mind if for nothing else. These individuals often find that their faith helps patch the holes in their belief in what occurs after death. Unfortunately, their faith is just that: faith, in what they are told by others, who also do not know.

Many of us would prefer not to think about this inevitable end-point to our lives and just look to our faith for answers so we can feel somewhat comfortable about the idea of eventually dying. When we do this, we find that we easily slip into a cloak of complacency, which some may interpret as a suit of armor which will shield them from any harm after death, if they follow specific rules. Typical of human nature, many of us fall short of keeping these rules, and as a result, suffer greatly, as our mind pays the price and becomes flooded with negative emotions, primarily guilt and fear. As we strive to drown out these emotions with the nonessential clatter of day-to-day living, we bury the burning questions about where we are going and what will happen to us, that is, until something bad befalls us and frightens us into allowing these questions to resurface. If we are lucky, "something bad" doesn't happen; and instead, we pick up on more subtle, synchronistic events that present themselves. Such occurrences allow us to methodically unbury those questions and slowly become seekers of truth. By making the choice to pay attention to these synchronistic events that help put us back on our intended life path, we begin to see the folly of looking outside of ourselves for answers and, as a result, we turn our thoughts inward. By doing this we begin to listen to our intuition, the voice of our soul, and seek answers there. In this way, we discover our true spirituality and find the spark of our Creator that resides in all of us. In this way, we determine that we are that suit of armor; we are indestructible beings that live forever.

We also come to realize that we are responsible for our actions, and that karma and reincarnation go hand in hand. Thus we intuitively know that we need to make some changes in our life, especially in the way we treat others. Only in this way can we come to know ourselves and therefore come to know our Creator. Only in this way can we live well and die well, carrying with us as full an understanding as possible of what lies ahead.

26

VISIONS OF THE AFTERLIFE

The succeeding paragraphs contain many varied descriptions of the afterlife as envisioned by my subjects under deep hypnosis during the regression experience following the death of the individual in that past life. The many descriptions are colored by these individuals' attitudes and belief systems and offer an interesting contrast. There are, however, many similarities that remain consistent.

* * * *

"I see gray and white outlines, some brighter than others... looks like glass... almost hear music... so many lights. See different pathways going far away. I see Masters or Elders; they're white, older, and larger. They are in the background, speaking telepathically."

* * * *

"I'm going higher and higher. The view is getting smaller." (Later I was told that the subject was in absolute awe over the exceptionally rapid rise of her soul to the light.) "It's white all around, feels good. I see occasional fleeting spirits; the impression of older faces stands out more, just see occasional faces, shadows. I asked where I was... I heard the word, 'transition.'"

* * * *

"I knew I was going someplace good, someplace I have been before. I'm now in the white light. I'm even made out of light; others appear as beings of different colors with no body... I'm communicating telepathically. I see 'Elders'; they're big, have form, no wings... shaped like a tall, caped figure made out of light. I don't see their arms, just what looks like a cape. The Elders are asking if I feel that I've completed my lesson by accomplishing it. I said, no, and I need to go back and complete the same lesson, which was to nurture and give and be happy without receiving in return.

"The Elders are now telling me that I'll stay a while and then return to Earth to complete my mission." I asked what's happening now. The subject hesitated and then said, "I'm resting and talking to other souls in my group." I then asked her to tell me if the Elders are different in any other way. She blurted out, "The Elders are high; young souls and troubled souls are closer to the bottom... I live in the middle."

"Who is above the Elders?" I quickly inquired.

"The Mountainous ones who are bigger. We can't see them; only the Elders can see or speak to them. God is above all."

* * * *

This subject is a very advanced soul; and as such, made exceptionally powerful and relevant statements following her description of the light and following her reflection upon what she had learned in a short life burdened with much suffering. She was a teenage girl arrested in Nazi Germany in 1943 for giving assistance to Jewish children. She was placed in a concentration camp with the children and tearfully described the atrocities and the desecration of the human spirit. She tried as hard as she could to comfort the children by soothing their mental anguish and allaying their many terrifying fears. As it turned out the Nazis continued their horrifying ethnic cleansing of these young, innocent human beings. The subject was crying profusely at that moment and uttered, "Once in rhythm, the Nazis do it more easily." She was forced into a big cart along with the children and taken to a place where they were all executed.

Following her death, she said, "I hung out and helped those souls in transition." In the light, she was greeted by angels, archangels, and cherubs, and could hear a choir. She felt that she was home and at complete peace, as she bathed in the light and in the sound of the

222

choir. "Everything is choice; we all make choices. The body is only a vehicle. You're not really being murdered. It is a choice for the soul to move on. It may look brutal and imperfect, but that relates to the body, and the body is not what is eternal. The soul can rise above any experience… it can resonate at the highest frequency, even in the lowest depths of life. You can express your being in your highest capacity. All that is required is your self. You can rise above all of it and create a place of peace and healing by spreading the light. You really live within; the wisdom there is eternal. Two polarities come together, the depths of destruction, and God's light and love. When you embrace such love, your soul is brought forth in full expression and you don't buy into the fear. Be that; radiate that in a place that looks like hell. Happiness is like the eye of a hurricane; it is created within and affects others in a good way, energetically. Sometimes others can't hear you when you're trying to calm them; they're having too much pain. Still, they are affected, and they will want to be around you and not know why."

* * * *

"Your level of vibration determines the level of afterlife that you go to. Souls gravitate to be with souls of the same vibration. The light intensity of the afterlife depends on the soul's level of vibration; those souls with a lower vibration gravitate to a darker area."

* * * *

"I see many souls in white tunics. The Elders are large spirits with white hair and beards and big foreheads; they sit in marble chairs. I cannot speak to them first; it's not my turn yet. The biggest spirit smiled and said he will tell me when it's my turn to incarnate. It's time… I'm going into a fetus." The subject could not advance to being born or beyond. Confirming my suspicion of a stillbirth, she then said she was fully developed but was born dead with the cord wrapped tightly, three times, around her neck. She had changed her mind; these people were not the right parents. She came back to the light, and her decision to return to different parents was supported by the Elders. She was again infused into a fetus and was born into her current lifetime.

The following is another rendering of the afterlife experience by the same subject, following her death as an old American Indian woman who had broken her hip and was left in a cave to die. Others in the tribe kept a fire going for her and brought her food and water once a day. She was happy but thought that she wanted to die so the pain would go away. She lay in the cave for three weeks until she died. The cave became bright as she floated above her body. Everything appeared beautiful as she continued to float toward the bright light. "It's taking forever to get into that light. A beautiful woman is greeting me; I feel I know her… she is giving me a big hug and producing a warm sensation in me. She's asking me if I want to stay or go. I feel and look young again… I have no pain. I want to stay here… the light is getting brighter; I'm walking toward it. The lady is smiling… I'm being sucked into a bright tunnel… I'm falling through it. It's getting darker… I'm in a beautiful place; others are here; I think this is where we wait."

The subject remained quiet for several minutes and then began speaking again. "Some are leaving through a door to a new life… I see two and three leaving at a time. Someone is speaking to me with his mind; I feel safe and secure. Look, there are animals, doves, dogs, cats, all white. I see trees and flowers, so vivid, such brilliant colors. It's an inside garden with pillars so tall I cannot see the top. There's a building far away, a large marble building. Somehow I know I can't go there until I'm ready. Those who are being guided into it are older-looking."

The subject again became silent; I waited without saying anything. She finally spoke. "There are double doors leading to other lives. I'm moving through the doorway and going down white stairs, everything is white." The subject then became excited as she said, "The stairs are turning pink; they're changing colors as you go down.

Now they're blue... I see an ocean...I'm underwater, I'm swimming, but there are no fish... it's so warm; I'm floating... I hear a drum beating... I'm a baby, something is squeezing me... I'm getting pushed out! No! I don't want to leave here... oh, it's cold! Too bright and noisy... I'm OK now; someone is holding me, it's my mother. I feel that I belong to these people."

In that lifetime the subject was a girl, born into an American family in the year 1921. At twenty years old, she married an American fighter pilot who served during World War II in the Pacific theater, fighting the Japanese. This was rather ironic, since the subject was Japanese. Thus we have here another example of why we gain a more global perspective in regard to our identity as we uncover more lifetimes.

* * * *

This subject openly cried when regressed to a past life in which she died in childbirth following a traumatic delivery and was forced to leave her newborn infant. As her spirit left her body, she felt extremely light, as if she was floating upwards. She entered and felt completely immersed in a bright light, and her sadness turned to feelings of peace and contentment. Hearing a voice saying, "Don't be afraid," she began to sense that someone very strong was there for her.

* * * *

This young female subject recalled a life as a Native American woman who died prematurely in her early 30s. Immediately following death she was greeted by a loving soul who had lived many lives with her, including her present lifetime. As she entered the light, she loudly uttered, "It's beautiful... so full of love and happiness... so bright, but not painful. It's bright with energy. I hear a musical, energetic hum, as love would sound. There are other souls here... it's alive with them. There are Masters, two of them; they must be a pair, like Yin and Yang, everything is a partnership. Ultimate love is the merging of two souls. Without that partnership to draw upon to keep the cycle continuous, creation cannot be achieved. In order to become infinite, you must have complete love for yourself and be completely loved by one who resonates on the same vibrational level."

* * * *

This subject was a young man who regressed to a life as a young American soldier who lost his leg in Vietnam. Before returning home to his loved ones, he endured flashbacks to terrible war atrocities that he committed while in Vietnam. These disturbing memories became too great a burden for him to bear, so he put a gun to his head and ended his life. His spirit remained by his body as the subject became progressively remorseful.

I asked the subject if he was proceeding towards the light.

The subject replied, "It's still dark…I see only a pinpoint of light."

This situation persisted as he continued to have difficulty in getting to the light. I then said, "I would like you to advance to when you are in the light, providing your spirit eventually goes to the light." Even though no spirits came to greet and guide him to the light, his facial expression transformed from tense grimacing to a peaceful, soft smile, as he made me aware of his being immersed in the light.

He then said, "My lesson was to not be self-absorbed. I did not accomplish this. Suicide was a cheap way out."

* * * *

This middle-aged woman incarnated as a boy in the 12th century. At thirteen years old, this young boy and his mother were killed by arrows from marauding soldiers. As both spirits headed for the light, which they described as white with many sparkling colors, the subject said, "I feel enveloped and embraced by the light, as if I'm becoming one with the light." The two spirits were greeted by the subject's present-day deceased father, who was described as a Master Spirit, taller in stature than the other spirits.

* * * *

This 49-year-old very advanced subject began her session from the spirit plane as she greeted souls arriving in the afterlife. "Welcome! Don't be afraid... you have completed your long journey. Welcome to the Hall of Souls. No need to grieve. First time here? Let me explain... here you will see those who have done random acts of kindness, held a door open, fed a hungry person, listened with compassion... they may include your friends, relatives, or acquaintances. Do not go near that door; they are the lost ones. They thought only of themselves and showed no acts of compassion. There is an observation platform where you can see the lost souls. Up there is the Master... feel his warmth and presence. "There are greeters and caretakers but only one God.

"The light is brighter; the order of sanctity is stronger there, in the Hall of Saints. In the Hall of Saints is our most revered saint. She is still taking care of people... she is a beautiful soul. She was a living saint on Earth and the patroness of India. She was revered and respected by everyone on Earth, also here, a little slip of a woman... she is a go-between for the saints and the Trinity...she is very close to the Blessed Virgin." (She was most likely speaking of Mother Theresa.)

"No, we don't fly around. People will know when we touch them. We don't manifest often; it scares people. Heaven is infinity; there are no pearly gates. You face yourself and you judge yourself. It is wonderful here... whatever you wish for, you will do it. You can be whatever you want."

27

THE TRAINING WORLD

On several occasions I have encountered a regression that was rather bizarre, both in location and in substance. When asked if this is Earth or another planet, the reply was always an abrupt, "No!" At first I was baffled by this three-dimensional yet completely unrealistic world that these subjects were physically living in; that is, until I heard, "We created this world." It then occurred to me that they were referring to a so-called "training world."

In one particular regression, the subject described a world that was peaceful and simple, with no need for education or jobs. The people were happy and loving. There was no pain or disease and no need for doctors. Reincarnation was so well understood and accepted that nobody mourned the passing of their friends and family members. Everyone there knew they were there to live together, share information, and practice love and communion before they went on. They knew they would once again see those who had died and would recognize their soul. Grieving over the dead was not an obstacle to happiness. The individuals there were given pet names or numbers and lived in family units. They had a romantic physical relationship but at a much higher level of spirituality. My subject explained that she was an Elder in training, teaching young souls.

This concept of training worlds was explored and discussed in depth by Dr. Michael Newton in his very original and brilliant work, *Journey of Souls*. In Chapter 10 he describes four so-called "training worlds," three of which are non-dimensional spheres of attention, or mental worlds, each for a different purpose. The fourth world, the world of creation and non-creation, is a three-dimensional, physical world, very similar to Earth, where individual souls learn and practice creating on a small scale, using only their own energy. The creative power increases as the soul advances. Training worlds are initially created collectively by the Master Spirits.

Newton's physical fourth world has many parallels with the very unusual world that my subject found herself in. Later in the regression she referred to it as a "training world." I have a feeling there are many such worlds created collectively by the Masters for many purposes.

One of the mental worlds mentioned in Michael Newton's book is the so-called 'World of Altered Time', where souls may carry on transient planetary study. Dr. Newton comments, "It is a timeless, mental world that is true reality, while all else is an illusion created for various benefits."[1] He had been told by subjects that souls could blend their energy into animate and inanimate objects and even into a specific emotional feeling. Dr. Newton further stated, "Some subjects tell of being mystical spirits of nature, including figures I associate with folklore, such as elves, giants, and mermaids." He also felt that some of our legends may have originated as memories of souls who came to Earth from other places.

These thoughts purported by Dr. Michael Newton have great merit and appear to form a splendid backdrop for the case of regression I intend to discuss next.

MYTHICAL FAIRY OF THE FOREST

This very unusual lifetime was recalled by an extremely enlightened woman who I feel tapped into this "World of Altered Time" to which Newton referred.[2] What the subject had to say about that life was both profound and poetic, and it appeared to fit perfectly into that timeless mental world.

"I am a mystical fairy in the forest. I'm both ethereal and physical. I am small and strong but not visible, and I'm here to inspire man,

---

1. Newton, *Journey of Souls,* Llewellyn, St. Paul, MN, 1994, p. 168.
2. ibid., p. 168.

even though he's not aware of my presence. I live in the forest, where I am befriended by animals and plants and nourished by the dew.

"I nourish those who are oppressed and come here to hide. They hear my silent song, they feel my breath on their cheek. I am harmony. I come from a tree... I am the soul of Nature. I have emotions but not reason. I can soothe the soul of mankind without making a conscious effort. I sense that I was human before, but now I am in another dimension, where I am unable to think rationally. My abilities are limited to emotional thinking, but my soul grows from the experience.

"I feel men's emotions and soothe their fears, hatreds, and negativity. I see people come to the forest and talk to the trees. I listen and bring them comfort. In doing so I help them think more clearly and see more good; this relieves their negative feelings and allows their love to come forth. I don't guide their thoughts; I just calm their soul through the use of the plants and trees... I am the soul of these plants and trees; I personify their energy.

"I am but a wisp, but I am Spirit; and it is my task to absorb human suffering and its disquietude and to see to it that Nature assists humans who seek solitude and peace in the forest by nourishing their bodies and souls through relaxing, soothing energy. I am the mythical fairy of the forest."

In his book, Dr. Newton methodically uncovers the many mysteries of life in the afterlife, within the parameters of what the Spirit Guides and more advanced entities of the spirit world would feel is appropriate for us to know at this time. He did this by regressing subjects into the afterlife and carrying on an exhaustive scrutiny of a soul's existence in that realm. I applaud him for putting forth this Herculean effort to so meticulously examine the many unusual facets of the strange hereafter, so foreign and yet so vital to our acceptance of what we believe to be true. His work adds greatly to the voluminous knowledge that has poured forth into the metaphysical cup of enlightenment, which we all need to drink from if we are to continue to raise our consciousness and properly prepare ourselves for the heretofore unknown called death.

28

SPIRITUAL WARRIOR

A remarkable case centered around Samantha, an attractive young woman who was referred to me for a better understanding of herself and because of her burning curiosity about past lives. She was rather nervous in the beginning; however, following a successful episode of relaxation, I was able to guide her into a deep state of hypnosis. She immediately began seeing shadows, which she described as "globes of energy." She felt that these entities did not seem to know each other and appeared to be waiting for a task to be assigned to them.

This description of her immediate environment led me to believe that she had been regressed into the afterlife. She immediately blurted out that she remembers feeling very sad. She then began to cry uncontrollably, saying "I'm scared!" I rapidly rose her above this scene and took steps to relieve this anxiety. Deciding on a different, less traumatic pathway to reenter into that lifetime, I had her return to the happiest moment in that life. Her response was rather unusual, as she returned to the day she was born. It was unusual in the sense that the happiness she remembered did not appear to come from the love of her parents, rather it appeared to originate from the love of God. She did, however, feel a great amount of joy toward her father, as she was born into this life as a boy. Coexistent with this joy was a feeling of jealousy that the mother manifested in relation to the father, because of his exceptional love for his new son.

As I advanced him through this lifetime, occurring in the 1950s, it became evident that this boy was very intelligent, academic, even nerdish, and had trouble fitting in. His father died early, leaving him with a controlling, unloving mother.

In his first year of college, he became so disappointed, so unhappy, and so removed from everyone, that he committed suicide. As his spirit rose from his body, he felt himself going through a tunnel and getting stuck. He felt disoriented as he could only see slits of light in the tunnel. This feeling immediately disappeared, as the slits of light became globes of energy, the same globes of energy that were encountered in the early moments of the session. Once again, these spiritual entities were patiently awaiting an assignment to be given to them by the elders. This subject thus related that she passed directly through the tunnel to this special place in the spiritual plane of the afterlife. It had not been necessary for her soul to go to the light, as other souls normally did. She further explained that the light was there, but it was not for her until she completed her assignment. She had no choice; she had to accept the assignment, which had been con-trived for her by the "Knowing," who she described as much larger, very advanced spirits in the hierarchy of the spirit world. Below the "Knowing" were the Elders, who gave out the assignments. Samantha then portrayed herself as one of this special group of spirits present-ing themselves in front of a semicircular panel of Elders, who, she said, resembled globes of light that looked like tips of a flame.

At this moment, the Elders were admonishing her, saying she did not accomplish her work, and therefore must make up for the work she didn't do. They were telling her she wasted a chance to carry out these good works in her last life. Samantha explained that the work had to do with helping others in a special way, but it was hard and exhausting. She now began to argue with herself. "I don't want to do the work, but I don't have a choice The Elders give us our assignments. They decide when we incarnate and when we die. Others like me want to do the work because they enjoy it; I can feel their anticipation. I don't like it as they do, and there are others like me who are rebellious, but we are few I haven't been doing this long, but the work is too hard. I know I am being selfish, but I don't want to keep coming back over and over for this purpose. I just want to have good time and die."

While remaining in front of the panel of Elders, Samantha now answered my question regarding her location. "This is not the usual place that souls gather, and there is no division of souls here. It is a very special place, high in the echelon of the afterlife." She then spoke of the Creator. "There is only one knowing being, one who is all knowing, all energy, all everything; never seen, just felt. I was taken back and somewhat confused by this entire sequence of events. I then asked if she could be more specific about why she was here and what work she was expected to do. Samantha then continued, "I know the reason why I and these other souls here are chosen for this life. We are totally different souls. We belong to a team of Spiritual Warriors. We fight the misdirected energies of souls with and without bodies and help them vibrate at a higher level."

This was the first time I had heard the term, "Spiritual Warrior." I was now making sense of what was being shown to me, and I felt very fortunate to be regressing this very special soul. I was being allowed to delve into this inner circle of very special beings of the spirit world and was being given a glimpse of how they function. Michael Newton made no mention of such spiritual entities in his extraordinary after-life work, *Journey of Souls*. I was beginning to feel an excitement, possibly similar to what Brian Weiss may have experienced when he first came across the Masters in *Many Lives, Many Masters*. My enthusiasm took on a chilling overcast as Samantha relayed to me what the Elders were telling her. They made it very clear that she was not to return to me. This came as a blow to my professional ego, but more than that, I felt like an intruder, someone who took advantage of a wayward, rebellious Spiritual Warrior, in order to gain access to very special, even sacred, information. At the same time I felt a certain degree of satisfaction in that this regression episode accomplished bringing this subject back to the reality of who she truly was, so she may once again be on her designated path, with clear vision and another opportunity to accomplish her mission.

In a fit of self-reproach, Samantha exclaimed, "I think I need to change my life-style. I'm too attached to my human form. I'm forgetting my mission, my assignment." She awakened spontaneously and then began to relate a strange story to me, one that occurred several years ago.

While she was on a trip to the Orient, an American stranger walked up to her while she was feeding birds in a town square. He spoke softly to her about her communication with the birds, stating "Oh, the birds speak to you as well." That day the stranger explained many things to Samantha. He told her that she was part of a special spiritual force, and as a Spiritual Warrior she needed to begin and consistently carry out her assignment. Samantha thought he may have been one of the panel of Elders that she had previously come across.

Following this unusual and moving encounter, Samantha began accomplishing these good works in both her dream state and her waking state. She related stories of transforming into another body in order to save lives. She healed souls with and without bodies by releasing their disorientation, their hurt, and their misplacement. By 1994 Samantha felt that her Spiritual Warrior work was becoming surreal. She then made a conscious decision to stop doing this work. Samantha ended the session by saying she knew where this man lived and that she needed to contact him so she may once again begin the work of a Spiritual Warrior.

Another subject mentioned certain things that I could not explain until I became aware of Spiritual Warriors. This subject was an older woman who relived a life in Rome in the first century A.D. She had a vision of Christ in the form of a light and felt that she must share what had been revealed to her. She was locked up and later hanged by the Romans. No one came to greet her as her spirit rose from her body. She felt that she was going to a special place and described it as light being all around her. She then felt everything become darker as she returned to another life on Earth and commented, "This is going to be another rough ride." She incarnated in China in the 1400s and was a fisherman who assisted the monks in preserving manuscripts and keeping them hidden from the ruling dynasty. Drowning in a storm at sea, the subject again felt that her spirit went to a special place, and there she was to wait for another assignment.

As a postscript to this episode, and after learning of Spiritual Warriors, I would like to relay what yet another subject brought out when telling me of her first incarnation on Earth. She spoke of being in Lemuria in spirit form and helping those on Earth in both spirit form and physical form. She went on to say that many beings from other places also help, mentioning angels, light-workers, and aliens. I then asked about Spiritual Warriors. She answered, "Spiritual Warriors are stronger; they do battle on an energy level, usually without coming into the third dimension; but when then do, they are born into an Earth life and usually remember who they are. They can now help people while in physical form, but they can also do this on other levels and higher dimensions due to a more advanced state of being. When they have completed what they need to accomplish, they go back to the source and receive assignments from the Masters."

29

A CHALLENGE TO CONVENTIONAL MEDICINE

One thing I have learned from this entire metamorphosis is that we never stop learning. Enlightenment is one continuous journey. Our spiritual growth is unlimited; its transcendence beyond our human boundaries is unimaginable. I feel as if I have barely scratched the surface of our understanding of immortality, yet many of my human brethren will remain narrow-minded, looking at my subjects with suspicion, disbelief, and ridicule. They will continue to walk the face of this Earth like trained robots, content with being whom they think they should be, according to what they have been taught by their parents, schools, governments, and religions. They even aspire to be what their friends, family, or coworkers feel they should be, or what TV commercials say is desirable or fashionable. What I have described here might very well be called "the human condition." It is a sad condition, for it portends a life on this Earth of unhappiness and unfulfillment, ending in an unenlightened death, filled with fear of the unknown.

Those disturbing questions that I began to ask myself many years ago still echo within my mind... Who am I?... What is life all about? ... Why am I here? ... Where do I come from? ... Where will I go at death? These poignant questions began to open my mind to the universe. My mind's eye was seeing for the first time. The more I learned, the more I needed to learn, and the more I wanted to learn. I truly felt my consciousness expanding as I packed more awareness into my physical brain. As my attitude, perspective, and thoughts became more positive, loving, and reflective of the increasing vibration of my soul's energy, I found myself changing. Life took on new meaning. I allow negativity to flow through me and not attach to it. I was looking at negative events as an opportunity to grow. I was squaring off with people in my life to shake off negative influences. I began to feel more comfortable about death and what lies beyond. I was becoming enlightened.

Now that I think about it, working day in and day out with life and death as a physician gave me a jump-start to seek the answers to those haunting questions. Most people are not involved with life and death to that degree; however, if they acquire a terminal illness or lose a loved one, these thoughts begin to pervade the hard veneer of their human condition.

As I sought the answers to these difficult questions, I found that I was indeed on a quest. I was becoming a seeker of truth, able to look at life in a whole new way, a way that brought me joy, order, and peace. Everything in life began to make more sense. I had the feeling that I was traveling the right path, doing what I was supposed to be doing.

My experience as a physician has led me to believe that negative thinking fosters a negative attitude, which in turn brings on a negative emotion such as fear, hate, jealousy, and so on. These types of emotions have been shown to be injurious to the physiologic functions of the body, including the immune system. If this sequence of events occurs often enough people become sick, both emotionally and physically. I further believe that once these illnesses manifest they continue to fester and maintain their destructive course due to the initiating cause, which is often buried in subconscious memory. If this cause is subliminal, it is most likely bathed in extremely powerful emotions which can affect the body in various negative ways without conscious awareness.

Hypnotic past-life regression therapy has been extremely successful in allowing the very protective subconscious mind to search for, identify, and bring these emotional sources of illness to the surface of conscious mind. My research has shown that emotional causes of illness can be traced either to an initiating event which occurred in one's present life or to a present-day situation that triggered subconscious recall of this occurrence from a past lifetime. Once causal events lying at the very core of an illness are brought forth from the subconscious, the conscious mind can then evaluate them for what they truly are, make a rational judgment, and with proper guidance, be able to release the negative effect on the body.

The many subjects that I treated hypnotically for emotional and physical problems were actually patients in my mind, for I was using a very powerful medical modality, the most important technological discovery in the history of mankind, the human mind. With it I was able to search out the causes of their problems, come up with correct solutions, and gain the satisfaction that only comes when one cures a patient of his ills. Having been on both sides of the fence and having seen the results from both perspectives, I feel that I am in a position to offer a challenge to my peers in the conventional medical field. The challenge is this: make good use of consultations with qualified hypnotherapists or physicians well-trained in this discipline. Allow them to be part of the therapeutic team involved in the treatment of these patients. Hypnotic regression therapy has been shown to work exceptionally well, and I am certain that using it in conjunction with conventional medical treatment would give patients a greater opportunity to participate in their healing and thus impact the remission and cure rate in a very positive way.

Under deep hypnosis, the well entrenched emotional cause of a serious illness such as cancer will easily surface and expose itself to the patient's conscious mind. Then the patient understands that the emotional turmoil that he has been carrying around and has unconsciously chosen to live with is really unnecessary baggage amassed through often faulty perception and interpretation of events and relationships in a present or past life. He comes to realize that he has been accumulating needless negative emotions which have, in turn, forged an attitude that has been literally destroying his immune system, the lack of which has led to his cancer. This is a sterling example of the mind/body connection carried over from past times. By unlocking this mystery, which continues to lead so many to their demise, the cancer patient's immune system will thus be revitalized, giving him what he needs to shore up his ongoing cancer treatment and help him win the battle of his life.

By taking spirituality seriously, physicians would be able to give their patients a much greater degree of thorough and comprehensive care, because by doing so they will be addressing not only the needs of the mind and body, but also those of the soul. Our creator has shown us the most masterful of designs in His unique creation of the human body. Its complexity defies description, while its miraculous functions define medicine. Should physicians not also recognize and show reverence for the power of its life-giving force, the eternal soul?

About the Author

Dr. Tramont received his Bachelor of Science degree from John Carroll University in Cleveland and his M.D. from New York Medical College in New York City. Returning to Cleveland, he completed his internship and a residency in obstetrics and gynecology.

After serving two years of active duty in the Air Force during the Vietnam War, he entered private practice in Chardon, Ohio. Positions held during his many years in practice included President of the County Medical Society, Head of the Department of Surgery, Chief of OB/GYN, and Vice Chief of Staff.

Dr. Tramont joined the Air Force Reserves in the early 80s and earned his Flight Surgeon wings following graduation from the School of Aerospace Medicine and also graduated from Air War College. He was appointed to Squadron Commander, promoted to Colonel, and served on active duty deployment during Desert Storm.

Following retirement, Dr. Tramont was certified by the American Board of Hypnotherapy. He has conducted extensive past-life research, and lectured to the university students of Dr. Raymond Moody's consciousness classes. He periodically lectures on past-life regression therapy for continuing medical education lectures to the staff at Sunrise Hospital in Las Vegas.

He presently carries on an active hypnotherapy practice in Las Vegas.

BIBLIOGRAPHY

Baldwin, William, D.D.S., Ph.D., *Healing Lost Souls*, Hampton Roads, Charlottesville, VA. 2003

Baldwin, William, D.D.S., Ph.D., *Spirit Releasement Therapy*, Headline Books, Terra Alta, WV, 1991

Boswell, Louis K., M.D., "The Initial Sensitizing Event of Emotional Disorders," *British Journal of Medical Hypnotism*, Vol. II, No. 4, December 1987

Deutsch, David, Ph.D. "Quantum Shmantum," *Discover Magazine*, September, 2001, Vol. 22, No. 9

Finkelstein, Adrian, M.D., *Your Past Lives and the Healing* Process, 50 Gates Publishing Company, Malibu, CA, 1985

Goldberg, Bruce, D.D.S., *Past Lives, Future Lives Revealed*, Career Press, Franklin Lakes, NJ, 2004

Mishlove, Jeffrey, Ph.D., *The Roots of Consciousness: The Classic Encyclopedia of Consciousness Studies Revised and Expanded*, Avalon Publishing Group, 1997

Moody, Raymond, M.D., Ph.D., *Life After Life*, Bantam Books, New York, 1975

Newton, Michael, Ph.D, *Journey of Souls*, Llewellyn Publications, St. Paul, MN, 2001

Paulson, Genevieve Lewis and Stephen J., *Reincarnation: Remembering Past Lives*, Llewellyn Publications, St. Paul, MN, 1997

Pearsall, Paul, Ph.D., *The Heart's Code*, Random House, New York, 1999

Robinson, James M., General Editor, *The Nag Hammadi Library*, Harper, San Francisco, 1978

Semkiw, Walter, M.D., *Return of the Revolutionaries*, Hampton Roads, Charlottesville, VA, 2003

Siegel, Bernie, M.D., *Love, Medicine, and Miracles*, Harper and Row, New York, 1986

Sutphen, Dick, and Taylor, Lauren Leigh, *Past Life Therapy in Action*, Valley of the Sun Publishing Company, Malibu, CA, 1983

Weiss, Brian, M.D., *Many Lives, Many Masters*, Simon & Schuster, Inc., New York, 1988

Weiss, Brian, M.D., *Only Love is Real*, Warner Books, Inc., New York, 1996

Woolger, Roger, Ph.D., *Other Lives, Other Selves*, A Dolphin Book: Doubleday, New York, 1987

Zukov, Gary, *The Seat of the Soul*, Simon and Schuster, New York, 1989

INDEX

GRANITE PUBLISHING L.L.C.

HAS THESE IMPRINTS:

WILD FLOWER PRESS
SWAN • RAVEN & CO.
LITTLE GRANITE BOOKS

TO RECEIVE A CATALOG OF MORE OF OUR BOOKS—
EMAIL: INFO@GRANITEPUBLISHING.US
OR
PHONE: 828.894.8444
FAX: 828.894.8454

VISIT OUR WEB SITE AT
HTTP://GRANITEPUBLISHING.US

TRADE ORDERS FULFILLED BY
BOOKMASTERS
800.537.6727
FAX: 419.281.0200

PERSONAL ORDERS FULFILLED BY
PATHWAY BOOK SERVICE
800.345.6665
FAX: 603.357.2073

TO RECEIVE OUR PERIODICAL EMAIL JOURNAL THAT TRACKS THE
EARTH'S TRANSITION TO WHAT
THE ANCIENTS CALLED THE 5TH WORLD
EMAIL US AT
5WJ@GRANITEPUBLISHING.US